TOWARDS A HUMANE ENVIRONMENT

RESPONSIBILITIES OF STATE, ROLE OF CIVIL SOCIETY AND RIGHTS OF CITIZENS

TOWARDS A HUMANE ENVIRONMENT

Responsibilities of State, Role of Civil Society and Rights of Citizens

Edited by
R. Rajeevan

KALPAZ

ISBN : 978-93-5128-069-9
Price : ₹ 990

First Published, 2015

Published by

Kalpaz Publications
C-30, Satyawati Nagar,
Delhi-110052
Ph. : 9212142040
E-mail: kalpaz@hotmail.com

Laser Typesetting : Rudra Computer Graphics, Delhi
Printed at : G. Print Process, Delhi

Cataloging in Publication Data—DK
Courtesy: D.K. Agencies (P) Ltd. <docinfo@dkagencies.com>

"Towards a Humane Environment: Responsibilities of State, Role of Civil Society and Rights of Citizens" (Seminar) (2012 : NSS College Nilamel)
Towards a humane environment : responsibilities of state, role of civil society and rights of citizens / R. Rajeevan.
pages cm
ISBN 9789351280699

1. Human ecology—India—Congresses. 2. Human ecology—Congresses. 3. Environmental policy—India—Congresses. 4. Environmental policy—Congresses. 5. Environmental policy—India—Citizen participation—Congresses. 6. Environmental policy—Citizen participation—Congresses. 7. Civil rights—India—Congresses. 8. Civil rights—Congresses. I. Rajeevan, R., editor. II. NSS College Nilamel. Department of Political Science.organizer. III. Title.

DDC 304.20954 23

Contents

Foreword 7
Preface 11
Editor's Prologue 13
List of Contributors 15

1. **Science and Spirituality in the Study of Environment and Development** **35**
T. V. Muralivallabhan

2. **Environmental Degradation – Beyond the Limits** **53**
N. Peethambara Kurup M.P.

3. **Traditional Knowledge, Intellectual Property Rights and Livelihood Sustainability** **59**
M. Rajesh

4. **From Skepticism to Trepidation: A Study on How the Social Media Youth Perceive the Mullaperiyar Dam Issue** **71**
Titto Varghese, D. Nivedhita and Santhosh Mathew Veranani

5. **A Public Space in the Urban Environment: The Case of Mananchira Maidanam in Kozhikodu** **91**
P. Sivadasan

6. **The Waste Management and Environmental Protection: A Concern for Human Existence** **107**
Abraham Mathew

7. Triggering the Environment: A Lesson from Kureepuzha 119
Rajan T.

8. Traditional Environmental Health Hazards and the Scope for Policy Intervention: The Case of National Rural Health Mission in an Island Community 133
Manju S. Nair

9. Development and Conservation with Special Reference to Wetlands 147
N. Unnikrishnan

10. Cropping Pattern Changes: A Threat to Sustainable Development 155
Maneesh B.

11. Eco-Feminism: The Role of Women in Environmental Management and Conservation 167
Kala Devi V.

12. Ecological Discourses on Thiruvathira 173
Yamuna D.S.

13. Physico-Chemical Characteristics of Water Sample from Parvathi Puthanar Canal in Thiruvanathapuram 179
Geetha R. Nair

14. Indoor Gamma Dose in the South West Coast of Kerala 187
Rani K. Pillai, Ben Byju S., Arunima S., Lekshmi R., Vishnu Prasad K. and *P.J. Jijo*

15. Dimensions of Global Environmental Politics 197
K.C. Sreekumar

16. Environmentalism in India: Issues and Initiatives 219
Rajeevan R.

17. Sustainable Environment: Rights of the Citizens and Role of the Court 235
G. Balachandran and *Hameema M.*

Index 247

Foreword

Environment belongs to all of us irrespective of caste, colour, sex, creed, religion, language or nationality. Environmental studies is a multi-disciplinary subject, in nature. It includes not only the study of physical and biological characters of the environment, but also its social, economic, cultural and political aspects. The earth which is the only known supporter of life is a small planet in the universe. This earth is experiencing an inhumane environmental degradation that is increasing day by day and makes its survival difficult. The prevailing inhumane practices create large scale ecological imbalances leading to serious consequences. This environmental crisis gets worsened day by day and will in near future become an overwhelming issue most directly related to the livelihood and survival of earth's flora and fauna, including human beings.

The genesis of the environmental problems can be easily traced to the life styles and developmental process adopted by man in the long path of his progress. "Has man a future?" asked the great philosopher, Bertrand Russel in the mid-sixties when the world was experiencing a possible nuclear tragedy under the pressure of cold-war situation. Today, unscientific and careless urbanisation, industrialisation and agriculturisation leads to major environmental challenges to our survival, than the nuclear holocaust. Today, we face serious crisis like pollution of air and water, exhaustion of non-renewable resources, poor management of soil, displacement of forest and water resources, unbridled consumption of fossil fuels, ozone layer depletion, climate changes, atmospheric warming and pollution in various other levels.

The impact of man on the environment is a major global issue and on the other hand man's fate depends largely on whether he succeeds in achieving a new equilibrium between the environment, he has conquered and the nature, in which he was created. And if this equilibrium is not maintained, man's modern socio-economic programme may turn out to be a programme of his own destruction. The issue has been put forward and discussed in various platforms from local government institutions to UN bodies. Remedial measures are being discussed, shaped and executed on the one side but the real problems remain as they are on the other side. Even four decades back, the Stockholm Conference suggested that "the protection of the environment is a major issue which affects the well being of people and economic development throughout the world."

The environmental issue was first seriously discussed in the UN conference on human environment at Stockholm (Sweden) in 1972. Indira Gandhi, the Prime Minister of India was the only visiting head of state to participate in the conference, which was attended by 113 countries. In the meeting Indira Gandhi stressed the point that "the global community must address the issue of global development in order to move towards an environmentally sound planet." She added that "the removal of poverty is an integral part of the goal of an environmental strategy for the world. Another major UN sponsored earth summit held in Rio de Janeiro, Brazil (1992) was attended by 115 heads of states, 10,000 government missions and about 20,000 NGOs and was inaugurated by our Prime Minister P.V. Narasimha Rao. No doubt it was the largest UN sponsored global conference both in number of participants and scope of the agenda.

In the UN conference on sustainable development held in Rio-de-Janeiro in June 2012, India emerged as the spokesnation of the developing world. Dr Manmohan Singh along with 125 crore Indian people has reason to be happy about the overwhelming support received from poor and developing countries in incorporating the principle of "common but differentiated responsibility" in the draft declaration submitted for adoption in the summit.

India is definitely a role model in the international arena to promote the idea of a humane environment. With this spirit India realised the need for international co-operation, bilateral and multi-lateral programmes and regional initiatives in dealing with issues of environment and development. At the government level, the ministry of environment and forests acts as a nodal agency for making relations with international agencies like UNEP, SACEP, IUCN, FAO, UNDP, World Bank EEC and SAARC. Independently, NGOs in India have also taken several initiatives towards global co-operation and exchange of ideas.

The shaping of a humane environment is not only the responsibility of UNO and national governments but it has an ethical and spiritual content representing the very basic values of human civilisation. It is the duty and responsibility of the civil society and every individual to contribute their own share in making the environment humane. For enlightening and awakening the civil society and the individuals, seminars, discussions and debates are notable exercises.

The book "towards a humane environment" has grown out of the deliberations of a national seminar entitled "*Towards a Humane Environment: Responsibilities of State, Role of Civil Society and Rights of Citizens*" sponsored by the Institute of Parliamentary Affairs, Government of Kerala and organised by the Department of Political Science, NSS College, Nilamel under the chairmanship of Dr Rajeevan R, who has edited this volume. There are seventeen topics in this commendable collection of articles related to various aspects of environment and ecology. The authors are well known environmentalists and experienced teachers and professors, who have had occasion to go deeply into the various dimensions of the subject. All the papers presented at the seminar were later revised in the light of the discussions that took place following the presentation.

It is definitely a thing of joy that several new studies on environmental issues are being brought out every year. A reading of this book will definitely provide a fresh look on environmental issues. Dr Rajeevan deserves to be felicitated and congratulated for his hard work to publish this volume. It is my earnest hope that the academic community as well as the environmentalists will make full use of this thoughtful volume, which will provide to accelerate the process of turning the environment more humane.

Dr. T. Varghese
Director General
Institute of Parliamentary Affairs
Government of Kerala
Thiruvananthapuram

29 August, 2013
Thiruvananthapuram

Preface

The magnitude of man's demand in pursuit of satisfying both his basic needs and greed is increasing proportionately to the continuing increase in world population. Environmental degradation is also aggravated by mismanagement of natural resources and a failure to invest and reinvest in their productivity, health and sustainability. Man's economic development coupled with technological and industrial development has made him blind about the resulting environmental degradation and harms he is causing for his own existence. The loss of ecosystem and the bio-diversity underpinning them is a challenge most directly related to the livelihood and survival of earth's flora and fauna.

We must keep in our mind that one day our natural system will collapse, leaving the humanity with acute shortage of adequate food, fresh air and pure drinking water and the greeneries. What we want today is to save our tomorrow through meaningful efforts to balance economic growth and environmental degradation. Efforts should also be made to balance the needs of the rich, who wants to maintain their exorbitant living standards without making any harm to the environment. Unless we cannot, we have no right to hope for a better tomorrow for our children and grand children. There is no second earth to go, when we make our planet uninhabitable. So designing appropriate policies and strategies that will lead to conservation of natural eco-systems and biological diversity and ecologically sustainable development—is not an option but a necessity.

This edited volume entitled, "*Towards a Humane Environment: Responsibilities of State, Role of Civil Society and Rights of Citizens*" is the result of a long felt need to shape some strategies to conserve our nature. This dream was partially materialised through organising a national seminar in my college on this theme. This book is the outcome of the papers presented in the seminar organised by Department of Political Science, NSS College Nilamel on October 2012 which was sponsored by Institute of Parliamentary Affairs, Government of Kerala. We regret that few of the papers are presented here do not cover full text due to non-availability. It should be mentioned here that it was not possible to standardise the various and differing research styles adapted in these papers.

This academic venture is the result of a lot of help extended by a number of individuals and institutions. At the very outset I am thankful to the governors and staff of Institute of Parliamentary Affairs, Government of Kerala for providing financial and other assistance, without which the seminar would not have been materialised. I extent special thanks to Shri Oommen Chandy, Hon'ble Chief Minister of Kerala and President of the Institute and to Dr. T. Varghese, Director General of the Institute. I am greatly indebted to each of the distinguished contributors to this volume who have been very responsive and helpful in making their contributions. The publication of this book would not have been possible without the unstinting help and encouragement provided by the management, Principal, staff and students of NSS College, Nilamel. My heartfelt gratitude is also due to them for their active co-operation and unending support. I am thankful to the participants of the seminar. I am also thankful to Manoj Computers, Kariavattom for typing the manuscript. I must acknowledge the indispensable aid and encouragement of my family and friends. My thanks are due to Kalpaz Publications, Delhi for their efforts to bring out the work in its present form.

R. Rajeevan

Editor's Prologue

Rajeevan R.

June 2013 flash floods, cloudbursts and landslips in Uttarakhand are the latest warning of the Nature. Nature's fury reinforced the fact that preserving the ecosystem and the harmonious balance with human beings cannot be compromised. A tremendous rise in human population integrated with technological advancement creates large scale ecological imbalance leading to serious consequences. The intensity of this crisis gets worsened day by day and will in near future become an overwhelming issue most directly related to the livelihood and survival of earth's flora and fauna including man. Designing appropriate policies and strategies that may lead to conservation of natural ecosystems and biological diversity and ecologically sustainable development is not an option but a necessity now.

The present day world is facing a severe environmental crisis, the magnitude of which extends from village life to the metropolitan capital cities. Nearly two-thirds of the globe's ecosystems are considered degraded as a result of mismanagement of nature and a failure to invest and reinvest in their productivity, health and sustainability. The crisis gets worsened day by day and will in near future become a severe environmental problem. The socio-economic fallout of the environmental crisis has virtually affected people all over the world resulting in wide spread poverty, displacement, loss of livelihood, health hazards, economic disruption, etc. The issue has been put forward and discussed in several platforms as an issue of the safety of the entire planet from local government institutions to UN bodies. Designing appropriate policies and strategies that led to conservation of natural ecosystems and biological diversity and ecologically sustainable development is not an option but an urgent necessity. A wide variety of theories and approaches have sprung up in recent times ranging from deep ecology to free-market environmentalism.

The Environment

Environment has different meaning for different people. The term 'environment' is derived from a French word '*environ*' means to 'encircle' or 'surround' and '*ment*' means 'to act'. So environment is the interaction between man and nature. The Webster's Universal College Dictionary (2000) defines the environment as "the air, water, minerals, organisms and all other external factors surrounding and affecting a given organism at any time." In Oxford Advanced Learners Dictionary, the environment is defined as "natural world in which people, animals and plants live." Einstein has rightly defined environment as "everything that is not me". So environment is the circumstances and conditions that surround an organism or group of organisms or the social and cultural conditions that affect an individual or community.

Environmental studies is highly interdisciplinary in nature. It includes information and knowledge from not only pure sciences like biology, geography or agriculture but also social sciences like economics or political science. It is all inclusive and holistic. It implies that we have a responsibility to be involved in and try to do something about the problems we ourselves have created. The subject deals with various issues such as safe and clean drinking water, hygienic living conditions, clean and fresh air, fertile land, plants, animals, human beings and other organisms and the harmonious interrelationships among themselves. The subject also deals with the behaviour of plants, animals and all flora and fauna in the earth. It also examines human behaviour and management of human societies. The subject also covers the rules and laws framed for environmental protection and management under the jurisdiction of national and international legislation.

Man and His Environment

The nature created the universe with definite laws and principles. Innumerable galaxies, suns, stars, planets, and their satellites are performing their function in accordance with an established order. At every moment, these bodies are changing their angles and positions. New stars are getting created and existing ones are dying. The earth which is the lone supporter of life is only a small planet in its universe. No other star of our galaxy has shown signs of life. This means that the living beings including man have no independent existence outside our mother earth.

Man is believed to appear in the planet barely a million years ago. During thousands of years of his early life, he lived as wanderer, hunter and gatherer of food resources. On those days he was in equal status with the other creations of the nature. He shared everything granted to him by the mother earth with his fellow beings. The mother extends to them air to breath, water to drink and multifarious items to fill her children's stomach and heart. Heavenly conditions are arranged for the flora and fauna on earth. As one of the children of nature, the relationship between man and this environment was so close.

Man's interaction with the environment became pronounced during the Paleolithic period (50 thousand to 1 million years ago) when he gathered the knowledge of fire and tools to bring about change in the environment. During the Neolithic period (10,000 to 6000 BC) man began to domesticate plants and animals. He began to settle in forests and grasslands, converted them to suit his needs and developed agricultural system. Ecosystems were gradually transformed into agricultural fields, human habitats, and permanent villages. Roads and irrigation facilities were constructed in an increasing manner. In this period, attempts were made by man to enslave the nature for his vested interests. During the next two ages, i.e., the Bronze Age (shortly after 3000 BC) and Iron Age (starting 1000 BC), man accelerated the exploitation of environment.

With the dawn of modern age, urbanisation, industrialisation and consequent growth in pollution began to take place. Air and water were polluted and land was degraded. The resources thus were depleted in an increasing manner. As a result of improving health care and development of medicines, population explosion took place. Consequently, the natural systems were stressed beyond their resilient capacity and ultimately are forced to a stage of collapse. All the water ways, rivers, inland and coastal waters are polluted. Forests, grasslands and wetlands have been razed down. All resources of the lithosphere have been mined and used in order to sustain industries and to produce more goods and services.

As a result of over exploitation of nature, the regeneration capacity has been totally reduced. So, man is reaching a stage, when he cannot exploit the resources any more unless he likes and begins to feel his limitations and helplessness. Fuel resources have been mined and used indiscriminately to run the industries. These actions in turn have triggered a series of chain reactions which man is unable to control. The problems arising out of exploitation of natural resources keep human society away from a humane environment.

The alarming increase in human population is the biggest threat that man poses to the environment. The human population is estimated to take 4200 years to reach 1000 million in 1804. Only after 1600 AD, the population growth attained a rapid speed. This trend followed uninterruptedly and on October, 1999 the World Population touched the six billion mark. It increased to 6.3 billion in 2001. It is reported that in the present day world about four to five children are born and two people die in every second. This means that every year the world population increases by 78 millions. It is estimated that this will reach about nine billion by 2050. These people will have to be fed, clothed, housed and supported by gainful employment. Virtually all of the increase will be in the developed countries, where birth rates are still much higher than death rates. In these countries about three billion people are experiencing severe poverty and lack of sufficient resources to meet their basic needs for food, clothing and shelter. Over 800 million-one out of every eight-remain undernourished.

The indiscriminate increase in human population is resulting in, over exploitation of natural resources. Phenomena like depletion of ground water, degradation of soil, over fishing from oceans, felling of trees, etc, are taking place all over the world. A recent report from the United Nations Project entitled 'Pilot Analysis of Global Eco-system' addressed those trends as it examined the status of the five major eco-systems which deliver the goods and services that support human life and economy: coastal/marine systems, fresh water systems, agricultural systems, forest systems and soil systems. The after effects of over exploitation of natural resources like forest, water and land shall be disastrous and make far reaching consequences for the environment.

A close examination of the culture and civilisation of human beings reveals the strong interrelationship between man and nature. In the past, everywhere in the world human beings extended love, respect and worship to nature. But modern man's environmental perception has been altogether a different one. His rational behaviour towards the environment and the society changes with the change in modern thought, attitude and culture. For humans involved in socio-economic revolutions, the natural environment is a source of whatever he can take. In order to meet rising demands of the people to raise their standard of living, and finally to enhance the power, mankind is engaged in a programme of self-defeat.

The Environmental Crisis Today

The genesis of environmental problems can be traced to the life styles and developmental processes of man specifically during the industrial revolution, started in the North and extended to the whole world. This revolution created the modern world with its world-wide commerce, factories, large cities and pollution. The industrial revolution and its technical marvels were energised by fossil fuels. Population increase and exploitation of natural resources took on new dimensions as the industrial world turned to the extraction of raw materials from all over the world.

The mounting demands of ever increasing population and rapid industrialisation led to the large scale replacement of natural systems by the human systems. The major crisis of the world today is the fast declining of natural resources. Nearly two-thirds of the globe's ecosystems are considered degraded as a result of mismanagement of the nature and a failure of invest and reinvest in their productivity, health and sustainability.

Together with these issues, the modern concept of development, which poses serious ecological and related problems such as the pollution of air and water, exhaustion of non renewable resources, poor management of the soil, displacement of forests and water resources, unbridled consumption of fossil fuels, global drying and rising salt pollution, problems related to the production and consumption of nuclear energy, uncontrolled urbanisation, the relegation of rural population to a marginal position, the increasing hold of multinational corporations and the crushing effects of globalisation through the destruction of traditional civilisation and culture. The issues of climate change, global warming, acid rains, ozone layer depletion, nuclear accidents and holocaust are serious issues which would upset the environmental balance with catastrophic consequences.

Green house effect is closely connected with the dangerous environmental phenomena like climate change, global warming, acid rains, ozone layer depletion, etc. As a result of increasing human population and impact of its activities on natural resources, earth's environment has been undergoing significant changes, especially during the 20th century. One of the most significant changes brought about by human activities is an increase in the concentration of carbon dioxide and other green house gases in the atmosphere. The Citizen's Fifth Report of

Centre for Science and Environment (1999), New Delhi revealed that the emission of carbon dioxide (CO_2) has been held as the most dangerous and most significant greenhouse gas emission causing global warming. The common greenhouse gases which cause global warming are carbon dioxide (CO_2), Methane (CH_4), Chlorofluorocarbon (CFC), nitrous oxide (N_2O), and Ozone (O_3). CO_2 are responsible for about half the global warming, other pollutants and other greenhouse gases account for the rest.

Global warming is the result of 'Green House Effects' created by greenhouse gases. Sunlight warms the earth's surface during day time and earth's surface radiates heat back to the space. Certain gases in the atmosphere absorb this radiant energy and re-emit the heat back to the earth. Those gases which are capable of absorbing and re-emitting the heat radiation are called green house gases. The heat from the surface of the earth warms up the greenhouse gases. These gases in turn emit some heat into the space and some back down to the surface. This fraction of the heat provides global warming in addition to the sun's direct heat. Without any green house gases in the atmosphere, the average gases radiate sufficient heat back to earth to give an average global temperature.

The global temperature has risen by only 4°C over the last 18000 years, but because of rapid industrialisation, it has increased by about 0.5-1°C since the last century. The rate of global warming during the past quarter century was greater than any previous period since 1880. During the late 1980s scientists began to suggest that the earth's energy flux was no longer in balance. Earth's surface was getting warmer, affecting the elements of the climate system. By 1995, it became evident that the main culprit was carbon dioxide emissions produced by the burning of fossil fuels-coal, gas and oil in factories, power stations and motor vehicles. When we burn coal, firewood and natural gas, huge amount of carbon dioxide escapes to the atmosphere.

The annual carbon dioxide emission from burning fossil fuels has been rising in recent years. The recent pace at which carbon dioxide levels has been rising to reach 400 ppm (Eight billion tonnes of CO_2 in the atmosphere equals 1 ppm). It is predicted that by 2030, CO_2 concentration will reach about 600ppm and average global temperature will rise by 1.5-4.5^oC. It is argued that as we reach 400 ppm and beyond, we are going farther away from safe levels of CO_2. Leading climate scientist James Hansen and others wrote that "if humanity wishes to preserve a planet similar to that on which civilisation developed and to which life on Earth is adopted... Carbon dioxide will need to be reduced... to at most 350 ppm, but likely less than that." ("Target Atmosphere CO_2: Where should Humanity Aim?" The Open Atmospheric Science Journal, 2008, 2, pp. 217-31). This paper provides the intellectual basis for the world wide campaign to reduce CO_2, headed by the organisation, 350 org. (Nagraj Adve, "*A Race Towards Climate Catastrophe*", *The Hindu*, Thiruvananthapuram, June 4, 2013).

Global warming will affect rainfall pattern. India witnessed an increase in rainfall by five per cent in summer and up to 15 per cent in winter. In Uttarakhand the powerful rain have killed about 300 people, damaged temple towns, and washed away almost all roads and 21 bridges in June, 2013. The level of sea water would rise by 20-140 cm in various parts of the world due to global warming. By the close of the 20th century sea levels have already risen by about 30 cm. A rise in sea level will hit the lower coastal regions of the world. Sure, low lying countries like Bangladesh, Maldives, etc., may be wiped out of the map. But this is not going to be spared. In 2005, hurricane Katrina killed thousands in the city of New Orleans in the U.S. Its devastation was likely accentuated by the loss of nearby wet lands which would have absorbed much of the storm's energy. In 2003, an unprecedented heat wave across Europe killed more than 50,000 people. Super hurricanes and cyclones are expected to become more common as the oceans warm up.

Ice and snow caps on mountains will melt as a result of global warming. Glaciers, considered as the thermometer of global warming, will undergo a big melt-down which would be difficult to track. According to R.K. Pachauri, Chairman of the

Energy and Resource Institute and Director General of the Intergovernmental Panel on Climate Change, "any evidence that glaciers are melting is a warning bell. We are seeing the phenomenon across the globe - the Arctics, the Andes, the Alps and now the Himalayas. It is likely to severely alter India's fresh water balance and to have adverse impact on food and energy production." (S.P. Misra and S.N. Pandey (2009) *"Essential Environmental Studies,"* New Delhi, Ane Books Pvt. Ltd, p. 567). IPCC's own evaluation predicts that average world temperature would rise by 1.4°C to 5.8°C by the end of this century. Such a rise would upset the environmental balance with catastrophic consequences.

The climatic changes affected the whole flora and fauna on earth. It is reported that spring flowers are blooming earlier than usual, at a time when their pollinators are not around. Migration patterns of birds and animals are changing. Tropical fish from the Caribbean islands are being sighted off the coast of England. Drought is hitting areas which have never experienced it and as a consequence animals are fast losing their traditional feeding grounds. Drought stricken forests are burning down, which is doubly harmful because forests are natural carbon sinkers. (Vasant Natarajan, "Be Warned! It's climate Weirding", *The Hindu*, Thiruvananthapuram, June 16, 2013).

As a result of this continuous increase in levels of green house gases, earth has been suffering from fever, and affect the whole flora and fauna on earth. This will affect the crop yield, cropping pattern, insect pests and diseases and the whole socio-economic systems. The influence of interaction of rising carbon dioxide and temperature with toxic air pollutants has become one of the prime issues threatening the sustainability of world's environment.

The rich industrialised countries of the North are mainly responsible for the crisis. They account for about seven out of every ten tonnes of CO_2 that have been emitted since the start of the industrial era. With just 15 per cent of the world population they account for 45 per cent of CO_2 emissions.

Developing countries, which are only in the way of industrialisation contributes comparatively low quantity of CO_2. In 1990 out of the 21 billion tonnes of global emissions, 14 billion tonnes were emitted by rich developed countries, home to only 1/5 of the world's population. Of these 14 billion tonnes, the US alone contributed five billion tons of carbon. India emits 159 million metric tons of carbon, which is only 10 per cent of the US emissions.

It is a reality that the world is going to face a catastrophe if it continues to emit green house gases in this proportion. Here global cooperation is the lone answer, while seeking solution to global warming issues. Global efforts have been made on these lines to solve the issue.

The environmental issue was first seriously discussed in the U.N. Conference on Human Environment held in Stockholm in June, 1972. The Conference resulted in the establishment of United Nations Environment Programme (UNEP). It also opened a platform of debate between rich and poor countries with their different perceptions of environmental properties. But the United States for its part, sought to derail the entire enterprise at several critical junctures by asserting its sovereignty, challenging any effort that could curb its economic growth. (Margaret P. Karns and Karen A. Mingst (2005) *International Organisations: The Politics and Processes of Global Governance*, New Delhi, viva p. 465).

The UN Conference on Environment and Development (The Earth Summit) held in June, 1992 in Rio de Janeiro, Brazil produced 'Agenda 21' trumpeted as "a plan of action to save the planet" (Jeffrey Haynes (2005) "Comparative Politics in a Globalised World", Polity, Cambridge, p. 160) and endorsed by representatives of all countries present. The notable feature of the conference was the establishment of important linkages between environment and development. It framed two international conventions on biodiversity and climate change. The conference led indirectly to the linkage of trade and environment in the WTO and to the 'greening' of the World Bank's Programme. (Margaret P. Karns and Karen A. Mingst, op.cit., p. 467) As it is in the Stockholm Conference, the United States followed a negative approach towards the Rio Declaration. The European countries, on the other hand, have far more been amenable and several countries have already met targets set for reduction of greenhouse gases. The talk initiated at the World Climate Conference in Geneva in 1979 to fight climatic change is in hanging fire. The Kyoto protocol in 1997 is for all practical purposes, a dead letter, which requested industrialised nations to specify legally binding targets for emission of six green house gases by seven per cent below 1990 between 2008 and 2012. Here also United States do not want to sign-up to ratify the Kyoto Protocol agreement on reductions. In a meeting the then US President George W. Bush said, 'we do not agree on the Kyoto treaty, but we do agree that climatic change is a serious issue and we must work together.'

The shaping of Asia-Pacific Partnership on Clean Development and Climate (APPCDC) in July 2005 pressurised United States to change its approach towards the issue. The pact signed by six nations – India, China, Australia, South Korea, Japan and United States representing 48 per cent of the World's Green House Gases emissions, attempted to create a voluntary non-legally binding framework for International co-operation on the transfer of technology to reduce GHG emissions. Though no agreements were signed, the meeting attracted a lot of international attention.

Though White House remained firm on its denial policy to cut emissions, the California state of USA passed the California Global Warming Solutions Act, 2006 for cutting GHG emissions to 1990 levels, which gave impetus to four other western states – Arizona, New Mexico, Oregon and Washington to promote clean energy. The moves of the state governments resulted in the framing of the US Climate Bill that aimed to cut industrial emissions by 20 per cent below 2005 levels by 2020, which had failed to muster majority support in the Senate. The US government's another move to push a modified bill (to reduce emission target to 17 per cent) also failed in the US Senate in April 2010.

The Rio+20: United Nations Conference on Sustainable Development held in Rio-de-Janeiro in June, 2012 was the latest international attempt to move the world green and sustainable. A key theme that dominated the Rio+20, is the so called Green Economy. It is a concept that has neither general acceptability nor academic acceptance. The United Nations Environment Programme (UNEP) clarified Green Economy "as one whose growth in income and employment is driven by public and private investments that reduce carbon emission and pollution, enhance energy and resource efficiency, and prevent the loss of bio diversity and eco-system services. (T. Jayaraman, Divya Singh Kohli, Sruti Mittal "Rio+20: What is at stake?" *Economic and Political Weekly*, Vol. XLVII, No. 23, June 9, 2012, pp. 10-13). The fact remains that any estimate of the net benefits of a green economy must include the impact of consumption of resources and environmental pollution. A major concern with the green economy language for developing countries include the fear that it will open the door to 'green' trade barriers and protectionism, while there would also be interference with domestic policies that take into account national circumstances such as subsidies for the poor in relation to fuel energy and bio resources.

It is a fact that in their search for sustainability, the developed countries look for solutions in terms that dictate to and impose on the rest of the world which would primarily safeguard their interests and which would offer little concession to the global south, especially the major developing economics. The growing globalisation of society might make the task of co-operation between the rich and the poor even more difficult because with globalisation, the rich have greater freedom to exploit the poor. The continuing ambiguity and lack of any meaningful solution on how developed nations proposed to fund green technologies and programmes of developing and poor countries was a major failure of Rio + 20 summit. The conspicuous absence of the two leaders of the first world nations, US President Barack Obama and German Chancellor Angela Merkal added to the confusion.

The fact remains that in principle US supports the extension of international environmental responsibilities, in practice it has often emerged as a major obstacle to global environmental agreements. An instance is that under the Kyoto agreement the European Union has agreed to cut green house gas emission by eight per cent while Britain has promised for a 12.5 per cent reduction but the U.S., the world's largest polluter, has rejected the agreement. It is often remarked that the U.S. government is unwilling to sign up to the central obligations because of domestic pressures to resist new environmental standards. It is observed that the Bush administration's environmental policy was strongly responsive to the preferences of its business supporters. It is also argued that Washington has refused to follow the Kyoto protocol and other green initiatives, fearing its citizens would never agree to reduce their consumption levels through compromising their luxurious life. What we want here for a humane environment is to find a balance to the needs of the rich, who wants to maintain their exorbitant living standards, and that of the poor, who wants to improve their abysmal living conditions.

It is a truth that United States of America supports the extension of international environmental responsibilities in principle but in practice the U.S. government is unwilling to sign up to the central obligations of environmental agreements. The U.S. stand is because of domestic pressure to resist new environmental standards. It is natural that business corporates are exerting a big pressure upon the U.S. government to do so. But at the same time the USA and the rich North can do a lot with in their limits. The rich and powerful nations like USA with their huge funds for research and development shaped a lot of green technologies which could be transferred to the poor and developing countries to reduce the emissions of green houses gases. The large quantity of carbon dioxide is emitted by these poor countries are mainly due to their outdated technology. New technologies can be implemented in these nations only if the rich nations share their responsibilities by recognizing that they are primarily to blame for the present environmental degradation.

To conclude every one must keep in mind that one day our natural system will collapse leaving humanity with acute shortage of adequate food, pure drinking water, fresh air or the beautiful greeneries. What we want today to save tomorrow's earth is meaningful efforts to balance development and environment. Unless we cannot do so, we have no right to hope for a better tomorrow of our children and grand children. There is no second earth to go when we make our planet uninhabitable. So designing appropriate policies and strategies that lead to conservation of natural eco-system and biological diversity and ecologically sustainable development is not an option but a necessity.

The present work is the result of a long felt need to shape some strategies to conserve our nature, which was partially materialised through organising a national seminar in my college on the theme *"Towards a Humane Environment : Responsibilities of State, Role of Civil Society and Rights of Citizens"*, with the financial assistance of Institute of Parliamentary Affairs, Government of Kerala. The book is the outcome of the papers presented in the Seminar. The 17 papers published in the volume present different issues and view points on environmental problems. All the papers presented at the seminar were later revised and edited in the light of the discussions that took place following the presentation.

Dr. T.V. Muralivallabhan in his paper *"Science and Spirituality in the Study of Environment and Development"* attempts to highlight the relationship between science, spirituality and development. He opines that most modern researches in science and technology are aimed at developing Green Technology or eco-friendly technology for solving the problems of the depletion of resources and degradation of environment. Moreover there are efforts from the Social, Political and Economic institutions to enact environmental laws and green policies of development. But still environmental problems are assuming the proportion of crisis. Therefore environmental experts are exploring the possibility of incorporating the moral principles, ethical practices, religious beliefs and spiritual values into the preventive and curative aspects of attaining sustainable development along with science, technology, politics and laws.

Sri Peethambara Kurup in his article *"Environmental Degradation - Beyond the Limits"* maintains that conservation of nature and natural resources is not solely the responsibility of the state but that of the civil society and the individuals. They are bound to protect it and hand it over to the future generations for their good life. As a staunch Gandhian and an able Parliamentarian, this environmental activist argued that Gandhian way of life is the lone solution of our present day ecological crisis. He believes that many of the Gandhian ideas can be profitably utilised for the betterment of our environment.

The best interests of our common future can be secured only by ensuring a harmonious linkage between traditional know-how and their modern application, argues Dr. M. Rajesh in his paper entitled *"Traditional Knowledge, Intellectual Property Rights and Livelihood Sustainability"*. He stood for sovereign states' rights over their bio-resources and any use of these resources by third parties should be based on prior information and consent. He points out the need and necessity to respect and preserve the knowledge, innovations and practices of traditional communities. The conservation and application of such knowledge may also be promoted with the active involvement of such communities.

The paper *"From Skepticism to Trepidation : A Study on How the Social Media Youth Perceive the Mullaperiyar Dam Issue"* jointly written by Titto Varghese, Dr. D. Nivedhitha and Dr Santhosh Mathew Vernani makes a content analysis of the posts and comments made in face book – a social networking site – by the youth on Mulla Periyar Dam issue. The authors went through the two opinions regarding the reconstruction of a new Dam because one party is skeptical of the strength of the existing Dam whereas the other doesn't have any doubt at all that the Dam will be safe for another 100 years. The first party is afraid of because if something happens to the Dam almost four districts of the state will be completely lost with its bio-diversity. The problem which started at the administrative level came down to be a political issue and again reached as a common man's emotional issue. Media also played their role in making the issue a burning one. The authors give a picture of the discussions which started in the traditional media, went up to the New media and how it reached the social media platforms giving it a fearful and life threatening face to it.

Dr. P. Sivadasan makes an important contribution in finding out the historical elements in the evolution of public spaces together with environmental concerns through his paper *"A Public Space in the Urban Environment: The case of Mananchira Maidanam in Kozhikkode"*. This paper discusses the evolution of public areas as a site of secular social interaction where people can get together and freely discuss and identify societal problems. The paper very interestingly discusses the historical evolution of this public space as the centre of art, literature and socio-political reformation of Malabar.

Dr. Abraham Mathew in his paper *"The Waste Management and Environmental Protection: A Concern for Human Existence"* makes a critical analysis of the inefficient and insufficient waste management system of Kerala. He has no hesitation to express the truth that if things are going to continue like this, Kerala will become the centre of all types of deadly diseases. He provides an alternative model of waste management programme by the government through collaborating Panchayati Raj Institutions with the effective involvement of civil society. He was confident that controversial matters can be amicably settled through the active co-operation and good will of the civil society and the government.

Dr. Rajan, T through his paper *"Triggering the Environment: A Lesson from Kureepuzha"* also discusses the problems of waste management. He revealed people's agitation over the question of spillage of waste by the Kollam Municipal Corporation (Kerala) in a place adjacent to a dwelling place. The paper gives an impressive narration of how the people of the locality formed an association named "Manushyavakasha Paristhithi Samrakshna Samithi" (Human Right Environment Protection Forum) and how their agitation helped them to escape from a severe health problem.

The article by Dr. Manju Nair deals with the inter linkages between health, environment and sustainable development in the paper entitled *"Traditional Environmental Health Hazards and the Scope for Policy Intervention: The Case of National Rural Health Mission in an Island Community"*. The paper examines the traditional environmental health hazards faced by people of an island in Kadamakudy Grama Panchayat and the role of NRHM as an intervention mechanism in ameliorating the health hazards. She identified deficiency of proper sanitation facilities, inadequate accessibility to safe drinking water and inaccessibility to medical services due to lack of transport facilities as the major environmental health hazards faced by the people of the island.

In his paper *"Development and Conservation with Special Reference to Wetlands"*, Dr. Unnikrishnan examines the ruthless conversion of wetlands for non agricultural purposes, which causes unaccountable damage to environment. To him the wetlands which are the eco-tones or transitional zones that occupy an intermediate position between dry land and open water, are the kidneys of nature. They remove or retain the sediments and excess nutrients in water. He identifies some major threats to this eco-system, which are reclamation and construction activities, pollution from sewage and industrial effluents, pollution by chemical fertilizers, herbicides and pesticides, unscientific tourism activities and plastic pollution, that pose major threats on the life of organisms like amphibian, reptiles, mammals, molluscs and thousands of other minor organisms.

Dr. Maneesh, B in his article *"Cropping Pattern Changes: A Threat to Sustainable Development"* shows the environmental issues of cropping pattern changes in Kerala, i.e., from food crops to cash crops. To him large areas of paddy land in the state has been diverted either to cash crops or to non agricultural purposes such as sites for construction of buildings or other infrastructural facilities like roads, railways or canals. To him the shift in cropping patterns from food crops to cash crops and also the shift from eco-friendly subsistence farming to profit-induced cultivation using chemical fertilizers and poisonous pesticides have accelerated the pace of bio-diversity loss, which will result in an acute shortage of drinking water, falling water tables, soil erosion and climate changes.

The article *"Eco feminism - The Role of Women in Environmental Management and Conservation"* brings out the role of rural women in conserving their environment. The writer V. Kala Devi remarks that women are more responsible to nature on which they depend for domestic food production. When women, who promote a non-monetised bio mass based subsistence economy of the household, get subjugated by men and thus the environmental degradation takes place. Man's dominance over women in turn results in his dominance over nature and natural resources. Also, as women are directly affected by environmental degradation, deforestation, pollution and over population, they are more concerned about environmental problems. Next, the author gives an account of the ecological movements initiated by women. The paper concludes with the recommendation that environmental education should be imparted to the rustics. Also women should be mobilised to participate actively in protecting and enriching the natural resources. Dr. Yamuna. D.S., in her paper *"Ecological Discourses on Thiruvathira"* examines the relations between man and nature in the folk festival of Thiruvathira. The author details how the entire biotic and abotic forms take part in celebrations. The pond, the season, the flora and fauna are found to be deeply influencing human living and have a role to play in their rejoicing. The games, dance and songs associated with the festival too precipitate a collective consciousness that has successfully comprehended the interconnection between natural phenomena and the human world.

Geetha, R. Nair's paper titled *"Physico-Chemical Characteristics of Water Sample From Parvathi Puthanar Canal in Thiruvananthapuram District, Kerala"* analyses the quality deterioration of water bodies of Kerala in the light of her experiments done in the water sample collected from two different locations of Parvathi Puthanar canal Thiruvananthapuram, Kerala. Her study provides that water qualities in the upstream stretches of water bodies of Kerala are generally good and potable, the quality deteriorates as the water bodies transverse through the thickly populated low land areas. Her analysis also shows high calcium content in the canal during summer and low, during monsoon.

In their paper *"Indoor Gamma Dose in the South West Coast of Kerala,"* Rani K. Pillai, Ben Byju, S, Arunima, S, Lekshmi, R, Vishnu Prasad, K. and Dr. P.J. Jijo reveal the fact that high background radiation levels are found in many parts of the world including South West Coastal regions of Kerala. This higher concentration is due to the presence of primordial radio-active nuclides in soil. Their study also reveals that indoor doses are found to vary with the nature of flooring materials used.

Dr. K.C. Sreekumar makes an important contribution in his paper *"Dimensions of Global Environmental Politics."* He described environmental degradation as a great challenge to the modern world. The prevailing development techniques create large scale ecological imbalance leading to serious problems related to the livelihood and survival of life on earth. In the paper he is trying to answer a few pertinent questions: How and when did environmental issues assume significance? What are the major global environmental issues? What are the measures adopted by different nations to solve the problem? What are the political dimensions of environmental agreements? He observes the trajectory of the global environmental politics as the result of the North-South divide politics and suggests that every nation, irrespective of it is being developed or developing has to know that it is going through a decisive moment in the history of humanity and that it needs to change itself before it can transform the world.

Dealing with the environmental issues in India, Dr. Rajeevan R. discusses the past, present and future of environmental conditions of India in his paper "Environmentalism in India: Issues and Initiatives". He deals with the causes and results of environmental pollution in India with special emphasis to Uttarakhand tragedy and indoor air pollution by biomass fuels. The article also goes through the initiatives made by India inside and outside the state for preventing environmental degradation. The article concludes with a strong warning that one day our natural system will collapse, leaving the humanity with acute shortage of adequate food, water and oxygen and the greeneries. There is no second earth to go when we make our planet uninhabitable. So designing appropriate policies and strategies that led to conservation of natural ecosystem and biological diversity and ecologically sustainable development is not an option but a necessity.

Dr. G. Balanchandran and Dr. Hameema in their paper entitled *"Sustainable Environment – Rights of the Citizens and Role of the Court"* beautifully narrate the nature as the perennial sustainable source of man's mental, physical, intellectual, moral, spiritual and social development. But over the years environmental pollution has been rampant. Man who ought to be the saviour has turned to be destructive cancer of nature. The authors remind us that "all is not lost; there is yet ample time and means to preserve our environs". They suggest that the primary step is to create public awareness and adopt important participatory legal methods. There are environmental Acts, environmental protection movements and public interest litigation which are the silver linings in the cloud of environmental pollution in India.

List of Contributors

1. **T.V. Murali Vallabhan:** Principal, SVR NSS College, Vazhoor (Mahatma Gandhi University), Kerala.
2. **N. Peethambara Kurup, M.P.**: Lok Sabha Member, Kollam, Kerala.
3. **M. Rajesh:** Regional Director, Indira Gandhi National Open University Regional Centre, Mumbai.
4. **D. Nivedhitha:** Professor, Department of Mass Communication and Electronic Media, Pondicherry University.
5. **Santhosh Mathew Veranani:** Associate Professor, Department of South Asian Studies, Pondicherry University.
6. **Titto Varghese:** Ph.D. Research Scholar, Department of Mass Communication and Electronic Media, Pondicherry University.
7. **P. Sivadasan:** Associate Professor, Department of History, University of Calicut, Kerala.
8. **Abraham Mathew:** Associate Professor and Head, Department of Political Science and Public Administration, St. John's College, Anchal, Kerala.
9. **Rajan T:** Associate Professor in Political Science, University College, Thiruvananthapuram, Kerala.
10. **Manju S. Nair:** Associate Professor, Department of Economics, University of Kerala.

11. **N. Unnikrishnan:** Associate Professor, SVR NSS College, Vazhoor, Kerala.

12. **Maneesh B:** Assistant Professor, Department of Economics, NSS College, Nilamel, Kerala.

13. **Kala Devi V:** Assistant Professor, PG Department of Environmental Sciences, St. John's College, Anchal, Kollam, Kerala.

14. **Yamuna D.S.** Assistant Professor, Department of English, Government College, Attingal, Kerala.

15. **Geetha R. Nair:** Assistant Professor, Department of Post Graduate Studies and Research in Botany, Mahatma Gandhi College, Thiruvananthapuram, Kerala.

16. **Rani K. Pillai:** Assistant Professor, Department of Physics, NSS College, Nilamel.

17. **P.J. Jijo, Ben Byju, S., Arunima S., Lekshmi R., Vishnu Prasad A.K.:** Centre for Advanced Research in Physical Sciences, Department of Physics, Fathima Matha National College, Kollam, Kerala.

18. **K.C. Sreekumar:** Visiting Fellow, Department of Politics and International Relations, M.G. University, Kottayam, Kerala.

19. **Rajeevan R.**, Associate Professor, Department of Political Science, NSS College, Nilamel, Kerala.

20. **G. Balachandran:** Assistant Professor, Government Law College, Thiruvananthapuram.

21. **Hameema M:** Assistant Professor, Government Law College, Thiruvananthapuram, Kerala.

1

Science and Spirituality in the Study of Environment and Development

T.V. Muralivallabhan

Abstract

Revolution in Science and Technology led to the revolution in industries, agriculture and the service sector. The inventions in S & T took the form of innovations in these sectors. But the consequent leaps in the economy in the form of development resulted in the destruction of the environment. Thus protection of environment while promoting development has become the core issue of modern development.

Most modern researches in S & T are aimed at developing Green Technology or Eco-friendly technology for solving the problems of the depletion of resources and degradation of environment. Moreover, there are efforts from the social, political and economic institutions to enact environmental laws and green policies of development. But still, environmental problems are assuming the proportion of a crisis. Therefore, environmental experts are exploring the possibility of incorporating the moral principles, ethical practices, religious beliefs and spiritual values into the preventive and curative aspects of attaining sustainable development (protection of environment and promotion of development) along with science, technology, policies and laws. This paper is an attempt to highlight the relationship between science, spirituality and development.

Key Words

Science, Spirituality, Environment and Development.

Introduction

Development

Development does not mean mere growth or advancement. It is a multidimensional concept which includes quantitative as well as qualitative positive changes. Development involves the natural growth due to natural instincts under natural conditions. Nature has a significant role in determining the pace of development in course of time.

Development is a term that is very popular in the subject of Economics. It is quite often used to denote the changes that are taking place in the developing nations of the world. The developed countries have already attained a particular stage of economic growth after having accomplished the various stages and processes of economic development. Their only concern is to maintain the already attained higher level of economic growth, high level of standard of living and the associated comforts and luxuries of life. The developing nations are accelerating their pace of development (which includes social-political-cultural and economical changes) to attain the status of developed countries. In this attempt, they seek the support of modern science and technology. Primary (agriculture), secondary (industry) and tertiary (service and infrastructure) sectors have undergone radical changes in the developing countries.

Environment

"The term 'environment' includes water, air, land and the inter-relationship that exists among and between water, air, land, human beings and other living creatures, plants, micro organisms and property".[1] So environment is a broader concept encompassing not only one habitat and its surroundings, but all habitats and all surroundings. For example, when the habitat of a pond in relation to its surrounding is studied, it is pond ecology and when the study is about the sea, it is marine ecology. The study of environment encompasses the study of many ecosystems. Also, it encompasses, along with the biotic relationships, the social, political, cultural, religious, economic and philosophical aspects of human life.

Hence environment is a broader term which includes the aggregate of surrounding things, conditions and influences. It is the total or the aggregate or the whole around which the process of ecosystems works.

Environment is the area in which everything lives, i.e., the house of human beings, the house of fauna and in the same way, the house of flora. Individually all the houses are the integrated parts of the 'one palatial house', i.e., the biosphere. This one house has its close contact with atmosphere, hydrosphere and lithosphere itself, on which it is resting. The house and its other sub-houses are being affected by all these spheres; rather the very existence depends upon these..... Thus, environment is an envelope in which every house is safe and intact, every house regulates its activity individually and collectively, affecting each other, being the integral part of the environment.[2]

Traditional Theories of Development

In the earlier societies, private property was justified only if it contributed to the welfare of the society. From this participatory position, economics gradually became more of a personal affair, utilizing the wealth for the benefits of the individual by way of accumulating profits. According to Fritjo Capra, it was with the scientific revolution that the enlightenment, critical reasoning, empiricism and individualism became the dominant values of the society. Then, the previous social dimension of economics was replaced by secular and materialistic orientation that led to the large-scale production of worldly goods and luxuries. This shift in emphasis at the end of the middle ages led to emergence of Capitalism in the 16th and 17th centuries. During that period, new values of individualism, property rights and representative governments became dominant in the society. By the time of the Mercantilists, the ancient notion of economics as the management of the household was extended to the level of the state-management of the economy of a nation as a whole. This extension of the notion of economics from the household level to the national level gave birth to the concept of 'Political Economy'. The treatment of the subject matter of economics was here descriptive and qualitative.

The traditional economics took into consideration only the scale of operations of individual producers and consumers. They considered these operations too small to exert any pressure on the natural environment. Adam Smith, David Ricardo and Thomas Robert Malthus were fully conscious of the natural limits to growth. While Smith predicted that economic progress would eventually come to an end, when the wealth of nations have (sic) been pushed to the natural limits of soil and climate, he felt that this point would be, too far, to worry about.

Adam Smith was a moral philosopher and his first book was on Ethics (*The Theory of Moral Sentiments*). From Ethics he reached economics and believed that social good is the sum of individual wants and that the market would automatically guide individual behaviour to common good. Therefore Smith's model was atomistic and mechanistic.

Ricardo and Malthus were worried about the ever-growing population and diminishing returns from the expanding scale of cultivation. Still they believed in the magic of technological progress to offset the diminishing returns. It was from the moral philosophy that the separate discipline of economics emerged in the 18th century. Then economics was deeply concerned with how individual pursuits affected larger social goals. But industrialisation succeeded in the wholesale harnessing of fossil-fuels into wealth which could create a hope that, union of science and technology would lead to the mastery of nature and thus an age of plenty.

The labour theory of value which attributed the entire value of a commodity to human labour also did not take into consideration of the role of natural resources and environmental factors in development. But Karl Marx who made labour theory the central idea of his Das Kapital had recognised the profound role of nature in development. In his Economic and Philosophic Manuscript (1844) he remarked, ".... the worker can create nothing without nature, without the sensuous external world. It is the material on which his labour is manifested, in which it is active, from which and by means of which, it produces."[3]

The Neo-classical economists were concerned only about the value in use and value in exchange. According to them, market price represents only the security price and it is unrelated to the use value of a thing. Natural resources like air, water, etc. were treated as 'free goods' which are outside the realm of economics, having no economic value or price. But now due to over exploitation, they are becoming more scarce goods than free goods.

Thomas Prugh deals with four cardinal points with regard to the ideas of Neo-classical tradition in treating the Environmental factor in economic activity.[4]

1. Environment is considered only a factor for economic production — a part of economy, not as economy as a part of environment. Hence economics is more important than environment.
2. There can be unlimited substitution for nature and natural capital with human made capital. Even the Nobel Laureate in Economics, Robert Solow, went to the extent of saying that, the world could in effect, get along without natural resources.
3. The doctrine of infinite substitutability leads naturally to the rejection of any limits on growth. Hence unceasing growth is believed to be the only solution to poverty and environmental degradation. In the 150th anniversary issue of the 'Economist' which speculated about the world economy over the next 150 years, conservative economist C Fred Bergsen predicted that

the standard of living would rise sharply almost everywhere, even as the global population would rise to between 12 billion and 15 billion. As technology continues to expand exponentially and virtually all regions will adopt the policy reforms that began to proliferate in the 20th century, and continued economic growth and population expansion are taken as merely the logical extrapolation of past trends.

4. It is also believed by neoclassical economists that the general good is promoted only through market and as individuals people can increase their welfare. Interactions, interrelationship, interdependence in community and the non-economic relations can be ignored while attaining human welfare.

The Keynesian model is also inappropriate in the sense that it concentrates on the domestic economics, neglecting the global aspects of economics. The globalisation combined with international institutions and agreements, multinational corporations, interrelated political conditions etc; make the Keynesian model inadequate and inappropriate in meeting social and environmental objectives of modern period. The Post Keynesians who advocated the Supply-Side Economics argue that supply of commodities should be stimulated "by investing more in factories and automation and by removing unproductive environmental controls. This approach is manifestly anti-ecological, likely to result in rapid exploitation of natural resources and is bound to aggravate our problems.[5]

In the 1950's, the theories of development treated environmental factors as externalities and gave importance to current consumption rather than resource conservation. While the economic theorists have been bypassing the ecological issues, the policy makers were busy in 'socialising' the costs of ecological protection created by private firms in their attempt to maximise profit. It needs to be noted that the so-called efficiency in production and the consequent profit to the private firms were at the expense of terrible ecological costs which were to be met by the society.

The Cost of Modern Development

A vicious circle of advertisement, demand, consumption and production which emerged in the era of industrialisation reached its zenith during the modern age. Also, an 'opening shortly' culture which demands a 'get ready' position from the consumers for consumption is the hallmark of the industrial development. These tendencies characterised the negative trend of man nature relationship.

Vicious Influences of Industrial Age Advertisement

Profit Demand

Production Consumption

The demand induced by advertisements further increases consumption and consequently production also is to be increased to meet the increased consumption level. As a result of increased production, the profit level also increases which in its turn encourages the producers to spend more on advertisement. Moreover, with the emergence of modern mass media, novel methods and designs of advertisements which are aimed at influencing consumers, reach the level of billions of dollars in the budgets of companies. Hence mechanisation of production, mechanism of advertisement and multiplication of wants have resulted in the wanton destruction of natural resources and disturbance of natural, ecological and environmental balance.

In the recorded human history, the period of great transition includes the Industrial Revolution, which encompasses roughly the last two hundred years and the next two hundred years. Many of the aspects of the Industrial Revolution are mostly contained within the second half of the twentieth century-the half-century of rapid and worldwide transition. The earlier period of this great transition is called the preparatory period and the later period is known as the aftermath or consolidation period.

The four important changes that took place during the period of great transition are:

(1) Demographic changes,
(2) Production pattern changes,
(3) Consumption pattern changes and
(4) Environmental changes.

These four changes had a tremendous impact on the ecology and environment of the world as a whole. The impact in its turn brought about radical changes in the political, economic, social, cultural and scientific approaches in the present century. The emergence of Ecological and Environmental problems can be traced to these changes.

From Problems to Crises

A problem is one for which we can find some solution but for a crisis, it is very difficult to find a solution. Ecological and Environmental problems are slowly becoming crises due to population growth pattern, production pattern and consumption pattern.

Biologists often apply the concept of carrying capacity, to questions of population pressure on environment. Carrying capacity is the largest number of any given species that a habitat can support indefinitely. The famous American wildlife conservation ecologist Aldo Leopold described carrying capacity in 1933 as a saturation point at which the numbers of a particular species of grazing animals approached the point where grasslands could support no more individuals. The size of population, the production pattern and the consumption pattern are the three important factors that forced mankind to surpass the Planet's carrying capacity. "The roots of environmental damage run deep. Unless they are unearthed soon, we risk exceeding the Planet's carrying capacity to such a degree that a future of economic and social decline will be impossible to avoid".[6] Climate change, global warming, ozone depletion, deforestation, desertification and pollution are destroying the nature beyond repair.

Science, Technology and Development

Seeking Truth is Science. It is an enquiry of the human mind that could be traced to over thousands of years. Searching the Truth in the external world and bodies with the stipulated methods is the Physical Science and the dynamics of framing the society to accommodate the theories and inventions of Physical sciences is the content of social sciences. But the scientific inventions and social innovations are only able to provide the material requisites of well being, not the eternal and sustainable requirements of welfare. Modern Science and the result of its research and application-technology are at the root of all modern development. From the invention of the wheel to the Nanotechnology, the impact is well documented and experienced.

Modern science, in its content and appearance is western. The physical science has often alienated itself from the moral and metaphysical aspects of the Universe. Dissenting voices from the established paradigms of modern science are either ignored or discarded as irrelevant. Descartes emphasised the 'usefulness' of science and Bertrand Russell described it as a "useful knowledge." But common people recognised and accepted science as they believed that it could unveil the true picture of reality at the micro level, by the reductionist method. But the sad truth is that "science brought out a view which was morally neutral or spiritually empty". This neutrality made science the enemy of man by making large scale manufacturing of nuclear arms, warplanes and ships and biological and chemical weapons. The scientific objectivity and certitude became the long ladders by which mass destruction reached the apex of human civilisation. The goodness and usefulness to humanity contributed by science, was neutralised by the destructive inventions and innovations of science. The mobile phone and its use by the people is the best example for the adverse impact of the neutrality of modern science. It can be used by a police man to pass on information about the hideouts of terrorists and the terrorists can use it for passing on information about the movements of the police. Hence ultimately it is the attitude and culture of the individual that determines the impact of the technology on the society.

Modern science regards the knowledge gained without any rational thought as unpredictable and beyond explanations. But Prof Barbara Me Clintock who won the Nobel prize for discovering the 'jumping genes' in 1983 opines that feeling, nurturing, receptivity, co-operation, integrity, etc., which are based on inter dependence, if incorporated into science, will not in any way decrease its accuracy and precision. "Inclusion and integration of the 'feminine' qualities in a balanced way would definitely help us see more of reality"

Science, Technology and Environment

As environmental problems assumed global dimensions and the impacts of problems spread to all countries, it became imperative for the developed countries to share technology that mitigates the impacts. In a conference in Bunos Aires in 1998 to implement a UN agreement to prevent global warming, the developing countries received commitments in principle from the advanced nations for finance and technology transfer. A majority of the countries who signed the agreement have consented to reduce their greenhouse gas emissions by 2012 to a level at least five per cent lesser than in 1990 by adopting suitable technology.

Canada has established an 'Environmental Technology Verification' (ETV) programme with a view to minimising cost and risks for users of different green technologies. Evaluation and verification of new technology and refurbished technology are considered essential in Canada. Some of the quantitative parameters for technology rating include value to the country of use, patent on IPR cover, obsolescence rate, safety, environmental friendliness, government support and quantitative cost.

About 10,000 technology transfer negotiations were held in the year 2001. The United Nations Asian and Pacific Centre for Transfer of Technology (UNAPCTT) has tried to bring up the negotiations to about 50,000 in 2002.

Eco-friendly (green) technology transfer is one of the important items in the agenda of development of UN. In the Agenda 21, Agenda 17 and 18 are respectively, biological diversity and environmentally sound management of biotechnology, (UNCED, 1992, pp. 67-70). Also in The Hague Declaration of

'Sustainable Development: From Concept to Action' forty leading thinkers of the world advocated an international policy for technology transfer. They argued that this will ensure the availability of environmentally sound technologies in underdeveloped countries; these technologies are not to be closely guarded like all other technologies, but should be made available more freely in the interest of the common good.

S & T for Sustainable Development

In order to make industry more Sustainable Development oriented, cleaner technologies are to be installed where re-cycling and re-use of resources are explored. 'Zero-Waste' technology is an innovation that assures sustainable industrial development. Environment clean up with plasma has been introduced by the MIT, Plasma Fusion Centre. High temperature of plasmas can convert solid wastes – soils, metals, combustible material and sludge – without combustion into lava like glass –which can be used in road construction. The process produces no toxic ash or dioxins and less gas emission than conventional incineration. Advanced waste treatment technologies are quite relevant and helpful for attaining sustainable development in countries where environmental degradation is rapid due to industrialisation.

Sustainable Means and Use of Energy

According to the scientists of the IISc Bangalore, 58 per cent of the Biomass production is excess, and is available for power generation. The biomass consisted mainly of coconut shell, areca nut franks and cashew nut stalk and all other forms of agricultural bio-waste. The advantages of biomass power generation are reduction of emission diversity, smaller size of operation, flexibility and employment generation potential.

Trees also can be used for oil production. Prof Srinivasa, who heads the Sustainable Transformation of Rural Areas (SUTRA) of the IISc Bangalore claims that Oil Seed bearing trees can help reduce import of petroleum products. When vegetable oil is used in engines the emission released are absorbed by the trees from the atmosphere. Hence pollution could be minimised. Diesel has been identified as the chief culprit for the undesirably high percentage of deadly particulate matter in the air. When the government in many countries are making diesel cheaper, they are following an anti-environmental policy. Studies have shown that as many as 40,000 and more people may be dying in our cities due to the atmospheric pollution caused by diesel.

The scope of 'Green engines to be used in vehicles also promise pollution-free environment. This is possible by converting the existing heavy-duty diesel engines to propane fuel. Japan, Canada, Austria and Netherlands are the leading nations where the conversion of Taxis and buses have taken a meaningful and 1996-2005' to promote and advocate ecologically sustainable energy use. This programme includes giving top priority to renewable energy projects like building up the solar industrial capacity in Africa to rural electrification projects in Asia and solar refrigerator production in the Arab region. Economists predict that by the year 2020 the energy consumption of a typical Chinese village will grow by 85 per cent and of its Indian counterpart by 145 per cent, assuming a high growth scenario. As developing countries concentrate on rapid industrial growth, they have to devour all the cheap and available sources of energy. Wind turbines can produce electricity at $0.5/kW at a good wind site with an average wind speed of greater than five meters per second. An advantage of wind power plants is that they are modular and can be sized to adjust to many situations and accommodate future growth in big or small increments, depending on the needs of a developing country. But in spite of all these positive efforts of the scientists, the environmental problems are assuming the dimensions of a crisis.

Social Sciences and Environment

Laws, regulations and policies are the steps taken in the society by the political authorities to protect the environment. At the international level, more than 300 conventions and summits have been held for the protection of the environment. The UN has accepted Sustainable development as the future policy of development. There are many NGOs working at the national and international levels for the protection of the environment while promoting development.

Internationally, NGOs could hold parallel meetings in the Rio Summit. With the Earth Summit in Rio in June, 1992, the environmental NGOs gained acceptance and recognition all over the world. Over 20000 participants of 9000 organisations from 171 countries were present at the summit and over 1000 meetings were held between NGO representatives in a forum parallel to official intergovernmental discussions. Thus NGOs gained a reputation for innovation for promoting local participation and raising regional issues at the international platforms.

Environmental NGOs all over the world are enthusiastically engaged in the protection of nature for attaining sustainable development objectives. This is clear from the various activities in which the NGOs are engaged at the international, national, and regional levels. To encounter the weak stand taken by the governments at the UNCED meeting, in Rio on deforestation, the World Rainforest Movement, an NGO, circulated its own proposals. It says that a solution to the forest crisis must incorporate ecological, social and economic elements taken together as a package.

Recently, the NGOs have made a new entry in professional Economics, by preparing and propagating alternative economic policies such as alternative budgets, Cairo Population Summit and in the Beijing Women's Conference on account of their consultative status. In the "Draft Declaration and Programme of Action" prepared by the preparatory committee for the world summit for Social Development, the Non Governmental Voluntary Organisations were allotted a leading role in achieving social development.

The International coordination of NGOs has recently called for the emergence of an "alternative paradigm of development based on indigenous systems" as a solution to Structural Adjustment Programmes of IMF and globalisation. The only answer projected by NGO ideologies to present problems is "the evolution of an alternative model of development based on environmentally sound principles and peoples' participation or what they call 'Sustainable Development'. So internationally, the recognition and acceptance of NGOs as a vehicle of social change, based on its popular character and democratic process, is clear from the above-mentioned roles it played. As a result, international NGOs like Green Peace and Friends of Earth could open new chapters of success in their books of world service.

Religion and Spirituality

Religion is also a science. "It is also an inquiry to know the Truth. As a discipline, it is more rigorous and perhaps more exacting. Like science, it is as clear as day light. At least up to a point, but beyond that point, it is possible that there is need for secretiveness because one does not want one's privacy encroached upon. Religion is essentially a personal affair.......Higher religion. However, is a different proposition: it is beyond reason. What a mystic sees and feels cannot be explained, but he himself is the proof of its validity. Religion basically is a science of the self".[6] The beliefs, experiments and practices of religion in one's life lead to inner experience of the Truth. Sharing of the methodologies of religions is possible, but sharing of experience is very difficult. The observation and experiments in religion result in an experience which is purely subjective and personal. But this experience is reflected through the actions of individuals as universal values. Hence religions are the means and spirituality is the end.

Real religion consists in the realisation of Truth and the experience of Truth at the personal level. Institutions, books, rituals, etc., are only secondary in the pursuit of Truth. These are all the tools of religion to make mind pure in order to understand and realise truth.

The Indian approach to religion gives four paths to understand truth.

1. Jnana-the path of knowledge/philosophy,
2. Karma-the path of duty/work,
3. Bhakti-the path of devotion, and
4. Yoga- the path of meditation and physical postures.

The Semitic religions are more inclined towards the path of Bhakti and Karma. But in the eastern religions, especially, in Hindu religion, these four paths are clearly distinguishable.

Whichever path is selected by an individual, he is able to reach the same state of mind. In the process of understanding Truth, an individual is free to choose either one or more than one path, as the choice depends upon an individual's taste and preference.

In the sustainable type of interaction between man and nature, it is spiritual or holistic outlook that guides the relation between human resource and natural resource. In such a society, human beings prefer a simple living. As a result, only limited use of resources and simple production with normal profit is the result. In this type of interaction both affluence and effluents are less and therefore depletion of natural resources and pollution of environment occur at comparatively low levels. The level of science and technology is also at the appropriate and normal levels.

The real religion will help a person to grow as a spiritual person who is less attached to worldly things and even if he is a wealthy person, he thinks of himself only as a Trustee of the properties. (Gandhiji) A spiritually motivated industrialist will not deceive the consumer for extracting more profit and he will not over exploit natural resources also. He will also distribute the excess production and profit among the members of the society. This type of a social system was visualised in ancient India.

Hindu scriptures in India recognised four goals in the life of a person. They are the fulfillment of desires (Kama), attainment of wealth (Artha), seeking basic principles of sustainability for individual and society (Dharma), and liberation or God realisation (Moksha). Among these four, Kama is considered the lowest goal, because this urge is found common to both men and animals. Artha is noticeable only in human beings and accumulation of Artha; is done due to the 'Karma' for 'Artha'. Dharma is superior to both, since without Dharma, Karma and Artha cannot be accomplished in a sustainable manner and hence they are to be regulated and controlled by the norms of Dharma.

Dharanat Dharma it ahu — Whatever sustains is Dharma. Also Indians believe that *Prithivim dharmana dhritam* — the world is sustained by Dharma. The principle of sustainability is the essence of Dharma. Dharma has various phases and stages — Dharma of an individual to himself, to his family, to the society and to the world as a whole. All these phases of Dharma, irrespective of time and place, will ensure and enhance the principle of sustainability by recognising the importance of interdependence and interrelationship among the living and non-living things in the Universe. Man cannot exist without acknowledging his indebtedness to other human beings and life forms on Earth. Wanton destruction is not permitted according to Dharma.

Ecological concerns are also found in Buddhism. The Buddhist monasteries were considered sanctuaries for wildlife because of the sense of interrelatedness of nature and belief in non-violence. Conservation is the core of Buddhism. As per the conservation techniques, there are sacred mountains in Sri Lanka and Japan. Compassion to beings is another ethical concept of Buddhism, which could help the modern concept of conservation and also a prerequisite for sustainable development.

The Jaina philosophy also is built very much upon the fundamental principle of 'Ahimsa'. Respect for other living beings and limiting the greed for worldly possessions are the two principles of sustainability embodied in Jainism. Nature is viewed in Jaina philosophy as a living organism — Cetana, or citsvarupa. This view takes away a Jaina from mechanistic thinking and familiarises him with the concept of limiting one's inordinate longing for worldly goods and this helps him to attain spiritual harmony and peace in life. Hence, even a householder has to reduce his wants and limit his desires, if he is to pursue his spiritual practice and not be altogether lost in the world.

Judaism is underpinned by a strong and clear ethical responsibility of human beings to care for nature. This responsibility arises out of the superiority of human beings over other beings. This superiority forms the basis of any conservation ethics on Judaism, as conservation arises out of the superiority of human beings.

In Christian thought, it is man who is endowed with great power to master the world. Such a masterly notion of himself has quite often led man to the brink of the destruction of nature and other living beings. Lynn White, himself a Christian recommended that Christians follow the medieval monk St. Francis of Assissi, who gave a more holistic and symbolic view of the relation of humanity to nature.

In the Quran and in the Shariah, man nature relationship is expressed in such a way that the supremacy of man must not result in the abuse of man's God-given powers. A modern Islamic commentary makes clear the position of Islam on environmental issues. "There is hunger, environmental destruction, and civil strike because humanity has broken the laws of Allah, not because it is His will. Allah has provided enough for the honest needs of all his creation. Thus, Muslims are forbidden to hoard beyond their genuine needs. To do so is to abuse Allah's creation.

Now as already seen, no technological magic or policy package is sufficient to solve the present environmental crisis. The spiritual understanding that calls for an active involvement in the affairs of the world should be able to stop any dissention and destruction of nature and its environment. It is spirituality or real religion that is strong enough to uphold truth, justice, and freedom inherent in the created order.

References

1. Government of India, "*The Environmental Protection Act of India*", 1986, No. 26.

2. Lodha, RM, "*Environmental Essays*" Ashish Publishing House, New Delhi,1991, p. 3.

3. Tucker and Robert C. (ed), "*Economic and Philosophic Manuscripts of 1844*", The Marx Engels Reader, New York, (1972), p. 58.

4. Thomas Prugh, "*Natural Capital and Human Economic Survival*", ISEE, Solomons,(1995), Ch.1, p. 8.

5. Ashtana Markul, "*What Science has Put Under?*", The Hindu, Sept. 10, 1995.

6. Swami Lokeswarananda, "*Science and Religion*" The Ramakrishna Mission Institute of Culture, 2003, Kolkata, p. 2.

2

Environmental Degradation — Beyond the Limits

N. Peethambara Kurup M.P.

Gandhiji said "*nature provides everything to the needs of man but not for his greed*".

Natural resources which sustain life are diminishing day by day. Rapid deforestation, unprecedented biodiversity loss, water scarcity, pollution of soil and water supplies, etc., pose a real threat to normal life. It is estimated that 60 per cent of the world's ecosystem services have been degraded or over used since the middle of 20th Century. The idea of a non-growing economy may be an anathema to an economist. But the idea of a continually growing economy is an anathema to an ecologist.

A humane environment is one which promotes the sustenance of life. Land, water and air are the basic needs provided by nature. Clean air, unpolluted water and land are the rights of every citizen. The state is responsible for providing and protecting air, land and water. As well all know law-making alone will not suffice.

India is one of the fast growing youngest democracies in the world. With robust domestic consumption and a growing middle class, India provides considerable opportunities as a consumer market and a global manufacturing hub. States in India are playing an increasingly critical role in the successful implementation of local and national reforms. Balancing the environmental impact of developmental activities and expanding consumption with sustainable solutions is a major challenge. Kerala is no exception.

Environmental imbalance that resulted from unsustainable developmental activities has stunning effects on the world's climatic conditions and water availability. The quality of air and water too has been affected many countries of the world over in general and many of them are facing scarcity of water. Indus is one of the great rivers of the world. Because of over exploitation, it no longer flows into the ocean at the port of Karachi. It's once fertile delta of rice-fields and fisheries has shriveled up. The lower Indus had been a lush ecosystem, supporting fishers and providing habitat to diverse species, including critically endangered Indus River dolphin.

Air Quality

Indoor air in China has high levels particulates ranging in size from visible dust down to viruses. Sources include outdoor air pollution, smoking, human skin cells, dust mites, pollen, volatile organic compounds (VOCs), and other harmful gases. Irritant lung and nose, asthma, allergies are caused by particulate matter. VOCs cause burning of the eyes, headache, and even cancer in certain cases.

Water Quality is Another Concern

Give me a tree and I will save the world – is the message conveyed by French Botanist Francis Halle in his Book "Dubon usage des arbres" (Making good of trees).

If a tree is not affected by diseases or by humans it could live for centuries. The history of our zoological species can be found in the life of a tree. Trees produce molecules to keep mice and insects at bay and in doing so provide man with taxol, an efficient anti-cancer drug. As we all know, lime, birch, and lemon trees are all used for medicinal purposes. A 15 meters tree in leaf would *cover a total surface area of 200 hectares. (It includes the trunk, branches roots and leaf surfaces together). The entire surface breathes and allows us to breathe. When trees breathe they clean the atmosphere. An adult human consumes about 700 gram of oxygen per day. In that time an average tree produces 15 kg to 30 kg. So the oxygen released by one tree is sufficient to provide oxygen to more than 20 people. The negative ions released by the movement of leaves are supposed to have beneficial effects on health and mood.*

Man cannot live without trees, and yet they are under threat everywhere. The UN declared 2011 as the International Year of Forests. Trees are home to 50 per cent of the world's biodiversity and provide subsistence to 1.6 billion humans.

From 2000 to 2005, 7.3 million hectares of tropical forests disappeared every year, i.e., 20,000 hectares a day.

• Trees are vital in preserving soil, containing floods, providing energy and producing healthy food stuffs. They make the surroundings cooler and more pleasant.

• According to Economist Pavan Sukhdev, study leader of Economics of Ecosystems and Bio diversity project, "if we halved the deforestation by 2030, the reduced carbon dioxide emissions would cut the cost of global warming by 2.6 trillion Euro" (3.5 trillion dollar).

The erosion of forests, soil and coastal areas leads to losses of between 1.3 trillion Euros and 3.1 trillion Euros a year. "It is the economic visibility of ecosystems that has led to this ecological Crisis", says Sukhdev.

A tree is invaluable. What we get from trees is priceless. We depend on trees for oxygen, shelter, food, clothes, bed, chocolate, medicine, etc.

Conservation of nature and natural resources is the responsibility of the State. Governments, world over are facing hurdles in developmental activities. Environmental impacts are irreversible. Since environment is part and parcel of the daily life, every citizen has a vital role to play. No government can fully ensure protection of environment by itself. Involvement and co-operation of the civil society is essential for the successful conservation of nature and natural resources. At the same time it is the right of the citizen to live in clean atmosphere. Every citizen has the right to avail water for sustenance. The State has to act as promoter of nature and natural resources. The land we live in and the air we breathe in and the water we drink are the gifts of nature. We are bound to protect it and hand it over to our future generations for their use. Each and every activity has to be eco-friendly or sustainable. Developmental activities as well as agriculture have to be sustainable.

Every natural resource is finite. Overuse or reckless use of the resource will definitely lead us to scarcity. It is estimated that if the whole human population consumes natural resources as the citizen of United State does, it will be exhausted within a year.

Civil society can do a lot through voluntary organisations by bringing to the notice of authorities concerned, the degrading water resources land and air pollution, etc., and get remedied. Involvement and participation of the public in this regard is one of the powerful means to remedy the grievances. This is what we see around us within and outside the country.

What is Sustainable Development?

Sustainable development meets the needs of the present without compromising the ability of future generations to meet their own needs. Seen as the guiding principle for long-term global development, sustainable development consists of three pillars.

- Economic development
- Social development
- Environmental protection

Rio + 20 focused on two themes: (a) a green economy in the context of sustainable development and poverty eradication (b) the institutional framework for sustainable development.

Humans have altered the face of the earth more than any other species. And the pace of change is increasing. We are not the only animals that shape our surroundings. Ants, beavers and elephants, among other creatures, remake their environments to suit their proposes. But no species has been a global agent of change as humans. Our most obvious impact is on the land, where more than 80 per cent of Earth's surface has been marked by human activity. Our terrestrial transformations go back at least to the beginnings of agriculture more than 10,000 years ago. Over the centuries, population growth and improved transportation have driven humans to control ever-widening tracts of land, with grave consequences for the species and habitats there. We have left our mark on Earth's air and water as well. Exhaust and emissions from transportation and industry have fundamentally changed our atmosphere. And oceans, lakes and rivers suffer from our pollution and over fishing. Human's impact on earth is not always harmful though. Parks, farm lands, and wilderness areas allow human use while preserving natural habitats. But our role in shaping the Earth is powerful, and the human foot print continues to expand.

• Average person living in the European Union today uses at least five times as many resources as the planet can support per capita.

• Consumption pattern is growing. In the European Union between 1990 and 2007 car ownership rose 35 per cent, meat imports rose 120 per cent and air travel jumped nine per cent, according to Oksana Mont of Lung University in Sweden, who is part of a coalition of European researchers investigating sustainable living.

• Most of the world countries— from India and China to Niger so far are consuming at a rate, per capita, below the world's carrying capacity. But if they achieve their development goals or even basic level of human development in some poor countries–many will rise above that line, dramatically increasing demands on world's fast-diminishing natural resources.

- Competition of scarce resources increases and much of the world is hit with higher food prices, water shortages and more extreme weather linked to climate change, many of the world's poorest may find themselves becoming ever poorer.

Let us protect our planet and ensure that people have a safer, more prosperous; healthier future.

3

Traditional Knowledge, Intellectual Property Rights and Livelihood Sustainability

M. Rajesh

Livelihood sustainability has been a major issue of discussion since the time of the Bruntland Commission report. With the passage of time, it is greatly felt that the human demand would be beyond reach the carrying capacity of earth, which the economist T.R. Malthus had predicted way back in the 18th Century and thereby, would put "our common future" in jeopardy. This time around, it is also perceived that technological progress may not provide all the answers.

However, man has from time immemorial looked at livelihood issues with concern. His synergy with nature and his efforts at obtaining a secure future for his subsequent generations has created a wealth of knowledge that sustained not only the environment but also made provisions for a stable environment. This wealth of knowledge is subsumed in the term Traditional Knowledge.

Traditional Knowledge

Traditional does not imply that the concept under question is antiquated. It only means that the knowledge is developed, sustained and passed on within a traditional community. It may keep on evolving as and when the community may respond to external realities that it may face time to time. (WIPO, Intellectual Property and Traditional Knowledge). In essence it may include know-how, skills, innovation, practices, etc., generated and handed over within a traditional community. Traditional Knowledge may be distinguished from Traditional Cultural Expressions or TCE, though the latter is one of the components of Traditional Knowledge. Traditional Cultural Expressions encompass songs, chants, narratives, motifs, designs, etc., (WIPO, Intellectual Property and Traditional Knowledge).

Traditional Knowledge by their very nature may not be well documented and therefore may be subjected to abuse and illegitimate exploitation by third parties. One of the most common forms of abuse takes the form of bio-piracy. Bio-piracy may be defined as the appropriation of knowledge and genetic resources of farming of traditional communities by other parties seeking monopoly over these resources (WIPO, Traditional Knowledge and Geographical Indications). The classic case in this regard is that of the attempt by US-based Indian nationals to patent Turmeric. The applicants sought to patent the wound healing properties of turmeric, which is a property that is known to indigenous communities in India for at least a couple of millennia. The patent was revoked on being challenged by CSIR.

The Convention on Bio Diversity (CBD) arrived at in the year 1992 as part of the Rio summit is a landmark in the field on providing the holders of traditional knowledge their due. It calls for equitable sharing of benefits arising out of the use of bio-resources, while ensuring the preservation of these bio-resources. It asserts that, nations have sovereign rights over their bio-resources and any use of these resources by third parties should be based on prior information and consent. The convention while calling for the protection of embedded intellectual property rights also clearly states that protection of IPRs should not run counter to the stated objectives of the convention (WIPO, Traditional Knowledge and Geographical Indications).

Two of the articles enshrined in the Convention of Bio-Diversity are of major importance. The first of these is Article 1, which states that the major objectives of this convention are sustainable use of biological components, fair and equitable sharing of biological resources and fair access to these resources. The other article of major importance is Article 8(j), which calls for respecting and preserving knowledge, innovations and practices of Traditional Communities those are relevant for the conservation and sustainable use of biological diversity (Gold, 2007). The application of such knowledge may also be promoted with the active involvement of such communities.

However, it may be noted that the Convention on Bio-Diversity has not yet been implemented in letter and spirit. Even though the CBD has explicitly stated that utilisation of genetic resources has to be on prior consent, the same has not yet been endorsed by the TRIPs agreement. The endorsement of the same by TRIPs would have made it binding on international private sector companies to obtain such consent. This is all the more important when we consider that most of the users of these genetic resources are companies from the Developed World while the holders of such traditional knowledge are mostly from the Developing World. It is in the light of the CBD that the discussion on the Plant Breeders Right and *sui generis* protection gets currency. Once Sui generis protection is granted, a new right is given only if, the new variety is "Distinct", that is distinguishable from the earlier varieties and secondly, if it exhibits "Stability", that is it retains its essential characteristics on re-production. The sad case of *Banisteriopsis Capi (BC)* indicates that it is not always that the "right" is upheld. The indigenous tribes of the Amazon delta have long known that Ayahuasca, a traditional wine could be made out of BC. However, in 1985, an American, Lorren Miller, obtained a patent for a variant of BC, for his product "De Vine" which was described as having been discovered in a domestic garden of Amazon (WIPO). Though initially the USPTO upheld the claims of the traditional communities that

"De Vine" was not distinguishable from prior art, during later appeals, the patent was upheld.

The approach of the CBD has however, been upheld by the Human Genome Organisation (HUGO) in its Statement of Benefit Sharing. In this "Statement", HUGO endorsed a model of benefit sharing based on compensatory justice. According to it, "the individual, group, or community, should receive recompense in return for [a] contribution" (Gold, 2007).

However, it is not always that Traditional Knowledge is abused. There have been instances through which the IPR regime has been used for the benefit of Traditional Communities. The most recent instance of this being the case of the Ayurvedic drug named "Jeevani". The scientists at the Tropical Botanical Garden and Research Institute used the tribal know-how of the Kani tribes of South India to develop a sports drug named "Jeevani" from the plant "Arogyapacha" (WIPO, Intellectual Property and Traditional Knowledge). The know-how was licensed to Arya Vaidya Pharmacy, and a trust was formed to share the benefits of the commercial exploitation to the Kani tribes.

Traditional Knowledge and Patenting

A patent is a right conferred upon an inventor to put to use his invention or authorise another person or entity to use the same under agreed terms and conditions without infringing the established rights and privileges of the wider society. Such an invention should meet three general conditions:

1. Non-obviousness, which essentially implies that it should not be an obvious piece of work for anyone possessing an ordinary understanding of the field under mention.
2. Capable of industrial or commercial application.
3. It should not be a general scientific principle, like the fact of the earth moving around the sun.

But when it comes to Traditional Knowledge, facts are not in black and white as envisaged by the law of patents. We may examine this aspect by analysing the case of the Neem Patent that had created much anger in the Indian sub-continent. Matters came to a head when in 1994, the European Patent Office (EPO) granted, Patent No. 0436257 to W.R. Grace and USDA for a neem-based extract for controlling fungi on plants obtained through hydrophobic extraction method (WIPO, Traditional Knowledge and Geographical Indications). It is seen here that while the patent application fulfilled all three conditions applicable for the grant of a patent, it had to be certified whether, it was at all an innovation. However, based on available evidence and based on their wisdom, the European Patent Office considered it a fit case for the award of patents. A challenge to the patent was made in 1995 by Indian Farmers bodies and by International NGOs, which clearly brought the fact to the notice of EPO that the state property of the neem plant has been known to Indian farmers since centuries and that it was a common practice throughout the Indian subcontinent. In 1999, based on the challenge, the EPO ruled that all aspects of the patent claims were known to the public prior to the filing of the patent application and therefore the claim submitted for the award of the patent did not constitute an "inventive step" (WIPO, Traditional Knowledge and Geographical Indications). It needs to be noted that the process of successfully challenging the patent application took not less than six years and therefore the commercial loss to traditional communities in the intervening period never got compensated.

Bio-technology is another area where patents hold great importance. Attention can be drawn to the patenting of numerous varieties of animal species. Even a bacterium that could eat crude oil and hence could be useful in oil spills has been patented (Watal, 1998). Similarly, the Harvard Oncomouse was also a major patent. However, the desirability of patenting living beings is an issue that is today more hotly debated than ever.

The issues related to patenting remains one of the most hotly contested areas about sharing of knowledge in the public domain.

Traditional Knowledge and Geographical Indications

Geographical indications are an important facet of the discussion on IPRs and agriculture. A particular agricultural product is ascribed a geographical indication if a peculiar defining characteristic of the product is ascribed to its specific geographic origin. The prominent example in this regard is that of Basmati Rice, which owes its rich aroma and taste to its specific origin in South Asia. Geographical Indications can only prevent the abuse of protected categories and does not protect the traditional knowledge embodied in the product directly.

A key element in implementing the clauses pertaining to geographical indications is disclosure of the origin of the genetic material of the biological product. Some national legislations have already incorporated these clauses. Let us examine the case of India. Section 10 of the Patent Act of 1970 and the 2nd Amendment to the Patent Act (2002) clearly mandates that the applicant must disclose the source and description of the biological material deposited. In the amendment, section 25 provides conditions under which the grant of patent could be objected to on the grounds of non-disclosure or wrong disclosure of the geographical origin of the product (WIPO, Traditional Knowledge and Geographical Indications).

One of the most celebrated cases pertaining to Geographical Indications pertains to that of the Basmati Rice case. As is well known, Basmati refers to the aromatic long sized rice grown in the plains of Northern India and Pakistan. However, in 1997, the USPO awarded the US commercial concern, Ricetek International patents on a number of attributes related to the Basmati Rice including, plants and seeds and a number of rice types similar to Basmati. India filed a suit to re-examine these patents in the year 2000 and in response Ricetek, withdrew their claim for patents on a number of aspects including those on Basmati type rice lines.

Another issue of significance in this dispute was the use of the term Basmati, which India argued was indicative of a belief in the consumer that the uniqueness of the Basmati rice could be obtained only if it were grown in the northern regions of India and Pakistan, due to the peculiar combination of soil, climate, agricultural practices and environment obtaining in this region. Consumers could be misled into purchasing a fake product if similar rice from other regions started being labeled as Basmati or similarly sounding names just as Ricetek had named its similar variant of rice, as Texmati. The action of India was indeed a delayed response. In the past two decades, the country had not opposed the gradual adoption of the name Basmati as a generic term, thus prejudicing the chances of Basmati being named as a Geographical Indicator (WIPO, Traditional Knowledge and Geographical Indications).

Traditional Knowledge and Basic Livelihood Issues

Traditional Knowledge can have an impact on the basic livelihood issues as well. The areas in which Traditional Knowledge commonly impacts can be conceived as follows:

- Health related issues through the use of Traditional Medicine
- Sustainable Agricultural Practices as envisaged in Traditional literature and oral tradition
- Preservation of Bio-Diversity using traditional know-how.

1. Traditional Medicine

Traditional medicines still form the mainstay of the medical systems of many developing countries. Most patented medicine is exorbitantly priced and hence out of the reach of the people of the developing and less developed world. This has put modern medicine outside the reach of 1/3 of the global population (Zhang, 2004). Modern western medicine is also widely noted to possess many side effects, which traditional medicine does not have. The most widely used medicinal traditional knowledge is acupuncture and herbal medicine (Zhang, 2004). Herbal medicinal knowledge as is applicable to the Indian case has been handed down from generations to generations. Very little of this knowledge is in the form of codified/written information.

Herbal Medicine

The major characteristics of Herbal Medicines, which makes it difficult to be protected, using modern plant protection laws, are:

One of the aspects to be noted is that herbal medicines take the forms of leaves, flowers, roots, stems or even mixtures and powders, with the result that the traditional concept of patenting cannot be applied claiming a discovery or the existence of an inventive step (Zhang, 2004).

Most of these products are prepared using basic techniques; those may not be considered as "novel" in the strictest sense of the word.

Further, it will be very difficult to keep such discoveries secret and thereby invoke protection under the trade secrets clause. In any case the process of assuming protection is so skill and resource intensive that Traditional Communities may not possess the acumen to obtain them (Zhang, 2004).

2. Sustainable Agricultural Practices using Traditional Knowledge

Needless to state, sound management of Traditional Knowledge and IPRs lies at the core of sustainable agriculture. Examples are not too distant to seek. The *Bela* community of Mali had developed a detailed understanding of the agricultural value of Oryza *Longistaminata* a variety of the local long rice. The Traditional Knowledge of the Bela community indicated that this local variety of rice had better resistance against common diseases like Blight. This Traditional Knowledge was used by scientists to create a new hybrid variety of rice known as Xa21, which was a resistant variety with higher yield (WIPO, Intellectual Property and Traditional Knowledge).

One of the prominent systems related to the management of agricultural systems is the UPOV system (The International Union for the Protection of New Varieties of Plants). Signed in 1961, the system calls for the uniform formulation of the scope of plant breeders rights. Over time the UPOV system has significantly strengthened Plant Breeders Rights most significantly through its amendment in 1991. The UPOV system states that in order that a variety is eligible for protection; it should qualify under 4 clauses:

1. Distinctiveness from known plant varieties,
2. Homogeneous,
3. Stable and
4. Novel, that is, it is not yet commercialised.

Protection is granted for a limited period only after which the variety moves into the public realm.

In the meantime, the TRIPS Agreement stipulated the introduction of either a "sui generis" system for the protection of plant varieties or for the introduction of patent system. It is in the light of this development that the UPOV system gained currency. In response to the TRIPS stand, India formulated its comprehensive Protection of Plant Varieties and Farmers Rights Bill 2001. This bill contained specific passages that conferred farmers with the right to save seeds for sowing and also with the right to sell seeds locally. These rights were sacrificed at the altar of Plant Breeders Rights under the UPOV Convention. However, for some unfathomable reason, the Government of India decided to join the UPOV in the year 2002, thereby hampering the rights of the traditional rights holders and therefore the sustainability of Indian Agriculture.

All this brings us to the moot point that domestic law must contain provisions that protect the Traditional Rights of people. Protection can be provided under two different patterns—Positive Protection and Defensive Protection (Srinivas). Positive protection refers to IPR and other legal rights being provided to holders of Traditional Knowledge (Srinivas), so that they can be guardians of their own futures and of sustainable development. It includes the right to refuse access as well (Srinivas). On the other hand, Defensive protection refers to protection through the legal system to prevent the misappropriation or inappropriate use of Traditional Knowledge (Srinivas). Defensive protection has two critical components:

1. The criteria for defining prior art applies to Traditional Knowledge. This implies that oral traditions should be taken as credible sources of Traditional Knowledge.
2. To ensure that Traditional Knowledge is readily available to Patent Examiners and other legal authorities examining patent applications (WIPO, Intellectual Property and Traditional Knowledge). There has been a general feeling that the Farmers' Rights Bill of 2001 could have worked better towards providing both Positive as well as Defensive protection.

It has often been suggested that a Compensatory Liability Regime can be effectively used to benefit the Traditional Knowledge owners. According to Reichmann and Lewis (Srinivas), a Compensatory Liability Regime can provide the following rights to the Traditional Knowledge holders (Srinivas):

1. Prevent second users from penetrating Traditional Rights holders market with a non-original imitation of the product.
2. To secure reasonable compensation from secondary users who have made improvements to the product.
3. To make use of the innovations of the secondary users to improve the original product.

Even though, the reasoning of the argument seems attractive, the difficulty lies in identifying the eligible beneficiaries of the system. Sometimes, in the field of agriculture, the right owners are so dispersed that it is a herculean task to identify the true owners of rights. In fact, Traditional Knowledge is mostly shared among communities (Srinivas).

A major convention on agriculture that agricultural policy makers in India often ignore *'The International Treaty on Plant Genetic Resources for Food and Agriculture'*, sponsored by the Food and Agriculture Organisation. Part III of this treaty calls for recognition of farmers' rights including for the protection of Traditional Knowledge related to plant genetic resources for food and agriculture. Taken to its logical conclusion, this treaty along with the Farmers' Rights Bill of 2001 could have gone a long way in protecting the rights of Indian farmers along with ensuring bio-sustainability.

3. **Preservation of Bio-Diversity Using Traditional Know-how**

Preservation of bio-diversity is an important concern of all societies. It is a matter of concern that regions which were once considered to be bio-hubs are now barren areas. This brings to the fore the overwhelming importance of preserving bio-diversity. Traditional Communities play a yeoman role in preserving bio-diversity. These can be visualised in two different ways:

1. The conservation of wild varieties of plants and domesticated animals by Traditional Communities contributes greatly to crop and animal diversity (Biber-Klemm, 2004). This has created a large genome pool that provides resistance against diseases and sustenance to yields.
2. Traditional Knowledge proves to be a vital cog in identifying genetic resources viable of commercial exploitation. This process leads to industrial innovation (Biber-Klemm, 2004).

Taking these aspects into consideration, the Indian Bio-Diversity Bill introduced in the year 2000 envisaged that Knowledge of traditional communities needs to be protected through registration of such knowledge and through the adoption of a sui-generis system of bio-diversity protection. Sections 19 and 20 of the said bill also stipulate that prior approval of the National Bio-Diversity Authority need to be taken for accessing bio-resources (Kaushik, 2004). Further, countries like India have for a long time envisaged at international forums that all applicants for patents must disclose the source of the genetic materials involved and that the legal provisions in the country of origin must be respected by every applicant (Kaushik, 2004).

Conclusion

From the above discussion, it is clear that it is the duty and responsibility of every country to protect its Traditional Knowledge. The best interests of our Common Future can be secured only by ensuring a harmonious linkage between Traditional Know-how and their modern applications. At the international level, frameworks like those instituted by the "Convention on Bio-Diversity" exist to guide individual nations in framing national legislations. However, the onus lies with domestic legislators in ensuring that all available Traditional Knowledge is used effectively to address emergent livelihood issues.

References

Biber-Klemm, S. (2004). *Protection of Traditional Knowledge on Biological Diversity at the International Level: Reflections in Connection with World Trade*. Geneva: UNCTAD.

Gold, D. C. (2007). Sharing the benefits of Genomics Revolution. In P.A. Chika, B. Onwuekwe, *Accessing and Sharing the Benefits of the Genomics Revolution* (pp. 65-81). A A Dordrecht, The Netherlands: Springer.

Kaushik, A. (2004). *Protection of Traditional Knowledge, Innovations and Practices: The Indian Experience*. Geneva: UNCTAD.

WIPO. (n.d.). *Intellectual Property and Traditional Knowledge*. Geneva: WIPO.

WIPO. (n.d.). *Traditional Knowledge and Geographical Indications*. Geneva: WIPO.

Watal, J. (1998). *Intellectual Property Rights in Indian Agriculture*. New Delhi: ICRIER.

WIPO. *Intellectual Property and Traditional Knowledge*. Geneva: World Intellectual Property Organisation.

WIPO. *Traditional knowledge and Geographical Indications*. Geneva: WIPO.

Srinivas, K.R. (n.d.). *Traditional Knowledge and Intellectual Property Rights: A Note on issues, some solutions and some suggestions*. Retrieved 2010, from SSRN: http://ssrm.com.

T.K. Mukherjee, R.R. (24-26 Nov. 2008). *Traditional Knowledge Systems, Intellectual Property Rights and their Relevance for Sustainable Development*, New Delhi.

Zhang, X. (2004). *Traditional Medicine: Its Importance and Protection*. Retrieved from UNCTAD: http://unctad.org/en/docs/ditcted10_ en.pdf.

4

From Skepticism to Trepidation : A Study on How the Social Media Youth Perceive the Mullaperiyar Dam Issue

Titto Varghese, D. Nivedhitha, Santhosh Mathew Veranani

Abstract

Mullaperiyar Dam is the hot topic of discussion for two southern most states of India these days. There are two opinions regarding the re-construction of a new Dam because one party is skeptical of the strength of the existing Dam whereas the other doesn't have any doubt at all that the Dam will be safe for another 100 years. The first party is afraid because if something happens to the Dam, almost four districts of that state will be completely lost with all its bio diversity. The problem which began as an administrative level issue came down to a political issue and now reached the level of a common man's emotional issue in such a way that the people who were living friendly in two neighbouring states became permanent enemies. Media played an anchor role in making this issue a burning one by propagating the doubtfulness regarding the strength of the Dam.

In the Media realm too there is a gradual transformation of ideas from one to another without surpassing the earlier ones. The discussions which started in the Traditional Media went up to the New Media and now reached the Social Media platforms which give a fearful and life threatening picture of the Mullaperiyar Dam. This paper is an attempt to make a Content Analysis of the posts and comments posted in facebook – a social networking site — by the youth on this particular issue. The study covers a period of two months starting from 20/11/2011.

Keywords: Social Networking Media, Youth, Teenagers, Mullaperiyar Dam.

Introduction

There will always be issues which media makes bigger than the real, to appeal to the audience. This is a technique played by all the media barons. It works well if it has something to do with the common man's sentiments. Governments and political parties make maximum use of this mode of journalism to cover up something or to divert the attention of the masses from some particular issues. Social Networking Sites (SNS) have started such kinds of propagandas as they have gained momentum as a youth media especially after the creation of facebook (Jones and Fox, 2009). Youth spend 80 per cent of their "internet time" on social networks. They spend roughly 2 hours and 20 minutes a day on the internet in which they spend 1 hr and 50 minutes for social networking sites (Roiworld, 2010). Youth spend a lot of time on these sites and thus SNS are an increasingly as an important tool for adolescents' and young adults' peer relationships (Szwedo,*et.al.*, 2011). They also help youth to have a voice in the society by expressing their opinions through posts in facebook, MySpace, twitter, blogs, etc. SNS make youth more social by assisting them in coping with shyness or loneliness. They provide opportunities for the youth to have a public voice and to share their creative ideas and thoughts (Davies and Cranston, 2008).

A study by Larsen in 2007 points out the opportunities a social networking site can provide young people as below:

(i) to easily find and interact with people with shared interests
(ii) to organise and co-ordinate political engagement and action
(iii) to build bridges between different groups
(iv) to promote ongoing collaboration (Larsen, 2007).

In the past, Youth in general have been referred to as 'problems of society', 'alienated from community or 'disengaged from democracy' at least in the minds of a large majority of people. This view assumes that being youth is vulnerable (Checkoway, *et.al,* 2003). Even now there are societies which think about youth like this. But the systems of beliefs and patterns of attitudes have been changed a lot and today. Youth are regarded as the building blocks of every nation. In the recent Egyptian Revolution many youths were actively leading and guiding the movement through SNS. The young activists used twitter and facebook extensively to create a sympathetic attitude of the international community towards the protesters. They could generate the attention and interest of the traditional and electronic media in large scale through their tweets, blogs and updates in facebook. They posted videos, pictures and information about the police torture of protesters and the world paid attention to it (Albon, 2011). These minute-by-minute updates through SNS made people even from abroad stay tuned to it (Baraniuk, 2011).

The computer-savvy activists use the Internet to initiate and organise a broad spectrum of dissention activities, including consumer boycotts and public protests and demonstrations (Langman, 2005). Many authors have pointed to social media like short messaging services (SMS), social networking sites (SNS) and blogs as an important new resource for the successful organisation and implementation of social movements (Wasserman, 2007). Social media technologies have been used especially in organising and implementing collective activities, promoting a sense of community and collective identity among marginalised group members, creating less-confined political spaces, establishing connections with other social movements, and publicizing causes to gain support from the global community (Eltantawy and Wiest, 2011).

Mullaperiyar Dam is the hot topic of discussion these days for the people of Kerala and Tamil Nadu, the two southern most states of India. From where four districts of Tamil Nadu are getting water for irrigation purposes. The agricultural lands of these districts depend on this dam for its water resource. Mullaperiyar was constructed in the year 1895 and is 117 years old. The guarantee period for the dam was 100 years. Now the area in which the dam is situated is continuously affected by earthquakes and tremors which measured up to 4.4 in Richter scale. People in the surrounding area are afraid to sit or sleep inside their houses because of fear of another earthquake which may cause the destruction of the dam. There are so many parts in the dam which are reported to have watei leaks. There are two opinions regarding the re-construction of a new Dam because one party is skeptical of the strength of the existing Dam whereas the other doesn't have any doubt at all that the Dam will be safe for another 100 years. The first party is afraid because if something happens to the Dam, almost four districts of that state will be lost completely with all its bio-diversity and the other is cynical about the availability of water for their cultivation if a new dam is constructed.

How the youth perceive this issue is our question especially in the social networking media. Are the youth are involving in the real issue? If yes, how? The paper is an attempt to find out the answers for these questions.

Theoretical Framework

Max Weber speaks about two different forms of action. According to him action can be either a basic action or an advanced social action. Basic action is an action that has a meaning. Social action has a meaning and is directed at other actors and causes action (Weber, 1991). The theory stresses the ability of the individual to exert control over their own actions. The individual here is not a passive receiver of someone else's ideas and directions. Instead he is the maker, creator and spreader of ideas. For Weber "it is society which is constructed by the individuals, and not the other way round". Social action perspective is called so because of this emphasis on people taking action and directing their behaviour.

Later Anderson and Meyer developed the theory further and proposed that media audience construct meaning from the content they perceive. Meaning for them is not delivered in the communication process, but it is constructed within it. Meaning, for them, arises in three different contexts: the intentions of the producer, the conventions of the content and the interpretations of the receiver (Anderson and Meyer, 1988).

Social Action Theory provides a community-oriented framework which leads to problem solving, achieving social justice, redressing the imbalance of privileges between the disadvantaged groups and the society. One of the key concepts of this theory is 'Critical Consciousness', which is defined as a "mental state by which members in a community recognise the need for social change and are ready to work to achieve those things" (Minkler, *et.al*, 2008). The authors further explain that the critical consciousness can be raised by engaging individuals in dialogues, taking part in discussions in different forums and thus seeking an amicable solution for the problem. "Facebook can be used to encourage social action and social change", says Jody Shulnak. Facebook creates facebook-specific social awareness through managing social information, helping direct and indirect communication, making efficient character assessment, construction of virtual identities, and performing them through profiles and facebook features (Shulnak, 2011).

Review of Literature

Internet usage has been classified by scholars under three categories: commercial, informational and communicative (Weiser, 2001). Now as the technological advancement is in fast track, there are other different categories or a category of two or more of these basic categories. The technological advancement has always been debated upon with polarised attitudes. On one side it was a 'moral panic' and on the other it was a 'digital faith'. New media is also not different from this (Green and Hannon,

2007). Eickelman and Anderson speaks about the impact of ICT in penetrating the cultural separation in the Middle East and giving the youth a chance to express themselves and to be active partakers in the democratic practices (Eickelman and Anderson, 1999). Fussell writes about the need for adjustments in the democratic field as the media savvy new generation has started taking part in the issues related to their existence (Fussell, 2002). Social Networking Media has created a revolution of itself as youth in a large scale joined the sites like facebook and twitter. According to a data collected in 2006 – '08 period, 65 per cent of the US youth were using social networking sites. 42 per cent of them were communicating with their friends through the SNS facilities (Jones and Fox, 2009). But today a third world country will have a better statistics than this. SNS allow young people to come to know about the luxuries, rights and freedom of their counterparts in other parts of the world. When they realise that they are denied of many things, they will come up in resentment towards their Governments (Schmickle, 2011).

Zhao suggested a division between the 'expressive internet' and 'instrumental internet' (Zhao, 2006). Expressive internet is defined as "the usage of internet to perform and realise social interaction, public performance, social monitoring and the production and maintenance of the social ties. In other words, it is a social ecology which includes other people, their values, norms and social contexts" (Petric, 2006). Authors are of the opinion that the expressive internet is the future internet without sidelining the instrumental internet. These social media tools which come in line with the expressive internet technology are on the path of rapid popularity as a tool for increased social interaction among people from different localities or even from different communities (Quan-Haase, 2007). Hampton and Wellman observe that people, especially youth, are making maximum use of the expressive internet in all the ways possible to complement their 'offline sociality' (Hampton and Wellman, 2003).

SNS help create communities which retain the interest of the members of the community by providing different kinds of services which in turn may expand their network of friends and well wishers (Mayfield, 2008). "SNSs replicate many of the functions of gossip or social grooming: users display their own bonds and observe those of others through profile 'friends', leave semi-public messages for each other (which serve mainly as acknowledgement), present a public self for their community, and watch and participate as all others also engage in these activities in an interlocked dance of community formation" (Boyd, 2006). These communities in turn may cause social movements as that happened in the case of 'Arab Spring', and the 'Occupy Wall Street' movement. Young users of SNS find it as a need (due to peer pressure) to adjust their profile or to join certain groups in which their friends are members (Lampe, *et.al,* 2007). Facebook allows users to provide status reports which will help others in their friends' circle to find out where they are and what they are doing or what they are up to. All of these activities are framed by 'semi-public comments' people leave on each other's profiles – short salutations, humorous repartee and more. "A profile on an SNS is thus not a static entity; rather, it is a locus of social interaction that evolves and changes" (Tufekci, 2008).

Research on the social influence on the purchasing behaviour of consumers found out that there is a 'neighbourhood effect' (Bell and Song, 2007) or 'contagion effect' (Iyengar *et.al*, 2008) when it comes to decision making regarding purchasing of low cost to high cost items. This is the case with online social movements too. But research conducted in Philippines and UK came to the conclusion that youth in those areas are not that much interested in formal political system; but they do really care about certain issues like social injustice, though they are not getting much chance to do anything for it (Santa, 2002; Edelstein, 2001). Through the SNS youth are always associating themselves with their peers whom they already know offline and share specialised and niche interests like organising a movement for a social cause online and thus gain new forms of visibility and reputation (Ito, 2008).

Jeff Jarvis was quoted saying that for some youth to be influential online they will have to be either a meme starter or a meme spreader (Bentwood, 2010). A meme starter, according to him is a creative man who forms opinions and expresses it well. The meme spreader will share it first. There are three other categories too. They are meme adapters (those who read what is going on outside and reform their opinion accordingly), meme commentators (those who take part in the conversations and shares their information basically through offline discussions) and meme readers (those who do not have the same reach as that of the meme spreaders because of less online activities). People can be mobilised through many methods. Denis Mc Quail is of the opinion that mass media cannot be considered as an effective tool of convincing, activating and mobilising people (Mc Quail, 1983). But there are evidences for mass media, making people convinced about seriousness of the issues as it happened in the case of India against Corruption movement led by Anna Hazare. A combination of traditional and new media especially the social networking media can create social movements online and offline at the same time.

Researchers argue that there is no point in asking more youth to join the political or democratic movement online; but to encourage the youth who are already civically minded and are engaged in such activities (Carpini, 2000). SNS have shifted the locus of content creation from the professional journalists to the common people. Now the public agenda can be set by the 'public' themselves. The SNS allow all citizens/netizens to change their relationships to the public sphere and they don't have to remain as mere spectators but can be the creators (Benkler, 2006). Previously, youth have been sidelined from taking active part in the democratic movements in many parts of the world. There has been shortsightedness with regard to the adolescents and youth even in the UN reports. Youth embody essential elements of both challenges: posing at once potential threats to peace and peace building resources (McEvoy, 2001).

Many worry that youth who spend significant time on fan sites or in online communities tied to hobbies, sports or other interests will become socially isolated. The study by Mc Arthur Foundation concluded the opposite to be true. Youth engagement in interest-driven online communities was associated with increased volunteer and charity work and in increased work with others on community issues. The Internet can serve as a gateway to online and offline civic and political engagement, including volunteerism, community problem-solving, and protest activity.

Youth today are regarded as the catalysts that can provide unique energy and insights to direct the community movements for social change (Checkoway and Finn, 1997). Now youth activism has become an integral element of broader struggles for social justice (Hosang, 2003). There was an elegant formula when youth started to join social movements saying: "Youth strengthening communities and Communities supporting youth" (Irby *et.al,* 2001). The formula clearly speaks about the way in which youth and adolescents are to be taken to the mainstream of the society. This will help them from being away from the anti-social or delinquent behaviour and at the same time provides the youth energy for all the needs of the society. Now racism and other forms of oppression both by the autocratic dictators and by the organisations are questioned because of the increased involvement of young blood (Ginwright and James, 2003). Youth are no more a passive group of receptors observes the famous media theorist Clay Shirkey (Shirkey, 2008). Another paper titled 'Egypt's Revolution 2.0: The facebook factor' also makes the observation that different from the days when the print media and television ruled the world's opinion formation process, the present day youth have started being the creators of online content which were crucial in the recent Arab Revolution movements (Herrera, 2011).

Many authors discuss about the facilities in social media in getting rid of the obstacles in organising a social movement. The internet savvy youth find it easy in such a way that the web is viewed as a new space to promote activism (Brooks and Hodkinson, 2008). Another interesting finding is that the youth are more interested in joining the non-institutionalised causes than the movements with direct links to the political issues (Putnam, 2002). It gives us an idea that the youth are no more interested in the dirty politics of their elder counterparts. But, many of these studies neglected to examine how the lives of the youth have been shaped by the use of new media technologies, especially the social media. Apart from the presence online and organising the movements online, how far the youth are really in to the actual issues in practical life is yet to be studied in detail.

Methodology

A content analysis is done on the posts, comments and pictures in the facebook page 'Save Mullaperiyar Dam' in order to find out the nature of the youth participation online and offline in the protest movement related to the controversial Mullaperiyar dam issue. There were many pages in the facebook. But the researcher selected this particular page just because it was the community with the maximum number of members. On 20 January, 2012, the number of members of this particular community was 60,205. There were more than 10 different groups related to this issue. Many groups were having around 1000 members each. All the posts and comments on all these days (two months from 20 November, 2011 to 20 January, 2012) were analysed.

Analysis and Findings

The Mullaperiyar Dam issue has been a topic of concern for at least a decade now. Recent earthquakes created panic at the location of the dam. The local newspapers took up the issue and later other medias and the TV channels started airing minute-by-minute coverage of the tension in the locality along with interviews of the local people. This led to a further attention of all the mainstream medias in to this issue. As the discussions on this issue gave way to anxiety and fear in the minds of not just the local people but at least the people of the four districts who are going to be affected by the calamity in the offing. It was in such a situation, the social networking sites, though had started groups earlier, were used by the people especially the youth to discuss about this issue. These online communities provided platforms for the like-minded individuals to come and join this group and post their comments for and against the basic theme. There were more than ten communities, formed by different groups of people in the social networking sites. There were different groups like (i) Save Mullaperiyar, save Kerala, save Tamil Nadu, (ii) Save Mullaperiyar Dam, (iii) Save Mullaperiyar, Save Kerala, (iv) Save Mullaperiyar , etc. But same individuals were members in these different communities.

The facebook page of 'Save Mullaperiyar Dam' is a community of more than 60,000 members. Within a short time period the community could witness such an enormous participation in the form of number of members. It is found that all the communities in the facebook related to Mullaperiyar were administered by Malayalees. No groups to support only Tamil Nadu were seen. But there were some groups like 'Save Mullaperiyar, Save Kerala, Save Tamil Nadu', which were speaking for the rights of both the states. One of the leading themes in many of the posts and comments was an accusation against the politicians of both the states. A member lamented in the page saying:

"what could have been settled in the administrative level was taken down to the political level by those nasty politicians......now they lost the grip on the issue because it has further went down to the emotional level of the common people.......somebody is getting mileage from all these gimmicks.......who is gaining from all these controversies is to be found out somehow."

This is a lamentation of a common man who wants to settle the issue in the way of justice. The agitation and pandemonium over this issue were created by politically motivated people opine many of the members of the facebook page. There were not many attacking comments on the Tamilians in the page; instead more than 95 per cent of the comments were for reaching at an amicable solution. Nobody was waging war there. The popular trend was like the following comment:

"Give water to Tamilnadu and give us our life back"

The social media youth succeeded in turning the direction of the discussions in the page and forming a sympathetic opinion towards the people of the locality. The youth organised different kinds of protest movements in the street only through the social media sites, especially the facebook pages. This shows that the online activism had led the youth to the actual protest out in the streets.

The social media could organise people from different walks of life to come together and raise their voices against the injustices done to the people of Mullaperiyar. The presence of thousands and lakhs of youth in all these movements gives us an idea that youth today are ready to come out of their secure life for some noble causes. The research on this particular issue reached at certain points which were the ways in which the youth could organise themselves and others for this cause. There were positive and negative elements in this online campaign. But, both were with the intention of having proper security for the people living at the dam site. Positively Social Media Youth did a wonderful job by:

1. **Posting the Event Invitations**: There were details of the events happening at different parts of the state in the facebook page. The details were given about rallies, candle processions and other gatherings. These were to organise people of that particular locality.

2. **Accepting Tamilians as Brothers and Sisters**: Many posts and comments in the page were like:

> *"we don't have anything against Tamilians. We just want to save our life"*
> *"Kerala and Tamilnadu are like siblings……we won't allow anybody to disrupt the harmony that exists between these neighbouring states whatever the situations be…"*

3. **Asking People to Wake Up and Join the Movement**: There were posts and pictures asking people to join some movements telling them that they may not get a second chance.

> *"life doesn't have a second take as in the film shooting….it's your only chance to be a part of this mass movement, because you may not be there tomorrow…."*

4. Posting the Comments of Elderly: There were participations in plenty from the part of elders who supported the youth for organising such apolitical movement. They congratulated youth from different parts of the state for organising mass movements especially through social media. Eminent personalities like Justice Krishnaiyer were active in the movement.

5. Posting the Comments of Tamil Youth: Some of the Tamilians posted in the wall of this community:

> *"we don't want water at the cost of the life of our brethren...Tamil Nadu is a state which had a Malayali CM, a Kannadiga CM and a Maharashtrian Superstar....——..."*

6. Giving the Scientific Facts Behind the Situation of the Dam: There were posts which had given the exact scientific analysis of the situation of the dam with pictures and graphical representations.

7. Cyber Activism Leading to Real Life Protests: Youth actively took part in the movement both online (through social media platforms) and offline (by taking part in the rallies and meetings) as a result of all the above situations.

8. Participation of People from Different Parts of the World: Youth made it sure that the pictures of people from different countries taking part in the Save Mullaperiyar campaign in different parts of the world. There were movements led by the Malayali community in different parts of the world where they asked their foreigner friends to attend the movement.

(i) They could make even the IFFK delegates to join the movement at Trivandrum Film Festival.

(ii) They could make the issue a matter of concern in different stages.

(iii) People from different parts of the world posed for photos with placards "Save Kerala" (may be at their Malayali friends' request).

(iv) Those who loved Kerala for its scenic beauty joined the movement in fear of losing the biodiversity of four beautiful districts of the state.

9. **Posting the Clippings from the Film Dam 999**: The posters and the story line of the movie were posted in the facebook page. Again there were video clippings from the movie which showcased the enormity of the collapse of a dam.

10. **Congratulating the Participants**: Social Media Youth were generous enough to lavish praises on those who participated in some way in this movement. They congratulated and appreciated Rima Kallingal, a film actress for boldly joining the movement without any fear of the potential loss of the Tamil audience, which made other film stars to keep away from this movement.

But, there was negative side for the story. The page and its content, knowingly or unknowingly created a kind of anxiety and unwanted fear in the minds of the people, especially of that locality. A 'larger than real' picture was given to this issue through the mass media. The news stories were giving a kind of anxiety in the minds of people that the dam is almost collapsed and the awaited tragedy can happen at any moment. This propaganda was so influential that the people of the locality were nervous to be inside their houses especially when there is a wind or when it rains. The social media also went in the same route creating unnecessary anxiety. There were no posts to show an element of "HOPE" in the midst of these turbulence and commotion. Nobody tried to alleviate the fear in the minds of lakhs of people at least through the social media. Instead every move was to pour oil into the fire.

There were also so many posts criticising Tamil Nadu for their double stands by comparing the protests at Koodankulam and Mullaperiyar. People of Tamil Nadu are struggling against the Koodankulam nuclear reactor project saying that the project will be a threat for the life of many in the locality. But the social media youth criticised the same people's attitude towards the

Mullaperiyar dam issue where they are not worried about the life of the 35 lakhs of people who will be affected by the collapse of the dam.

Another main feature was the criticism on the Government of Kerala for being in snail pace to an issue which is really a life threatening one. Many posts were there stating that "*Mullaperiyar is not the issue of Kerala Congress*" (a regional party which raised their voice sternly for the construction of a new dam) alone. There were also posts criticising the politicians for not having unity by telling them:

> *"Respected Politicians of Kerala please do your job or resign from the posts in which you are now. You are in that post because of us and for us. At least show some unity now. Or please learn from Tamil Nadu politicians who are united for this cause."*

Conclusion

The longevity of Mullaperiyar Dam and its endurance are to be time tested. But the issue had made the Youth of Kerala; especially those were members of the social media sites, a much more united lot through their online activism. But, the specialty of this movement was that the online activism in this particular issue didn't stop there. The youth could take it further to the real life situations where they demonstrated what they can do on this particular problem. This is an indication that the Social Media Youth are not mere spectators in the social issues but are active partakers of the movements. They organised protest programmes in different parts of Kerala and even in other parts of the world. They could easily join the movement with other ecological movements and get the support from many human rights activists. Another important factor about this movement was that it was a non-aggressive movement. There was no physical violence involved in any of the movements they organised. There were peaceful and silent protests which spoke a lot. Though we cannot say that the Social Media platforms provide the youth a real democratic awareness or social consciousness, there are instances like this where the youth themselves can join together to form movements in protest of something they feel is unjust. We cannot conclude that the social media youth are all connected with the Mullaperiyar issue all the 365 days a year. But somehow the social media forums and communities instill in them an attitude which made them sympathise and empathise with those people who were in trouble in Mullaperiyar. Instead of making a generalised statement that the social media youth are politically or socially motivated always, what we can conclude here is that at least for a particular period of time and at least for a particular social issue, the youth in Social Media come forward to do their part. This is more common when it is something related to ecological problems. The way the social media youth promoted this issue is noteworthy and to be appreciated because this may be the first of this kind and could serve as the *numero uno* motivator for the rest of the youth movements for a positive cause.

References

1. Albon, C. R. (2011, January 31) 10 must-follow Twitter feeds for Egyptian protests. *UN Dispatch*. Retrieved from http://www.undispatch.com/10-must-follow-twitter-feeds-for-egyptian-protests#

2. Anderson, J.A. and Meyer, T.P. (1988) *Mediated communication: A social interaction perspective*. Newbury Park, CA: Sage.

3. Baraniuk, C. (2011, January 25) Watching the revolution on Twitter: Egypt #Jan25. *The Machine Starts Blog*. Retrieved from http://www.themachinestarts.com/read/20

4. Bell, David, R. and Sanyoung, Song (2007) *"Neighborhood effects and trial on the internet: evidence from online grocery retailing," Quantitative Marketing and Economics*, 5 (4), 361-400.

5. Benkler,Yochai. (2006) *The Wealth of Networks: How Social Production Transforms Markets and Freedom*. New Haven, CT: Yale University Press, 272.

6. Bentwood, Jonny. (2010) *Distributed Influence: Quantifying the Impact of Social Media*. An Edelman White Paper. Retrieved from the blog -technobabble2.0.

7. Boyd, D. (2006) 'Friends, friendsters, and My Space Top 8: writing community into being on social network sites', *First Monday*. 11(12).

8. Brooks, R. and Hodkinson, P. (2008) 'Introduction', *Journal of Youth Studies,* Vol. 11:5, pp. 473 – 479.

9. Carpini, M.X.D. (2000) Gen.com: Youth, Civic Engagement, and the New Information Environment, *Political Communication* 17, No. 4 (October 1, 2000): 341–49.

10. Checkoway, Barry. and Finn, Janet. (1997) *Young People as Community Builders.* Ann Arbor, MI: Center for the Study of Youth Policy, School of Social Work, the University of Michigan.

11. Checkoway, Barry, Schuster, Katie Richards, Abdullah, Shakira., Aragon, Margarita, Facio, Evelyn, Figueroa, Lisa, Reddy, Ellen, Welsh, Mary, and White, Al. (2003) Young people as competent citizens. Oxford University Press: *Community Development Journal,* Vol. 38 No. 4 October 2003 pp. 298–309

12. Davies, Tim., and Cranston, Pete. (2008) *Youth Work and Social Networking* Final Research Report. How can Youth Work best support young people to navigate the risks and make the most of the opportunities of online social networking? September 2008.

13. Edelstein, W. (2001) *The rise of right-wing culture in German youth with some suggestions for prevention.* Berlin, Germany: Max Planck Institute for Human Development.

14. Eickelman, D.F., and Anderson, J.W. (1999) *New media in the Muslim world: The emerging public sphere.* Bloomington: Indiana University Press.

15. Eltantawy, N., and Wiest, J.B. (2011) Social Media in the Egyptian Revolution:Reconsidering Resource Mobilisation Theory. *International Journal of Communication* 5, Feature 1207–1224. Retrieved from http://ijoc.org/ojs/index.php/ijoc/article/viewFile/1242/597

16. Fussell, E. (2002) Youth in aging societies. In J. Mortimer, and R. Larson (Eds.), *The changing adolescent experience: Societal trends and the transition to adulthood.* New York: Cambridge University Press.

17. Ginwright, Shawn. and James, Taj. (2002) "From Assets to Agents of Change: Social Justice, Organising, and Youth Development." *New Directions in Youth Development* 96: 27-46.

18. Green, H and Hannon, C. (2007) *Their Space: education for a digital generation* (Demos). London: Magdalene House.

19. Hampton, K. and Wellman, B. (2003) 'Neighboring in netville: how the internet supports community and social capital in a wired suburb', *City and Community*, Vol. 2, No. 4, pp. 277–311.

20. Herrera, Linda. (2011) Egypt's Revolution 2.0: The facebook factor, retrieved from http://www.jadaliyya.com/pages/index/612/egypts-revolution-2.0_the-facebook-factor.

21. Hosang, Daniel. (2003) *Youth and Community Organising Today*. A Paper For The Funders' Collaborative on Youth Organising Occasional Paper Series on Youth Organising.

22. Irby, Merita, Thaddeus, Ferber, and Karen, Pittman. (2001) *Youth Action: Youth Contributing to Communities, Communities Supporting Youth. Community and Youth Development: Complementary or Competing Priorities for Community Development Organisations*. The Forum for Youth Investment.

23. Iyengar, Raghuram, Christophe Van den Bulte and Thomas W. Valente. (2008), "*Opinion leadership and social contagion in new product diffusion*," Working paper, University of Pennsylvania.

24. Ito, Mizuko. (2008) *Building the field of Digital Media and learning*. Chicago: MacArthur Foundation. Retrieved from www. digitallearning. macfound.org/ethnography.

25. Jones, S., and Fox, S. (2009) *Generations online in 2009*. PEW Internet and American Life Project. Retrieved from http:// www. pewinternet.org/media/Files/Reports/2009/PIP_Generations_ 2009.pdf

26. Lampe, C., Ellison, N. and Steinfield, C. (2007) '*A familiar Face(book): profile elements as signals in an online social network*', in Proceedings of the SIGCHI Conference on Human Factors in Computing Systems, ACM Press, New York, pp. 435–444.

27. Langman, L. (2005) From virtual public spheres to global justice: A critical theory of interworked social movements. *Sociological Theory*, 23(1), 42–74.

28. Larsen, M.C. (2007) *Understanding Social Networking: On Young People's Construction and Co-Construction of Identity Online* (Paper for the conference Internet Research 8.0: Let's Play, Association of Internet Researchers, Vancouver). Retrieved from http://malenel.word press. com / publications/ 39523.

29. Mayfield, Antony. (2008) '*What is Social Media?*': e-book by from iCrossing Updated on 01/08/2008.

30. MacArthur Foundation. February 23, 2011. Does the Internet make for more engaged citizens? Digital Media and Learning Grantmaking, Grantee News, Press Release. MacArthur Foundation. Retrieved from http://www.macfound.org/site/apps/nlnet/content3. aspx?c =lkLXJ8MQK.

31. McEvoy, Siobhan. (2001) "Youth as Social and Political Agents: Issues in Post-Settlement Peace Building", *Kroc Institute Occasional Papers*, 21: OP2.

32. Mc Quail, Denis. (1983) *Mass Communication Theory: An Introduction*. London: Sage.

33. Media Effects Theories. Retrieved from http://oregonstate.edu/instruct/comm321/gwalker/effectsmedia.htm

34. Minkler, M., Wallerstein, N., and Wilson, N. (2008) "Improving Health Through Community Organisation and Community Building." Glanz, K. *Health Behavior and Health Education: Theory, Research, and Practice*. San Francisco: John Wiley and Sons, 291-298.

35. Petric, G. (2006) 'Conceptualising and measuring the social uses of the internet: the case of personal web sites', *The Information Society*, Vol. 22, No. 5, pp. 291–301.

36. Putnam, Robert, D. (2002) *Comunidade e Democracia: a experiência da Itália Moderna*, FGV: Rio de Janeiro.

37. Quan-Haase, A. (2007) 'University students' local and distant social ties: using and integrating modes of communication on campus', *Information, Communication and Society*, Vol. 10, No. 5, pp. 671–693.

38. Roiworld. (2010) *Teens and Social Networks Study; Networks Study*. Retrieved from http://33751159-Teens-Social-Networks-Study-June-2010.pdf

39. Santa Maria, M. (2002) *Youth in Southeast Asia: Living within the continuity of tradition and the turbulence of change*. In B. Brown, R. Larson, and T. S. Saraswathi (Eds.), *The world's youth: Adolescence in eight regions of the globe*. New York: Cambridge University Press.

40. Schmickle, Sharon. "Behind the Turmoil in Egypt: Angry Young People Who Expected More."*Minnesota Post*. January 31, 2011. Web.

41. Shirkey, C. (2008) *Here Comes Everybody: How Change Happens and People Come Together*. New York: Penguin Books.

42. Shulnak, J. (2011) Social Action Through Social Media. Retrieved from https://docs.google.com/viewer?a=v&q=cache :Fiat 65VTwqMJ :www.clark.edu /Library/Powerpoint/social_ action_ social_ media.ppt

43. Szwedo, David.E., Mikami, Amori.Y., and Allen, Joseph. P. (2011) Qualities of Peer Relations on Social Networking Websites: Predictions From Negative Mother–Teen Interactions. *Journal of Research on Adolescence*, 21 (3), 595 – 607. University of Virginia.

44. Tufekci, Zeynep. (2008) GROOMING, GOSSIP, FACEBOOK AND MYSPACE: What can we learn about these sites from those who won't assimilate? *Information, Communication and Society,* Vol. 11, No. 4, June 2008, pp. 544–564.

45. Wasserman, H. (2007) Is a new worldwide Web possible? An explorative comparison of the use of ICTs by two South African social movements. *African Studies Review*, 50(1), 109–131.

46. Weber, Max. (1991) *The Nature of Social Action* in Runciman, W.G. *'Weber: Selections in Translation'* Cambridge University Press, 1991. p. 7.

47. Weiser, E.B. (2001) *'The functions of Internet use and their social and psychological consequences'*, *Cyber Psychology and Behaviour*, Vol. 4, No. 6, pp. 723–743.

48. Zhao, S. (2006) 'Do internet users have more social ties? A call for differentiated analyses of Internet use', *Journal of Computer-Mediated Communication*, Vol. 11, No. 3, pp. 844–862.

5

A Public Space in the Urban Environment : The Case of Mananchira Maidanam in Kozhikkode

P. Sivadasan

The 'public sphere' has become increasingly central to theories and studies of democracy, media, and culture over the last few decades. Scholars have attempted to read the bourgeoisie public sphere in the context of the evolution of capitalist society in the industrial society of Europe. The modern industrial society wanted these changes to enable the society to live with the interests of the market. Partly as a result of national response to the colonial rule, the public sphere in its nationalised form developed in India in the 19th and 20th centuries. There are historical elements in the evolution of public spaces along with the concerns of environment. The Mananchira Maidanam in Kozhikkode evolved due to the integration of these two factors linked with the everyday life of the urban population. A scrutiny of all these factors would help us to discuss the evolution of public arenas as a site of secular-social interaction and the challenges emerging against the public spaces today.[1]

The public sphere can be defined as the sphere between the civil society and the state. It refers to the common and publically accessible spaces such as market places, newspapers,etc., which have the purpose of framing public opinion. The public sphere mediates between the 'private sphere' and the sphere of public authority. It is an area in social life where people can get together and freely discuss and identify societal problems and these discussions influence political action. Geard Haises says that the public sphere is a space for discussion in which individuals and groups congregate to discuss matters of mutual interest and were possible to reach a common judgment.[2]

The Indian public sphere has been decisively shaped by the experiences of British colonialism and the national movement. The cultural particularities prevalent in India also created the emergence of the public sphere. The establishment of British colonialism in Bengal by the eighteenth century enabled the European capitalists to promote an Indian elite to work for a new society favourable to the development of Indian capitalism. Thus, the development of the modern public sphere was essential to the birth of Indian capitalism. Sandria Frietag debated this issue in connection with the Cow Protection Movement of the late nineteenth century and she preferred to use the word 'public arena' in India, in the place of 'public sphere'.[3]

The word 'public' carried at least four different and interrelated meanings in the contemporary language. First we speak of physical spaces, such as city squares and parks, as being public when they are open to all people. Secondly, we distinguish between public and private concerns. We identify the former with issues that are common interests to all members of a polity and therefore the legitimate concern of governmental institutions and the latter with areas of life that should be left do people private discretion and remain their personal secrets. Thirdly, we employ the term 'public' as a social category. We use it in both relatively restricted sense to describe everyone who participate in particular public events or forms of expression, as in the phrase 'reading public' and in a more general sense to character the collective of citizens. Fourthly, we describe the aggregate of individual views that emerge among a public of citizens on issue of the days as 'public opinion'.[4] These multiple uses of the term 'public' constitutes the idea 'public sphere' or the 'public space'.[5]

The city in the capitalist society was an important place of public activity. It linked the public and the market in the presence of the state. An important element of the city is the space meant for public interaction. The open ground guarded by the laws and regulations of the state regulated the public interaction. This space was used for exhibitions of products and skills both by private and public agencies. The state also used the space to demonstrate its authority over the people. This was a new development in the modern industrial town though it later spread to all towns and cities. The open space became integral to the life in the city. In the Indian colonial context, this open space was called the *maidanam*. The administration of this *maidanam* was an important responsibility of the city administration and it wanted to control the population wherever they assembled. As the city grew, the administrations became ever more sensitive about the *maidanam*. In the late nineteenth century when the city was recognised and refurbished with an increasing Victorian look, the importance of the *maidanam* also increased.[6]

These concerns and protests provided the widening of ideological base that informed the connections between nation state and the individual. Sandria Freitag recorded that the first was participation in collective rituals informed by an ideological framework that came to equate 'communities' and nation. Secondly, the creation of a public sphere in which citizens of the nation helped to shape it through the exercise of public opinion. This shift in the organisation of community around the local community to one in which individuals identified with the nation was accompanied by the creations of a public sphere, which was fully elaborated and institutionalised in the Nineteenth Century.[7]

The *maidanam* was very integral to the imperial administration in colonial India. In 1902, the Government of India expressed its eagerness to reconsider existing arrangements for the control of the *maidanam*. The *maidanam* had another identity and that too carried its contradictions. The natives perceived the *maidanam* as a metaphor for British occupations and identified the space with the European way of living. But as a significant number of natives imbibed English educations and culture, they also started making incursions into this space. Over the years well-to-do sections also started enjoying the flavour of this open space.[8] The *maidanam* was the place to visit in the afternoon for a leisurely walk or a coach rite, for gawking at the sahibs and the memsahib or to watch the sahib's cricket play or football. The *maidanam* was the place to go for enjoying circus shows, bioscopes do marvel at the launching of hot air balloons, etc.

The *maidanam* lends itself as a mirror which reflected the growth and evolutions of the feat of power of the empire. As the empire grew, evolved and natures; it had to spare attentions to the issue of mental and physical spaces necessary for the wellbeing of the colonizers. Their needs neither were no longer satisfied by the existing spaces, which included the attach sites, pigeon fight enclosures, pooja grounds and religious processions on the streets. Thus, the *maidanam* provides a deep insight into the working of the mindset of the colonial ruler. The project of modernity could only be implemented in a limited form within the colonial form of power and in this case was limited to the physical space of the *maidanam*.[9]

The history of public space is the history of the people who live around it. The discussion on the urban spaces in Kerala is incomplete without a discussion on the *maidanam*. The *maidanam* is a space integral to the urban and semi-urban spaces in Kerala today. Kozhikkode's first serious move towards urbanisation happened in the later part of the Seventeenth Century after the English gained firm control over the town in 1793. The city of Kozhikkode was a busy trading centre where people from all parts of the world flocked in the medieval period. This activity never necessitated the birth of an open space for public activity in the town. The palace of the Samoothiri was the centre of the town and the Tali Temple attracted people of higher castes to live around it. The market was also adjacent to the palace and the people involved in it lived away from the town or in the market itself because of the rules of caste restrictions.

The invasion of Mysorean army in the middle of the seventeenth century changed the entire structure and thereby the palace also disappeared from the city. The open space appeared in the site of the palace was occupied by the Mysorean forces and they required facilities including mosque and temporary sheds for their activities. This site became Palayam. The open space gradually developed into an arena of public activity in the town and people of all castes and religions were free to use it. The administration of the Mysorean forces necessitated the emergence of public offices, police station or *Qasaba,* etc., around this open space. This was a major change in the social structure in Malabar. The social system emerged under the Mysorean rule was totally different from the traditional system existed in Kozhikkode and Malabar. Gradually, new public spaces began to emerge in Malabar which violated the caste rules of pre Mysorean Malabar.

The defeat of Tipu Sultan in 1793 enabled the East India Company to undertake the administration of Malabar. The whole of Malabar region up to the boundary of Kochi was kept under the Bombay Presidency and later shifted to Madras Presidency by 1800. The East India Company followed the administrative system of the Mysorean rulers in Malabar. They selected Kozhikkode as the centre of Malabar District and necessary offices were erected in the same place chosen by the Mysorean rulers in the city. This was the newly developed public space called Mananchira Maidanam.

The arrival of Christian missionaries in Malabar in the Nineteenth Century changed the character of social life in Kerala. The intervention of industrial capitalism, labourers, the printing machine, factories, schools, churches and training centres, railway and expansion of city life, new middle class, etc., necessitated busy activity in the urban life. The Mananchira Maidanam became a site of busy popular activity in the nineteenth and early twentieth centuries. It included the enjoyment of city life, business activity, exhibitions and publicity of new products, circus and cinema shows. Being a strategic town in the commercial life in South India, capitalists stayed in the town during the colonial period. They wanted to create amenities necessary to them including recreational and sports activities and related spaces in the city. The Mananchira Maidanam in the central part of the city helped them to organise such activities for the elite people in the town. Like the Mysorean authorities, the British also used the Maidanam for army parades and trainings. During the time of emergencies special army parades were conducted in the *maidanam* to threaten the people of Malabar. Such parades took place during the Malabar Rebellion and First World War.

Nationalist demonstrations took place in the *maidanam* to exhibit the power of the nationalist forces. The conferences of associations like the Indian National Congress also wanted to show the number of people in Malabar opposing the colonial government. The Second Malabar District Political Conference was planned in the Mananchira Maidanam in April, 1917 according to this idea. This District administration denied permission to it, to help the imperial view point. Subsequently, the conference was held in the Tennis Court of K.P. Raman Menon as the 'Tennis Court Conference'. The colonial government established control over this public space by erecting a fence around the *maidanam* with public subscription to prevent the assemblage of masses in the open space. It was followed by rules and regulations and monitoring of the police to control the mob assembling in the public space.

In Kerala, the sphere of public activities emerged by the nineteenth century. The most important change during this period was the development of colonial institutions instead of the feudal *swaroopam* and the temple of the pre-colonial period. It changed social relationships during this period.[10] The growth of public sphere was not unique in the case of Kerala. It developed as a partner of capitalism, enlightenment, and the middle class.[11] During these days Kerala experienced modernity in the context of protests against the oppression of upper classes. These movements resulted in the formation of caste organisations like the Nair Service Society, Sree Narayana Dharma Paripalana Yogam, etc. All these changes occurred in the context of the evolution of the modern public space. This public space was also the platform of exhibitions, demonstrations, gatherings, cinema shows, circus carnivals, political meetings, etc. In this context, the debate of the evolution of the *mananchira maidanam* as a public space in the urban history of colonial Malabar becomes very important. The *maidanam* became the space for several cultural and political events during the late nineteenth and early twentieth centuries. During the national movement political meetings, public speeches, etc., were organised in the *maidanam* and the space became the site of conflict between national and colonial interests. In this context, the public space and the public opinion were confronted by heavy pressures of various interest groups. The public exhibitions and the print media actively engaged in the public space to intervene in the public opinion. The space of *Mananchira Maidanam* played an important role in the formation of public opinion in Malabar. The social life in all respects in the Kozhikkode city was influenced by the events in the *maidanam*.

The Manachira Maidanam had become a public ground under the Mysorean rule in Malabar. The site was subjected to physical changes under the administration of the East India Company. Cannolly, the Collector of Malabar granted a piece of land near the *Maidanam* to the Muslims to construct a mosque which became an expanded form of the Old Pattala Palli.[12] Moreover in September 1871, a part of the *Maidanam* was donated to the Basel Evangelical Mission School, the Municipal Council Hospital, etc.[13] This space was the 'Parade Ground' to the public in the city in and around 1845. The British military conducted drills (*kavath*) in the *Maidanam* which shared a new experience to the people in the town.[14] The *Maidanam* was a free space to them and up to the arrival of the British. When it was undertaken by the colonial police, in the name of security and restriction, the public space became a great concern in the city life. Thus in 1906, the *Maidanam* was separated by a fence built around it. This fence was donated by Rarichan Mooppan, a landlord in

Kozhikkode in connection with the visit of the British Prince. The public was told to celebrate the visit of British Prince and a 'Royal Visit Committee' was formed including the elites in the city under the instruction of the colonial authorities.[15]

In course of time with the evolution of the Municipal Council of Kozhikode, the city administration undertook the custodianship of the *Maidanam*. The British authorities framed rules for the administration of the municipality in 1850. After 15 years, the Town Improvement Act was implemented in selected towns and on July 3, 1866 Kozhikode became a Municipality which was then the biggest one in the Malabar District. The people of the Kozhikkode Municipality were given the right to elect members of the council.[16] In 1896-97, the right to elect half of the members of the council was given to the voters in the Municipality and this Indian elite in the Municipal administration also supported the government to restrict the public use of the *Maidanam*. Thus, the *Maidanam* became a site of conflict during the national movement in different levels. If the British Government was using the space to demonstrate their imperial power in the form of military drills and parades, the capitalist forces intervened in the society by using the *maidanam* space for exhibitions. The camping of touring companies and cinema shows also influenced the people to shape their understanding of the society. Along with this the nationalist forces in Malabar began to concentrate their activities in Kozhikkode as the headquarters of the Malabar District. The jurists, merchants, lawyers, clerks, teachers and journalists camped in the city to take part in the movement against colonialism and they undertook the duty of propagating new ideas for social changes in the society.

The national movement in Malabar became powerful by the beginning of the Twentieth Century, especially with the outbreak of the First World War. The Indian National Congress, the Ramakrishna Mission, the Theosophical Society, masonic orders, clubs, the Sree Narayana movement, and other Christian missionary agencies began to represent their interests in the public sphere in the city life. This naturally created contradictions in the national movement. C. Krishnan attempted to revive Buddhism in Malabar and he had also supported British rule instead of the Brahmin raj of the early phase of anti-colonial struggle.

An important incident connected with the development of conflicting interests in the place was the plan to host the Second Malabar District Conference in Kozhikkode in 1917.[17] This Conference was controlled by the Theosophical Society which had branches in Kozhikkode and other parts of Malabar. Controversies piled up with the nomination of the president of the Conference. C.P. Ramaswami Aiyer was invited by the Reception committee to deliver the Presidential Address. The new nationalist middle class wanted a leader like Bal Gangadhar Tilak to lead the Conference in 1917. Few people expressed their dislike in the selection of the President and said that Tilak was not an apt person to preside over the conference. It shows the commencement of the conflict of opinions and the war of ideas began to fill the pages of newspapers in Malabar. Another demand of the public debate in Kozhikkode was that the proceedings of the Conference were to be done in Malayalam. Most of the conferences of the educated middle classes used English language in its proceedings. And these pro Malayalam activists demanded that the president was to be one who understands the language of the District. Some people demanded that Rama Varma was to be invited to preside over the conference. According to them if a plebiscite took place in Malabar on this subject, majority of the votes would go in favour of Rama Varma.[18] To these people Rama Varma, a natural leader and King of Thiruvithamcore was a thoughtful attention to every Malayali. This debate shows that the Congress Movement in Malabar was under the control of the Home League.

The Second Malabar District Political Conference commenced at Kozhikode on 23 April, 1917. C.P. Ramaswami Aiyer, the Secretary of All India Congress Committee, presided over the conference. P. Achuthan, K.P. Keshava Menon, T.V. Sundarayyan, K.P. Raman Menon etc., were in charge of the Reception Committee.[19] The organising committee requested the District authorities to sanction the Mananchira Maidanam to conduct the proceedings. It was a time of the World War and the government was trying to control public opinion and was intervening in the public space in increased strength. This forced the government to reject the demand because of the political and geographical and communal importance of the Kozhikkode city. The city became crucial to the colonial authorities because of the presence of the German Basel Mission and its factories, labourers in the industrial units, the presence of anti-colonial spirit among the members of the Muslim community and the influence of Home Rule League in Malabar.[20]

The meeting of the nationalists at Kozhikkode was a challenge to the colonial government in Malabar during the First World War. When the *maidanam* space was not allotted, the Reception Committee decided to conduct the Conference in the Tennis Court of K.P. Raman Menon's residence. This became a chance to the nationalists to point out that the Conference at Kozhikkode was the beginning of a movement like the French Revolution against the despotic rule of the British in India.[21] C.P. Ramaswami Ayer attended the Conference and portrayed the character of colonialism in India with special emphasis on the colonial policies in Malabar. He stressed the drain of wealth from India and the help offered by the Indian people to the British in the World War. The denial of the *maidanam* for a nationalist activity was seriously discussed in the public space in Malabar and it compelled the nationalists to talk about the requirement of nationalist public spaces in the society. Because of the attitude of the government towards the Conference, the proceedings gave care to organise revolutionary activities like conducting *misrabhojanam* and launched a movement to open the approach road towards the Tali Temple for the use of the underprivileged classes in the city. This was an important change in the nationalist political activity in Kerala.

M.P. Narayana Menon's speech at this conference emphasised the requirement of an anti-imperialist movement of the people in Malabar. This Conference also denounced the practice of untouchability and restricting some section of people to walk through the public roads. In course of time people like

K.P. Kesava Menon presided over weekly meetings of the Congress branches. The Congress activists met on all Sundays and began to discuss political and social issues. These gatherings naturally became study classes and they produced a gang of trained activists in the national movement. The most important result of the District Conference held at Kozhikkode was the commencement of the participation of young people in the anti-imperialist and social reform activity in Malabar. Large number of young people became active in the movement when they realised the absence of freedom in using the public spaces in India. Young people like M.P. Narayana Menon, Moyyarath Sankaran, K.P. Kesava Menon, etc., began their political career with the Conference held at Kozhikkode in 1917.

The Tennis Court Conference as it was called became the reason for these changes in the political life in Malabar. T.M. Nair, the leader of the Non Brahmin Movement in Madras and a native of Malabar criticized the Conference as a work of the Brahminical forces. He ridiculed the conference as 'the Tennis Court Conference'. The fame of Tennis Court Conference and French Revolution began to spread with the Kozhikkode event. Kesava Menon spoke in English at the conference, though there were criticisms against the use of foreign language in discussing the issues of the society in India Madathil Rarichan Moopan presented a resolution arguing for the representation of middle class and landlords in the Conference. Later in the Madras Legislative Council, C.P. Ramaswami Ayyer moved a resolution in favour of the War Fund. The nationalists of this period were not bold enough to attack the imperial authorities and they offered all assistances to the British government in the War. All of them expected certain rewards to India after the War. Young people like M.P. Narayana Menon opposed this stand of the moderate nationalists[22].

The lower caste people were not allowed to walk along the roads adjacent to the Tali Temple Kozhikkode. The consciousness of the right to use public spaces without the distinctions of caste and class compelled the nationalists to speak for opening the Tali Road to the untouchable classes. During the Conference, C.

Krishnan, K. Madhavan Nair, Manjeri Rama Ayer, K.P. and Kesava Menon used the road in violation of the restrictions and began a new movement for social change in Malabar. It was the first civil disobedience event in Malabar.

'Our Day' was celebrated in the Madras Presidency by the British Government to ensure the participation of the Indian people in the World War on 12 December, 1917. It was celebrated to collect funds for the Red Cross work, particularly amongst the troops in Mesopotamia. A procession was held in the Kozhikkode town with portraits of the British king and queen and Union Jack flags were carried in the procession headed by an elephant carrying the emblems of the Red Cross society[23]. The procession passed through the principles streets from the Huzur Office attended by many people. This procession was led by C. M. Rarichan Moopan, P. T. Raman, etc. They sold miniature Union Jacks and collected money for the Red Cross Fund. There were student processions from different institutions in the town. Our day flags and Button holes were also sold in different parts of Malabar. A fair was also held in the *maidanam* to attract the people.[24] In Trichur the supporters of the government collected an amount of Rs 16,046 to the War Fund. This shows that the concept of public space began to develop into newer areas of work and it began to have fresh interventions. All these activities concentrated around public spaces and the Mananchira Maidanam became a busy site of public activity of various pressure groups.

During the Non-Cooperation Movement, the British government declared orders prohibiting K. Madhavan Nair, U. Gopala Menon, Moideen Koya and Yakub Hassan from delivering public speeches at the Mananchira Maidanam. By negating the government order they came to Mananchira for the speech and were arrested by the police in 1920.[25] It was in this time youngsters like Moyarathu Sankaran began to challenge the rules of the British government. The Congress movement was turning into a mass movement exhibiting their strength in the public space in the form of the military drills of the colonial authorities. Moyarath Sankaran and other were inspired by the leadership of nationalists like K. Madhavan Nair[26].

The Celebration of Independence Day in August 1947 was the culmination of the national movement. This celebration on the evening of 14th August 1947 was conducted at the Mananchira Maidanam. The celebrations in the Kozhikode City commenced with the erection of a stupa in the north side of the Mananchira Maidanam. The place where the stupa was erected was later called the Tagore Park. In 1994, the Mananchira Square came into being as a developed form of the *maidanam* in the post-independence period. It represented the pain and agonies that the people of Kozhikkode city felt in connection with the anti-colonial movement in Malabar.

The public space or a public *maidanam* is not a free gift of the colonial rule. It is a result of the collective work of the public who made the public space accessible to all. The Mananchira Maidanam regulated the opinion and interests of the people through public debates, conflicts, gatherings, shows and exhibitions. The government met this challenge by using the space to demonstrate their power. Manachira had an important role in the cultural life of the people and it became a centre of literary activity. S.K. Pottekkat, M.T. Vasudevan Nair, Thikodiyan, Urub etc., used their evenings at the Manachira Maidanam.[27] They collected facts, figures and imaginations from the space for their activity in the literary world.

This investigation gives evidence to say that the emerging national elite in the town also wanted to occupy the public space and wanted to distance the common masses from it. Those who were against the British attached special importance to the *maidanam* as a symbol of British domination. When they could become the members of the Municipal Council, they endorsed the regulations of the colonial government. By this period investment capitalism had begun to intervene in the democratic institutions in India. These forces wanted to bridge the interests of the elites of colonialism and the Indian society. Those who paid taxes to the British became voters. According to property qualifications the elite in Indian society began to occupy these democratic bodies. Irrespective of religious and caste differences people gathered in the public grounds. The enclosure becomes necessary for the British to prevent the birth of public opinion among the ordinary masses. Any programme conducted in the Mananchira Maidanam could easily change the taste and interest of the people. Thus, Mananchira Maidanam became integral to the daily life of the urban population and the visitors from various villages.

References

1. Sandria Frietag tried to bring out the link between public sphere activities and the national movement in the Indian context and prefers to identify it 'public arena.' See *Collective Action and Community: Public Arenas and the Emergence of Communalism in North India,* Oxford University Press: New Delhi, 1990.

2. Geard Haises, *Vernacular Dialogue and the Rhetorically of Fublic Opinion,* University South Carolina: Colombia, 1998, p. 86.

3. See Sandria Freitag, *op.cit.*

4. Jostein Gripsrud, Hallvard Moe et.al (eds.), *The idea of the Public Sphere: A Reader,* Lexington Books, 2010, p. 43.

5. *Ibid.,* p.114.

6. Sarmishta De and Bidisha Chakrabarty, '*Maiden: The Open Space in History' in Social Scientist*, Vol. 38, January-February-2010, p.11.

7. See Sandria Freitag, *op.cit.*

8. Sumanta Banarjee, *The Parlous and the Streets: Elite and Popular culture in Nineteenth Century Calcutta,* Seagull: Calcutta, 1989, p.23.

9. Sarmishta De and Bidisha Chakrabarty, 'Maiden: The Open Space in History' in Social Scientist, Vol.18, Jaunary-February, 2010, p.18.

10. M.G.S. Narayanan, *Charithrakarante Kerala Darshanam (Mal.),* Trivandrum, 2011, p. 99.

11. K.N. Ganesh, *Kealathinta Innalakal (Mal.),* Trivandrum, 1997, p. 386.

12. T.B. Seluraj, *Kozhikodente Paithrakam (Mal.),* Mathrubhumi Books: Kozhikkode, 2011, p. 98.

13. *Ibid.,* 2011, p.100.

14. *Ibid.,* p.101.

15. The "Kallingal Madam" was a wealthy Thiyya house in Kozhikode. The senior member of this family was given to the title 'Moopan' by Tippu Sultan. Later Samuthiri Rajas also conferred the

same title to the senior member of Kallingal family. In the Nineteenth Century Sakthan Thampuran sanctioned the title, 'Moopan' to two senior members of this family, Rarichan and Kunchikkoru and thus it became a hereditary title. In course of time the people identified the senior member of this family as Moopan. The Moopan had the privilege to use turban, umbrella, manchal, dolly etc., even in front of the Samuthiris. C. Sankaran Master, *Nammude Mahanmar (Mal.),* Trissur, 1913.

16. Nagara Sabha Vikasana Rekha (Mal.), Vol.165, Kerala Ditrict Planning Board, August 17, 1997, p. 26.

17. K.P. Kesava Menon, V. Parukuttyamma, Thiruvananthapuram, 1988, pp.75-76.

18. MNNPR No. 10 of 1917, for the week ending on March 10, 1917, West Coast Spectator, March 13, 1967.

19. K. Madhavan Nair, *Janmasatabdi Smaranika (Mal.),* Mathrubhumi Books: Kozhikode, 1982, pp. 21-22.

20. T.V. Sundara Ayar, *'The Tennis Court Conference'* in Mathrubhumi Weekly, October, 1946.

21. *Ibid.*

22. V. Parukutti Amma, K.P. Kesava Menon (Mal.), Department of Culture, Kerala Government: Thiruvananthapuram, 1988, pp. 75-76.

23. T.V. Sundara Ayar, *'The Tennis Court Conference'* in Mathrubhumi Weekly, October, 1946.

24. W-24, *The Madras War Fund: Illustrated Record,* Higgin Bothams: Madras, 1919, Regional Archives, Kozhikkode.

25. Moyyarth Sankaran, 'Uthama Netavu, 'Indiyum Keralathineeyum Rashtriya Guru' in Mathrubhumi Weekly, 15th January, 1934, p. 27.

26. *Ibid.,* p. 28.

27. M.T. Vasudevan Nair, 'Kozhikodinte Paidrakam' in Dr. P.B. Salim, N.P. Hafis Muhamed, M.C. Vashishit, (ed.), Malabar Paithrukavum Pratapavum (Mal.), Mathrubhumi Books, Kozhikode, 2011, p. 30.

6

The Waste Management and Environmental Protection : A Concern for Human Existence

Abraham Mathew

The advancement of civilisation along with industrial development has caused a great damage to natural beauty of mother earth. Things have worsened because no or very little attention has been paid towards protecting the environment. Land, water and air are being polluted in every minute. Exposure to water and air pollution can cause serious health problems for both man and living beings. Waste dumped along water bodies will endanger the very existence of man. The State of Kerala has a big heap of garbage owing to total collapse of waste managing system. Even coastal areas are not free from this menace. According to pollution control board, one million cubic meters of sewage is generated in the state coastal areas, of which 30,000 cubic meters reached the surface of water bodies. The back waters alone receive 60 tonnes of sewage from the city. Thus, Kerala now became a place of garbage. The quantity of waste created is increasing due to extreme consumption habit and affluence of the people. The ever increasing rates of pollution are mainly because of the lack of enforcement of laws at the local level. The Planning Commission of India's 10th plan document reports sewage alone is responsible for 80 per cent of water pollution. Current malfunctioning in municipal solid waste management is more managerial failure, rather than a technological break down.

The Maladies of Kerala

According to an international study, Kerala has been listed 'the first 50 must- see destinations of a life time'. Are we going to welcome the tourists from the top of heavy garbage dumps? Here, we are deliberately turning Gods own country into a devils backyard. Kerala is undergoing various threats from various diseases like Chikungunya, dengue fever, swine flu, malaria, viral fever, etc. Recently, rat fever is also increasing in Kerala at an alarming rate. Under this gloomy situation how we boast of health standards at par with the west? If things are going like this, Kerala will become a centre of all types of deadly diseases. This is mainly because of inefficient and insufficient waste management programmes at State and local levels.

In addition to it, there are serious threats from e-waste. Over the last few decades the world has witnessed a revolution in the electrical and electronic industries. The electronic products have become an inevitable part of modern life. However, the discarded or unused and outdated e-products are increasing at an alarming rate. As per the UNEP reports, the year 2020 e-waste in India will soar by 500 per cent. A major share of it may be the contribution of the State of Kerala. Another problem faced by the State of Kerala is, the lack of environment friendly e-waste reprocessing or recycling system. There are no clear cut e-waste management regulations at the central or state levels. Unrestrained dumping and improper waste re-cycling methods generate considerably dangerous emissions, with severe impacts on environment and health.

Plastic bags, thin plastic film sheet and all kinds of plastic waste forms another major source of pollution across the state. Plastic break down result into the formation of toxic particles that pollute the soil and water bodies. A good portion of marine wastes is being generated out of plastic products. The survival and growth of unique marine species are affected by the above problem. The possible impact of toxic materials from plastic wastes in the ocean affects human health, is a matter of rising concern. The consumption of plastics is increasing in Kerala shall be viewed very seriously. However, little measures have been followed to recycle, reuse and safely dispose plastic wastes, and little regulation have been enforced at management level. The garbage collection or disposal facilities are not well designed, hence tonnes of plastic materials dumped in the soil, blocks, rainwater seepage into the ground. The existing rules and regulations to prevent the menace of plastic wastes are very little. Even those rules are not being implemented properly by the authorities.

Man-made Disaster

The quantity of waste materials of different types is increasing due to increase in human population and increase in standard of living. It means waste materials are produced as a result of human activity. No doubt, the problem of waste is a manmade disaster. However, the authorities and the civil society are not aware of its adverse consequences at its right magnitude. The government and the Panchayati Raj institutions are lethargic or afraid of addressing this issue. For the protection of environment and to control pollution and the waste management, the Government of India has framed many laws. After independence serious efforts have been made in the form of legislation for the protection and conservation of environment. However, the policies and the decisions taken by the authorities in this regard in most cases are half hearted or having insufficient force to address such issues permanently. Interestingly, when one policy is being taken to address an issue, another issue hitherto unknown is cropped up. This is a serious challenge with regard to environmental protection and waste management, at all layers of governance. As if now the waste processing facility is available only in three corporations out of five in Kerala. The other corporations have land for waste dumping, but no facilities for collection or processing. In case of municipalities, out of 53, only 17 have land and treatment facilities. Of a total of 1000 and above village panchayats, only 126 village panchayats have land for waste treatments. All facilities for waste treatment are available only in 7 panchayats, while partial facilities are available in 105 village panchayats.

In Kerala the per capita generation of waste is relatively high compared to other parts of India, due to the higher per capita income, as well as difference in the consumption patterns. The source of solid waste in Kerala and the percentage contribution from the each source is given below:

1. House hold waste–49 per cent
2. Hostels, marriage halls and institutions–17 per cent
3. Shops and markets -16 per cent
4. Street sweepings–9 per cent
5. Constructions–6 per cent
6. Slaughter house, hospitals–3 per cent

Major Waste Management and Environment Issues in Kerala

A major endeavour for waste management, Malinya Mukta Kerala was launched on 1st Nov. 2007 with a mission of clean Kerala. If we consider the situation of waste management, despite success in a few areas, there is considerable dissent among people especially, those surrounding the waste processing centres. Efficient disposal and management of waste is still an issue in Kerala. To site an example, the Vilappilsala plant in Thiruvananthapuram, despite being handed over to government by the private party is not functioning in a proper manner. It causes numerous problems to people living in surrounding areas and they are still protesting against it. One of the main issues pointed out in waste disposal was lack of suitable model for effective waste management.

In Kerala, public-private partnership was tried without much success by Thiruvananthapuram Municipal Corporation in their Vilappilsala plant. The agreement to efficiently process 300 metric tonnes of municipal solid waste was not done by POABS, the private company. It resulted in improper dumping of unprocessed waste in the premises. This led to complaint from the neighbourhood about foul smell and contaminated discharge polluting water bodies. TMC accused POABS of inefficient operation of the plant. People near the Vilappilsala plant were protesting for the closure of the plant. The air pollution and the water pollution in the area is a serious threat to the health and well-being of people living in that area. The failure of POABS was mainly attributed to the lower capacity of the plant, difficulty in segregating and processing waste, lack of technical know-how which resulted in lower conversion of efficiency. Moreover, uneven demand of organic manure and lack of space to store manure which resulted in dumping of untreated waste and subsequent problems.

The case of Plachimada Coca-Cola plant was more or less the same of the Vilappilsala. The large-scale cadmium pushed out of the plant created environmental pollution and many related issues. The depletion of ground water caused due to the plant was another serious havoc faced by the villagers. The protest, spearheaded by the people living in the area ultimately found success and led to the closure of the plant.

The issues related with the proposed airport in Aranmula, Pathanamthitta district and those related with the implementation of 'Swaminathan Commissions' recommendations to rectify the problems of Kuttanad, are still inviting strong opposition from different quarters. Environmentally hazardous ventures must be stopped throughout the State for the larger interest of the society and sustainable development. Besides, almost all rivers and water bodies have been in the verge of either extinction or becoming sewage flowing centres. For example, Ashtamudi lake, Vembanad lake and many other water bodies including major rivers are facing serious threat in the form of waste and pollution. The ecology and the living conditions of the people will be affected badly if we could not take ardent steps to revive the rivers, the very life blood of our State. Rules and regulations must be initiated and implemented sincerely to achieve this end.

However, these sorts of issues are very often politicised by political parties for achieving their petty interest.

In Kerala, a large portion of the waste are generated by biodegradable substances. Following facts will show the alarming state of affairs existing in a small State like Kerala.

1. Biodegradable (71—83)

2. Paper (3.5—5)

3. Plastic, rubber, glass, metal (5.0—9.0)

4. Domestic hazardous (4.9 — 11.5).

The Role of Civil Society in Waste Management

The civil society and citizens can play a pivotal role in this regard because they are closely connected with the environment. They are knowledgeable about their own communities and its problems. Their day to day observations give them access to information about environmental conditions that the government could never obtain. The civil society and NGO's are very active nowaday to study such problems. The intimate connection between individuals and their own communities enable the citizens to concentrate on localised environmental problems. A federal or even a state government agency might not consider such "small scale threats" to the environment serious enough to justify action on the national or regional levels. Citizen participation in environment enforcement thus broadens access to enforcement resources. They can thus contribute in a more realistic and responsive manner, in environment enforcement strategy.

However, there is an apprehension on the part of the government that citizen involvement in environment enforcement will disrupt its own enforcement efforts. There are lots of such burning issues live in the air. There are instances of efficient waste management programmes chalked out by the government and Panchayati Raj institutions, for the larger interest of the society are very often scuttled by the involvement of civil society on trivial reasons. They often suspect government agencies of not properly fulfilling their enforcement responsibilities. It is understood that many conflicting matters can be amicably settled through the active cooperation and good will of the civil society and the government.

The citizen participation and cooperation is being utilised in a full-fledged manner by the western countries, in environmental protection. Avenues for public participation and its enforcement are many and varied. Some requires special expertise and some require only energy and common sense. Methods of collecting valuable environmental data are numerous; one way is to gather information from physical observation or verification. Violations identified through these information gathering activities can then be reported to environmental organisations or government. In USA, a citizen can file a law suit against an alleged violator. Citizens can also gather about environmental violations through the use of information collected by the government. The citizens may be able to use the information they have collected by going to court themselves to enforce environmental controls. One approach to encourage citizen involvement in environmental enforcement would be to permit citizens to enter into private property to undertake environmental monitoring when warranted by a serious threat to public health.

Innovative Waste Management Programmes

It is the responsibility of the civil society and the government to formulate or introduce innovative programme to tackle the issues related with protecting the environment and waste disposal. An innovative concept, 'harmonious society' popularised by Hue Gintao, the former President of China has been well appreciated by everybody. According to this formula, the well-being and prosperity of the society, good neighbourliness, and peaceful life situation can be maintained properly. Studies about such innovative ventures can help a greater extent to introduce such things in our situation too. Another option would be to allow the citizens to assist the government in carrying out its own environmental monitoring activities. In Argentina, private participation in inspecting violations of water quality legislations is being carried out efficiently and proper mechanisms to publish the violations in the press or through community assembling are practiced. This could create pressure on industrial polluters to find out alternative mechanisms. The approach adapted by the USA in gathering information through both formal and informal citizen monitoring can be adapted in our system. The lessons from USA are most useful and practicable in our situation too. The recycling of waste materials in India is not developed up to the international standards and various measures of such mechanisms can be adapted to strengthen environmental protection.

Measures for Protecting Environment

(a) Protect Water Bodies and Invent Non-conventional Energy Sources

The first and the foremost thing is to preserve the sources of water and water bodies properly at maximum possible extent. Strict rules should be introduced to check water pollution by men. The growing menace faced by water bodies and rivers in Kerala is the waste dumped from industries and sewage from other centres. Clean drinking water is a rare commodity in Kerala while we have plentiful and rich source of water.

Another area where much attention is required with is the use of petroleum products. Alternative energy sources must be found to address the growing demands of energy. For that non-conventional energy sources can be properly utilised and tapped. Sometimes the initial cause of installing projects related with such endeavours may be costly, but the hazards associated with atomic energy and petroleum products can be minimised considerably.

(b) Stop Deforestation and Start Afforestation

Strict measures should be taken to stop deforestation and at the same time forestation and social forestry be promoted among the people. Planting trees in large numbers everywhere on a war footing basis is the need of the hour. It would help to keep the ecosystem in the proper manner. The example of King Ashoka of ancient period in India shall be followed by the democratic rulers of the present century. King Ashoka popularised the planting of tress on way sides and protected it in serious manner, is an example to everyone. The planting of trees must be popularised among the younger and old generations, is the responsibility of the government.

(c) Promote Nature Friendly Constructions

The construction of houses, business establishments, industrial centres etc. must be done on environment friendly manner. If the mode of construction in the pretext of development is taking place in Kerala on a fast scale like this it may convert the God's own Country into a concrete jungle. The finest example of environment friendly construction is the 'Baker model'. It was the pioneer model in the realm of house construction on environment friendly manner. This has been initiated by Lary Baker, a famous architect came from the western continent. The models of technology introduced by Baker are environment friendly and sustainable. Many institutions in Kerala were designed and constructed accordingly. This programme which initiated in Kerala about forty years back, can be experimented and popularised widely in the present situation.

(d) Regulate the Use of Plastic and Toxic Materials

The use of plastics and such toxic materials is increasing in an alarming manner that causes serious hazards to environment and living beings. The steps taken to control the use of plastics and toxic materials have not found tangible results because efforts of the government are not having sufficient strength or force. The Government and authorities are not sincere in dealing with such issues and are reluctant to pressurise the civil society to follow the rules strictly.

(e) Deep Ecology and Green Politics

The time has come to know the importance of environmental protection. Serious threats are being faced by humanity in the pretext of development and it created irreparable problems to them. The political parties and the party in power are not taking this issue as serious and always think and act online with their petty party interest.

The large scale land mining, sand mining and quarries causes serious threat to ecological balance. The uses of strong pesticides have also created large scale problems to the environment. Following blindly the western model of cultivation causes huge threat to the ecosystem. The auto control capability and regeneration capability of the environment shall be maintained at all costs. The principle of 'Deep Ecology' is a programme initiated to protect the environment in its virginity and purity shall be popularised and it may help all living beings to live peacefully on earth. The bio-diversity of the earth system should be maintained even though serious threats against it increasing in the backdrop of 'pseudo' development. The principle of green politics is getting momentum in all corners of the world since the threat to environment and ecology increasing. This situation warrants the relevance of 'Green Politics' that aimed at the well-being and prosperity of humanity in the present and future.

Conclusion

Lessons learned and best practices shall be promoted by the society and the authorities concerned. Increased awareness of proper solid waste practices are the need of the hour. Both formal and informal activities like public meetings, media programmes, literature and website promotion, workshops and educational expose, etc., shall help the waste management programmes. Examples of success that could be brought up would include the recycling programmes at schools, churches and communities; and ongoing efforts to engage and work with the NGOs and the business community. In addition, there are institutional strengthening programme which facilitates training opportunities for government agencies dealing with solid waste management. Efficient waste management must start from every home in the state. Every household must ensure proper segregation of waste into: sharps, degradable, electronic. Waste, thus, segregated must be handed over to collection personnel in strong paper bags. The practice of throwing away wastes in open must be dealt with firmly. The onus for efficient waste management lies with the local governing bodies. However, the citizens cannot wash their hands of this responsibility. Thus, the policy related with waste management should be pro-active rather than reactive.

Appropriate strategies and action programmes have to be developed and implemented with genuine public participation on a war footing basis. It is proved that, the waste collection and disposal can be done effectively through *Kudumbasree* units in Kerala. The role being played by them in corporations and municipalities are quite commendable. The collection of waste is conducted in an effective manner by these groups. But they are not provided with sufficient protection, in terms equipments for collecting and disposing wastes. It is a fact that disasters related with environment are manmade. For the survival of the present and the future generation, we have to preserve good drinking water, good air and healthy surroundings. We will not hand over debris to the next generation. Conservation of resources has therefore, economic, aesthetic and scientific value.

Environmental conservation is an integral part of the socio-economic development of a state. Thus, policy-makers should give topmost priority in this regard. A systematic assessment of the impact of ecosystem – service-based approaches on both the people and nature's well-being are highly critical. So let us fight together to achieve the above goals.

References

1. A.D. Koushik and Rituraj, *Managing resources for disaster reduction*, IJPA New Delhi, Oct-Dec 2008.
2. Satendra and A.D. Koushik, *Water resource management for disaster mitigation*, IIPA, IJPA, July-Sep. 2003.
3. "Human development report", 1999 and 2000 UNDP.
4. www.unep.or.jp
5. B.B. Hosetti and A. Kumar, *Environmental impact assessment and management*, Daya Publishing House, New Delhi 1998.
6. Matrubhumi Yearbook 2012.
7. sanitation.kerala.gov.in
8. The Hindu, *Living in an extreme world*, July 13, 2013, p. 10.
9. The Hindu, *turning garbage into gas,* July 18, 2013, p. 10.

7

Triggering the Environment: A Lesson from Kureepuzha

Rajan T.

Is there any other world for the future generation to live in or do they have the resources to sustain their life? - are questions that haunt the minds of any prudent man of the present day world. Alarming progression in population, concurrent growth in world economy and intensive use in energy and raw materials[1] have ignited the intelligence and provoked the thought of the best of the creations of God in this direction. That is why concern about sustainable environment the world over in general and Third World countries in particular has become the focal point of the rhetoric and thinking of the present and consequent transition from 'ecological modernisation' to 'ecological sustainability'. The crisis on the question of 'ecological modernisation' versus 'ecological sustainability'[2] though not fully settled, strived at a stop gap arrangement at simultaneous realisation earlier, now switched over to a shift from the former to the latter in the light of emerging circumstances and accumulated experiences.

Development for growth and profit, unscrupulous constructions of convenience and unprincipled exploitation of natural resources to the very end of total destruction of nature's equilibrium are coincidental to industrialisation, urbanisation and globalisation which play havoc with sustainability of the environment and survival of the future generation. Mahatma Gandhi foresaw the intricacies of this growth and profit oriented development when he perceived: "It is imperative that the developmental process in a community is compatible with its environment as well as with the particular culture of that community."[3]

Obviously the earth is unique in the sense that it is the only place that sustains and nourishes life. Right from evolution to this day of development men started exploiting nature unscrupulously. Every human activity, in the pursuit of development conceived as incompatible with environment,[4] puts pressure on the environment. It causes environmental degeneration when the limit exceeds. Giddens, for example, has commented that "industry and capitalism have transformed the world of nature in ways that were unimaginable to earlier generations, leading to the formation of a created environment—one that is physical but not natural".[5] This phenomenon has transgressed the limits of all frontiers and boundaries imposing up on itself a universal dimension. Further, the process has augmented a new pace and speed of its own in the wake of globalisation.

Even before the fanfare of globalisation environmental issues tended to be international in character though its scope was limited compared to the present. That is why on issues like global warming, ozone depletion and acid rains peoples of the world come in togetherness. On such issues "state cannot claim any exclusively state centered approach to the business of bringing about environmental sustainability".[6] Similarly, an apparently domestic issue like waste management, because of its inherent dangers[7] and omnipresent nature, has come to transcend the boundaries of states. A clear symptom of this beyond the territorial transition is the suspected involvement of foreign NGOs in domestic environmental issues as alleged by home governments.[8] This boundary escapism is opposed to the West Phalian system of territorial states. Consequently, the question of sovereignty becomes incongruent with territory. What unites the peoples of the world in this context of boundary escapism is their concern for human rights. In fact, all environmental issues violate human rights which in turn unite the people and in this process the very classical concept of sovereignty gets undermined.

Every environmental issue is peculiar in terms of its origin. An environmental problem arises either on account of the failure of the state to check it effectively[9] or due to lack of vision, foresight and planning.[10] Absence of policy as such does not contribute positively to environmental problems.[11] In this connection a distinction is to be drawn between government and governance. It is government that forms and formulates policy. Implementation or governance comes only at the latter level. That is why Barry said: "The institutionalisation of green values within collective ecological management should be thought in terms of governance as opposed to government"[12]. Contextually, those who suffer in the two aforesaid instances are the people themselves. It is their right to life and survival, the very core of human rights that stand violated.

Therefore, a pertinent matter of debate on environmental issues is the doubt about the status of the state vis-a-vis the citizen. Is state the protector or the violator of citizens' human rights? The state is built and rests up on a consensual foundation which subsequently transformed in to and crystallised in the theory of legitimacy. The use of power by the state is legal and justifiable only if and when it is derived from the people or society over which the power is exercised. Here recourse may be taken to John Locke. To him "society and government are two things. The second exists for the wellbeing of the first, and a government which seriously jeopardises social interests is rightly changed."[13] Again, he openly speaks out that "the grant of community divests the people of power so long as the government is faithful to its duties."[14]

This background provides a common platform against which assessment of any environmental issue should begin. Either development or its ill- effects are not remote to any part of the globe. In India also "nature-based conflicts have increased in frequency. They revolve round competing claims...and have generated a new movement struggling for the rights of victims of ecological degradation."[15]

Kureepuzha, a suburban centre of the Kollam city in Kerala, just five kms away from the riddles of the main centre, is the best test case in this regard. It forms a part of the Kollam Corporation. The present stage in the history of its environmental degeneration goes to the days of the erstwhile Kollam Municipality when it was used as a site for a compost plant for treating human excreta. Twelve years back with the inauguration of the Kollam Corporation this place was added to the Corporation as its fifth ward and the original compost yard of four acres was enlarged by adding another twelve acres of nearby land. The strategy of location of the present yard is such that 2.5 acres out of the subsequently acquired 12 acres either shares boundaries with or lying adjacent to four historically important temples. Again, the yard was constructed by the corporation in total disregard to or ignoring Coastal Regulation Norms which totally bars any construction within 100 meters landward from High Tide Level (HTL).[16] The Corporation also failed to consider its proximity to two schools.

Even after the inauguration of the Corporation, the place was continued to be used by the local body to dump wastes. But the dumped waste in the yard could not be processed due to lack of skill, expertise technology and planning. Therefore, the Corporation constructed a new plant with improved capacity of 45 MT per day. But it is not commissioned till date on account of lack of planning in storage and segregation of wastes.

As per the statistics provided by the Corporation the total waste produced by the city is 64 MT per day.[17] Each resident of the city generated solid waste at an estimated quantum of 200 grams per day. The sources from which solid waste are generated:

(a) Domestic waste which constituted a major chunk of the total,

(b) Waste from shops and establishments,

(c) Waste from vegetable and fruit markets,

(d) Waste from meat, fish and slaughter houses and

(e) Waste from construction and demolition.

Provision for collection and storage of waste was done by the Corporation at primary and secondary levels. At the primary level collection was effected by the Corporation staff themselves. Conservancy staff of the Corporation, on convenience basis, identified certain open places at the secondary level. These are open spaces where waste is openly stored prior to being collected and transported for disposal. There are no temporary dumping yards in the city. Therefore, the waste is directly transported to the dumping site at Kureepuzha. A total of 30-35 MT of unsegregated waste is transported to the site daily of which only 15—20 MT converted into compost. Thus, there is an untreated quantity of waste to the tune of 15—20 MT every day. This is dumped in the open space in the yard. During rainy season rain water carries dirt and filth to the nearby water sources including the Ashtamudi Lake, causing contamination of both under water sources and the waters of the Ashtamudi Lake which is included in the Ramsar List. Moreover, stray dogs and birds often found entry in to the yard for their livelihood causing their left-over's to be spread and spilled in the areas nearby. It was against this background that the Corporation went ahead with the plan of a new plant with improved capacity which didn't materialise. The non-commissioning of the plant, subsequent accumulation of waste up to a height of 14 meters, contamination of water sources and the noxious, nauseating and mephitic smell emanating from the dump site caused the people to suffer a lot.

An Assertion for Survival

The ill- effects that it left on the lives and hopes of the people of Kureepuzha is beyond imagination, explanation and comparison. The survey conducted in this regard shows that the vast majority of the respondents to the tune of 98.57 per cent considered the effect of the waste disposed pollution as severe.

Among the respondents 97.14 per cent spoke of the nature of pollution as environmental. But its manifestation varied from person to person. Lung disease affected 57.14 per cent; intestinal diseases 20 per cent and those suffering from skin disease constituted 21.42 per cent. Unanimity was maintained by the locals in their attitude towards the impact of pollution on social status. All of them agreed that their social status was badly affected. People from other places were hesitant to contract marriage with them. There was an instance of a marriage proposal coming to a cease at the engagement ceremony itself because of the untimely leak of filth and consequent mephitic smell from the yard. With the aggravation of pollution and the problems that it left, property value had decreased considerably in the locality. Similarly, on the question relating to the violation of human rights also, there was cent per cent unanimity that the Corporation sponsored pollution violated their human rights. Again, cent per cent described the extent of human right violation as absolutely intolerable. On the question whether the corporation would be allowed to continue disposal 94.28 per cent responded in favour of no disposal at all. To the question "Were all your agitations within the limits of law," 95.71 per cent opined in the affirmative. Again, "What will you do if the corporation goes ahead with the disposal either under the cover of law or up on a court verdict," 98.57 per cent replied that they would agitate till death.

Thus, the Kollam Corporation and its waste dump site had deprived the people of Kureepuzha of their human rights. The local body sponsored pollution totally denied them of their right to life guaranteed by Art. 21 of the Constitution.[18] From the beginning itself no political party was willing to argue for them. Therefore, the people quite in disregard to all political affiliations and ideological commitments got themselves united under the banner of 'Kureepuzha Poura Samithi' in 1992. For the period from 1992-2002 the frequency of agitation was comparatively lesser and its intensity moderate. It was in 2004 that the people started an intensified agitation over the question of spillage of waste into the dwelling place of those who lived in the Puramboke land adjacent to the dump yard. The issue was finally settled at the instance of the then District Collector, B. Sreenivas in the presence of the then Kollam Mayor, Sabitha Beegum. But the increased rate of dumping and its worst effects brought the people together to form the 'Manushyavakasha Paristhithi Samrakshana Samithi' (MPSS) in 2011.

The issue assumed a serious dimension with the publication of a joint study report by the Zoology Department of the Fatima Mata National College, Kollam and Environmental Sciences, Department of the Kerala University, Trivandrum. The study found high physico-chemical and bacteriological contamination in the waters of the Ashtamudi Lake near the dumping yard. Apart from this, the study report also highlighted the bacterial contamination of wells caused by leakages from garbage. The report also brought to light the absence of any waste treatment system in the yard and the accumulation of collected waste in the past several years.[19]

Against this wanton dumping of waste by the Corporation, the people once again started an agitation in October, 2011. The agitation had brought the waste collection to a standstill for ten days. A truce was arrived at the instance of Shibu Baby John, the Labour Minister, Prasanna Earnest, the Mayor and people's leaders. But the peace was short lived. Again, on 30 October, 2012 the people blocked the entry of vehicles loaded with waste to enter the yard and unload which lasted for three days. The City Corporation held that the MPSS had been blocking trucks in violation of High Court Orders. People's version was that the Corporation was allowed by the High Court to empty trucks subject to the condition that the waste carried should not contain any plastic. Further, they said that the Corporation had not implemented the earlier agreement arrived at in the presence.

Meanwhile temple authorities and devotees began to express their dissent at the way in which Corporation authorities dealt with the matter. All the wells in the vicinity of the yard including the wells of the temples got contaminated due to leach ate from the yard. Consequently, they were forced to change the schedules of rites (poojas). "After human beings, it is the turn of Gods to suffer the ill effects of the garbage plant at Kureepuzha," commented a leading English Daily.[20]

On 20 June, 2012 the Corporation, in the wake of escalating vector diseases, had decided to transport the waste to the plant which had come to a standstill due to stiff resistance from the public under police escort. The MPSS held a demonstration on 2 July, 2012 in front of the Kollam Main Post Office as part of widening their agitation. N. Sathyapalan and Manalil Santhosh, President and Secretary respectively of the MPSS said that though the Corporation had constructed and inaugurated a garbage treatment plant several months ago, it had not started functioning till date. They also complained of accumulated waste lying untreated for several months in the yard polluting the lake and the wells in the locality and also foul smell emanating from the dump yard disturbing and degenerating normal human life.

As usual the agitation had brought forth much litigation. There are 13 cases pending against the locals and office bearers of the MPSS in the Kollam West Police Station and three cases in the Sakthikulangara Police Station. The MPSS itself filed a case in the Hon'ble High Court of Kerala in 2011. The Corporation also filed a case in the very same year seeking police protection. While hearing the above petition filed by the Corporation on 22 January, 2012 the Court directed the Pollution Control Board (PCB) to file a report regarding the functioning of the plant within two weeks. The PCB submitted that defects directed to be rectified were not rectified by the Corporation. It also brought to the notice of the court that there was no treating and processing of waste but only dumping. On the basis of the above assessment on 5 July, 2012 the Hon'ble Court passed an Order constituting a judicial commission headed by the District Judge, Kollam. This Commission visited the yard and the surrounding areas on 12/09/2012 at 4 P.M.

Conclusion

Kureepuzha would not have been in the news had there not been any pollution that endangered the life of the people in the last ten years. In yester years she was called up on to bear the burden of the waste of the Calamities. The same practice continued even after the formation of the present Kollam Corporation. Fed up with this she started agitations after agitations followed by arrest and detention. But the consequences of the agitation were less severe than the ill-effects of the burden of waste itself for the people of Kureepuzha.

The present dreary situation forcing the people to agitate is the sole creation of the Corporation. The Corporation couldn't initiate, evolve and implement a strategy viable enough to cope with the tremendous hike in the quantity of waste. It is practically not possible for the present plant with 15-20 MT capacity to process 30-35 MT waste collected daily. Contextually and consequentially this led to accumulation of waste at the dumping site. Even the stated second plant with an improved capacity of 45 MT couldn't be commissioned by the corporation for its failure to segregate waste which could have been done and originally envisaged to be done at the collection centre. This had resulted in large scale heaping of wastes in the yard causing leach ate from the yard in to the Ashtamudi Lake and suburban wells. A single sight of the yard itself is more than enough to infer the gravity of the problem. In the survey also 94.28 per cent respondents perused this. Therefore, it could be understood that lack of proper planning, clear vision and inexpert implementation triggered the issue and defeated the mission.

Moreover, both circumstances and conduct on the part of the Corporation speak voluminously on the neglect of pollution safeguards by itself. Acquisition of additional land to the tune of 12 acres in the Coastal Regulation Zone by the Corporation for enlarging the yard itself is a matter of serious concern. Moreover, the inability of the Corporation to initiate steps in advance to segregate waste at the collection centres itself, causing to bring the entire waste into the yard and putting it in heaps in the open space was blatant violation of pollution safeguards. The report of the Pollution Control Board which it submitted to the Hon'ble High Court of Kerala also endorsed the omission of the Corporation to adhere to pollution safeguards. The very same fact in all its seriousness had been perused by 62.85 per cent of the respondents. Lack of a viable sustainable strategy in tune with pollution safeguards is incidental to lack of vision, foresight and planning on the part of governance. This augments significance especially when it is learnt that there was clear cut policy (Kerala Sustainable Urban Development Project, ADB aided project) laid down by the government in the matter of waste disposal.

The nature and dimension of all environmental issues are such that they ultimately tend to be international in character. This character transition is only a matter of time both in terms of its nature and the changing international scenario. Consequently, distinction between an international environmental issue and a domestic one is getting thinner as is seen at present. In the instant case, on being petitioned by the agitating people the Asian Development Bank withheld the loan which it made available to the Government of Kerala for modernising waste treatment plants. This is clearly indicative of the fact that the Kureepuzha agitation caught the attention of an international agency. Not only that such a response from an international agency should be viewed as symptomatic of the seriousness that the problem came to have at the international level itself. Therefore, definitely the Kureepuzha issue transcended the boundaries. However, further internationalisation depends on ground work by the aggrieved people.

Forcing the people to live in an intolerable situation amidst pollution, consequent health problems to which they were subject to, subsequent social inhibitions imposed up on them—all of them are inseparably connected with the people's right to life and survival. Therefore, what has been done by the Kollam Corporation, as a 'constitutional local authority' is a sheer instance of state deprivation of the basic human rights of the people.

In such circumstances it is quite natural for the people to retaliate. History is conversant with innumerable examples of man's organised endeavours to protect their rights. Their agitations were tried to be suppressed by brutal force by the state. That itself forms another instance of violation of human rights by the state. A state that incessantly violates the human rights of the governed, under whatever cover, cannot take recourse to make any claim for its authority as being built up on a consensual foundation or legitimacy as philosophically and juristically perceived. What is lawful may not be legitimate always. But the legitimate is always lawful. For example, a hike in tax may be lawful from the stand point of a government. But the people may think it arbitrary and in such an instant the probability for an agitation against the government is preponderant. On such serious occasions people will not render obedience to the state and its agencies. The way in which the people conducted their agitation in Kureepuzha in the instant case is parallel to event in Vilappilsala, Thiruvananthapuram were already validated the contractual proposition from which the later theorists in Political Science developed the theory of legitimacy. Therefore, no stretch of reason, except reason vitiated will justify state's use of force then. Such a state, whatever is its claim to democracy, is a mere power monger.

Even at this belated hour the state should have the minimum courtesy to learn that 'growth' and 'progress' are not 'development' as properly conceived in terms of sustainability. 'Development' has a philosophy and psychology of its own. It is this philosophy and psychology that the Mahatma Gandhi had bequeathed to us. Hence it is well written: "Here, one stumbles in to a complex world where, despite the advent of the cyber space and its seamless fantasies, Mahatma Gandhi and his 'village society' hold greater attraction."[21] Let this thought be humanity's premium mobile for the future.

References

1. There was a growth in world population at an alarming rate especially between 1900-2000 at a fourfold rate and a corresponding increase in gross world product by fourteen fold. This period also witnessed an intensive use in energy and raw materials which generated more waste per unit of wealth. Carbon dioxide emissions rose to thirteen fold and energy use increased sixteen fold. See Mahesh Rangarajan (ed) Environmental Issues in India-A Reader, 7th impression, 2011, Longman: Pearson, pp. i-ii.

2. 'Ecological Modernisation' challenges the idea that improvements in environmental quality or the protection of nature are inimical to economic welfare. As a powerful idea economic modernisation links ecological sustainability and modernity in a way that appears to make them realisable simultaneously.

See Andrew Dobson States, Citizens and the Environment in Quentin Skinner and Bo Strath (ed) States and Citizens: History, Theory, Perspectives. Cambridge University Press, 2003, pp. 208-209.

3. M.K. Singh (ed) Encyclopedia of Great Indian Political Thinkers, Vol. 4, Anmol Publications, New Delhi, 2008, p. 270.

4. Development should not be equated with growth. Growth can bring in prosperity and money. But it never accommodates the multi dimensional needs of the individual. Development has to be compatible with environment. See Gyanarangan Swain, Environment and Sustainable Development in Tapan Biswal (ed) Human Rights, Gender and Environment, Viva Books, Delhi, 2006, pp. 371-372.

5. Giddons quoted by Ahluwalia, S.K. Environment Problems in India, ADB Publishers, Jaipur, 2005. p.1.

6. Supracited Note 2, p. 210.

7. Danger is posed by the presence of e-waste with radioactive properties and chemical substances.

8. In Plachimada (Kerala) and Kudankulam (Tamil Nadu), Government of India alleged the involvement of foreign NGOs behind people's agitation for conservation of environment.

9. The present trend set by the sand mafia in Kerala bears exemplary likeness to this category. Both political patronage and political nurturing put pressure on governance not to take any action against the violators.

10. The way in which waste management is done by the various local bodies in Kerala form the subject matter of this proposition.

11. It is despite the existence of a specific policy called the Kerala Sustainable Urban Development Project (KSUDP), an Asian Development Bank (ADB) assisted project that the recent issues at Kureepuzha emerged.

12. Barry quoted by Quentin Skinner et al, Supracited Note 2, p. 210.

13. George H. Sabine, A History of Political Theory, Oxford, New Delhi, 14 ed, 1975, p. 493. *See also Chester C. Maxey, Political Philosophies,* MacMillan, New York, 1950, pp. 405-410.

14. *Ibid.*

15. Madhav Gadgil and Ramachandra Guha, Ecological Conflicts and the Environmental Movement in Mahesh Rangarajan (ed) supracited note 1, p. 385.

16. Order No. 43/A3/11/S and TD dated 27/04/2011.

17. www.kollam corporation gov.in/solid waste management.

18. The Constitution of India, Art. 21.

19. Hindu, dt 13 August, 2011.

20. The Times of India. dt. 2 June, 2012.

21. A. Damodaran, India, Climate Change, and the Global Concerns, Oxford, 2010. Preface, p. x.

8

Traditional Environment Health Hazards and the Scope for Policy Intervention: The Case of National Rural Health Mission in an Island Community

Manju S. Nair

People experience the environment in which they live as a combination of physical, chemical, biological, social, cultural and economic conditions that differ according to the local geography, infrastructure, season, time of day and activity undertaken. The varied environmental health threats that people face classified as traditional hazards, associated with the lack of development or modern hazards linked with unsustainable development are inextricably related to these facets of environment. When environmental health risks are poorly managed, the 'traditional risks' are not eliminated in all parts of society and remain important health threats among the poor and disadvantaged, while the 'modern risks' continue unabated. But if environmental health risks are managed well, the 'traditional risks' can be eliminated completely. Public policy definitely has a role in reducing the environmental health hazards and promoting development. Against this background the paper examines the traditional environmental health hazards faced by people of an island Panchayat, Kadamakudy, in Kerala and the scope of intervention mechanisms in moderating the health hazards.

The paper is organised into five sections. Section I deals with the interlinkages between health, environment and sustainable development. Section II examines the various traditional and modern environmental health hazards and its impact on development. Section III focuses on policy intervention to promote public health with focus on National Rural Health Mission (NRHM). Section IV deals with the traditional environmental health hazards faced by an island community in Kadamkudy Grama Panchayat and the role of NRHM as an intervention mechanism in ameliorating the health hazards. Section V concludes the study.

Section I

Interlink between Health, Environment and Sustainable Development

Wherever people live and work is called their environment. The environment encompasses people's surroundings and the circumstances relating to their surroundings, so it includes physical, biological, social and cultural factors. People constantly interact with their environment, it helps to shape their lives and it affects their health and in turns their development. The definitions and linkages between health, environmental health and sustainable development are provided below.

Health

Health is viewed differently by different people all over the world. The WHO defined health as 'a state of complete physical, mental and social well being and not merely an absence of disease or infirmity.' Hence good health is a synthesis of physical, mental and social well being. As stated in the first five year plan, 'Health is a positive state of well being in which harmonious development of mental and physical capacities of the individuals lead to the employment of rich and full life.' It implies adjustment of individuals to his total environment—physical and social. According to WHO the conditions required for health not only include the availability of resources to meet basic human needs and provide protection from all environmental hazards, but also requires a sense of security and well being. If the environment in which one works or lives is deficient in some way, this can lead to both physical and psychological problems. Health is no longer seen as being solely the responsibility of doctors, nurses and other medical personnel, but now is also the responsibility of individuals, households, communities, governments and multinational agencies. These groups have the knowledge and power to make changes in their environment and living conditions, and therefore can affect the health of the population at large.

Environmental Health

WHO defines environmental health as those aspects of human health, including quality of life, that are determined by physical, biological, social and psycho-social factors in the environment. It also refers to the theory and practice of assessing, correcting, controlling and preventing these factors in the environment that potentially can adversely affect the health of present and future generations. (WHO 1993)

Breakdown of the Global Burden of Environmentally Related Disease

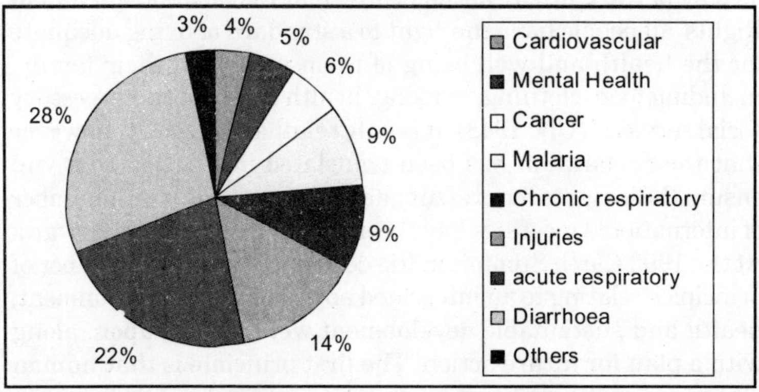

Source: Cairnross *et.al.* (2003).

Global Burden of Environmentally Related Disease

The role of the environment on the burden of disease is significant; the environment has been implicated in 21 per cent of the overall burden of disease worldwide. Most of this burden falls on developing countries.

Figure shows a breakdown of the global burden of environmentally related disease. Twenty eight per cent of the burden of disease is from diarrhea. The second largest health burden is acute respiratory disease; followed by injuries.

Sustainable Development

The World Commission on Environment and Development define sustainable development as 'meeting the needs of the present generation without compromising the ability of future generations to meet their needs' (World Commission on Environment and Development, 1987). These needs include food, work, shelter and health care for all the population and they must be provided and in a manner that prejudices none of them and preserves the environment and its resources. Sustainable development is also about addressing equity within the present generation. It is often the poorest groups in society who are most exposed to environmental hazards, including dangerous working conditions and restricted access to adequate and safe food and water. In addition, low quality housing is often situated in the most polluted areas, such as contaminated land near roads and industrial plants. The importance of this has been enshrined as part of the United Nations Universal Declaration of Human Rights 'all people have the right to a standard of living adequate for the health and well being of themselves and their family, including food, clothing, housing, health care and the necessary social services' (UN, 1948). It is only relatively recently, however that the declaration has been translated into action that will ensure these rights for present and future generations. A number of international meetings have been held to discuss ways forward. At the 1992 Earth Summit in Rio de Janerio, Brazil, a number of principles relating to an integrated approach to the environment, health and sustainable development were agreed upon, along with a plan for future action. The first principle is that human beings are at the centre of concern for sustainable development.

They are entitled to a healthy and productive life in harmony with nature. In the years since the Earth Summit, commitment to securing human health and a healthy environment has become widespread, as evidenced by a number of declarations and statements that have emanated from recent international conferences. Many countries have formulated or are in the process of formulating national plans for sustainable development that give increased weight to health and environment concerns.

Section II
Traditional and Modern Environmental Health Hazards and its Impact on Development

It is a well documented fact that environment hazards act as a deterrent to improved health status of exposed people. A hazard is defined as 'a factor or exposure that may adversely affect health' (Last 1995). This is basically a source of danger, it is qualitative term used to express the potential of an environmental agent to harm particular individuals. The different environmental health hazards can be divided into 'traditional hazards' which were associated with lack of development, and the 'modern hazards' which are associated with unsustainable development. Traditional hazards are related to poverty and insufficient development. They include lack of access to safe drinking water; inadequate basic sanitation in the household and the community; food contamination with pathogens; indoor air pollution from cooking and heating using biomass fuel or coal; inadequate solid waste disposal; occupational injury hazards in agriculture and cottage industries; natural disasters, including floods, droughts, and earthquakes; and disease vectors, mainly insects and rodents. Modern hazards are related to rapid development that lacks health and environment safeguards and to unsustainable consumption of natural resources. These hazards include water pollution from populated areas, industry, and intensive agriculture; urban air pollution from automobiles, coal power stations and industry; solid and hazardous waste accumulation; chemical and radiation hazards due to introduction of industrial and agricultural technologies; emerging and re-emerging infectious disease hazards; deforestation, land degradation, and other major ecological change at local and regional level; climate change; stratospheric ozone depletion; and pollution. One of the differences between traditional and modern environmental health hazards is that the former are often rather quickly expressed as disease. A person drinks polluted water today and develops severe diarrhea tomorrow, for example. The incidence of diarrhea can accordingly be a relatively useful measure of the risk. For many modern environmental health hazards, however, a long period may pass before the health effect manifests itself. A cancer-causing chemical released into the environment today may not reach a person until it has passed through the food chain for months or years, for instance, and even then may not cause development of a noticeable tumor for decades. Similarly, environmental change, caused by human activities, that occurs over several decades such as stratospheric ozone depletion due to chlorofluorocarbon emissions, may undermine the life-supporting functions of Earth.

Clearly, the relation between human health and the environment is complex. Each of the traditional and modern hazards is associated with a variety of aspects of economic and social development. Driving forces create the conditions in which environmental health hazards can develop or be averted or that are generated by large numbers of people in their pursuit of the basic necessities of life or in their appropriation and use of consumer goods. Driving forces include policies that determine trends in economic development, technology development, consumption patterns, and population growth. The driving forces in turn generate different kinds of pressures on the environment, in such forms as waste from human settlements and depletion of natural resources or emission of pollutants from activities such as energy production, manufacturing, transport, mineral extraction, agriculture, forestry, fish harvesting and tourism. These pressures can lead to changes in the state of environment, as seen when land use is changed (deforestation or drainage problems) or when discharges of toxic chemicals or other forms of waste increase concentrations of chemicals in air, soil, water or plants. The pressures are potentially associated with all stages in the life cycle of industrial products, from initial resource extraction and transportation of raw materials, to processing and distribution, to final consumption and disposal. Whether a resultant altered state of the environment creates a hazard to human health depends on many factors, including the degree to which humans may actually be exposed. Exposure requires that people are present both at the place and at the time when the state of the environment changed and became hazardous. Exposure, thus, refers to the intersection between people and environmental hazards. Levels of exposure may range from harmless and acceptable to dangerous and unacceptable, depending on the potential for physical harm. Given known exposures and the knowledge of dose-response relations, estimates can be made of the health risk of specific hazards to the extent that current knowledge allows. Environmental hazards in turn, can lead to a wide range of health effects. These may vary in type, intensity, and magnitude depending on the type of hazard to which people have been exposed, the level of exposure, and the number of people affected. Most important diseases are associated with more than one type of exposure, and environmental hazards interact with genetic factors, nutrition, life-style hazards, and other factors in causing disease.

Section III
Role of National Rural Health Mission (NRHM) as an Intervention Mechanism

Improvement in the health status of the population was one of the major thrust areas in the social development programmes of India since independence. Over the past six decades India has built up vast health infrastructure and invested massive amounts on five year plans in medical education and research. Even after these programmes and initiatives, an unacceptably high proportion of people die out of new diseases apart from the existing ones. Also the public healthcare system was not able to meet the growing demand, the gap between demand and supply has to be bridged by private players, and this has facilitated the growth of healthcare industry in India. The private healthcare was not a perfect substitute to the public healthcare system as it intended on the professionalisation and commercialisation of the industry.

On the flipside, the rural population who constituted the majority was deprived of quality health services and at the best they received only rudimentary healthcare. Accessibility towards quality health services is the right of every citizen and health being a state subject as in the Entry 6 in the state list (List II) in the Seventh Schedule of the Constitution reads "Public health and sanitation hospitals and dispensaries," it is the duty of the state to ensure that their subjects are provided with accessible, affordably quality health services. For this very reason Government of India introduced many schemes and policies like Reproductive Child Health (RCH), Pradhan Manthri Swasthya Suraksha Yojana (PMSSY), Malaria Eradication Programme (MEP), AIDS Control Programme, etc.

Tenth Five Year Plan (2002-2007) portrayed a dismal picture of health service and infrastructure and emphasised on restructuring and developing the health infrastructure especially at the primary level. As a large segment of population in India was poor the need for a multipronged and multi-sectoral approach on issues relating to rural health care system was thought of. A task force was set up by the Ministry of Health and Family Welfare (MoFW) with public health experts, civil society representatives and government servants to identify the areas which sought government intervention. The task force had referred to the Report of National Commission for Macroeconomics and Health and the Mid-term Appraisal note on the Tenth Plan prepared by the Planning Commission to arrive at the robust framework for centre-state partnership to improve outcomes in the health sector. It was as a result of these consultative processes that the framework of the National Rural Health Mission (NRHM) was designed. NRHM was, thus launched on April 12, 2005 to provide accessible, affordable and accountable quality health services to the unprivileged and vulnerable sections of the society especially women and children in the remotest rural region.

NRHM (2005-12) seeks to provide effective healthcare to rural population throughout the country with special focus on eighteen states, which have weak public health indicators and/ or weak infrastructure. These eighteen states are Arunachal

Pradesh, Assam, Bihar, Chhattisgarh, Himachal Pradesh, Jharkhand, Jammu & Kashmir, Manipur, Mizoram, Meghalaya, Madhya Pradesh, Nagaland, Orissa, Rajasthan, Sikkim, Tripura, Uttarakhand and Uttar Pradesh. The mission is an articulation of the commitment of the Government to raise public spending on health from 0.9 per cent to GDP to 2—3 per cent of GDP. NRHM aims to undertake architectural correction of the health system to enable it to effectively handle increased allocations as promised under the National Common Minimum Programme and promote policies that strengthen public health management and service delivery in the country. It seeks to revitalise local health traditions and mainstream AYUSH into the public health system. It further aims at effective integration of health concerns with determinants of health like sanitation and hygiene, nutrition, and safe drinking water through a District Plan for Health. It seeks decentralisation of programmes for district management of health and to address the inter-state and inter-district disparities, especially among the eighteen high focus states, including unmet needs for public health infrastructure. It also seeks to improve access of rural people, especially poor women and children, to equitable, affordable, accountable and effective primary healthcare.

The core and supplementary strategies of NRHM include training and enhancing capacity of Panchayati Raj Institutions (PRIs) to own, control and manage public health services, promoting access to improved healthcare at household level through the female health activist (ASHA), setting up Health Plan for each village through Village Health Committee of the Panchayat, strengthening sub-centre through a untied fund to enable local planning and action and more Multi Purpose Workers (MPWs), strengthening existing PHCs and CHCs, and provision of 30-50 bedded CHC per lakh population for improved curative care to a normative standard (Indian Public Health Standards defining personnel, equipment and management standards), preparation and implementation of an inter-sectoral District Health Plan prepared by the District Health Mission, including drinking water, sanitation and hygiene and nutrition, integrating vertical Health and Family Welfare programmes at

National, State, Block, and District levels, providing – Technical support to National, State and District Health Missions, for Public Health Management, strengthening capacities for data collection, assessment and review for evidence based planning, monitoring and supervision and formulation of transparent policies for deployment and career development of human resources for health.

Section IV

Traditional Environmental Health Hazards Faced by an Island Community in Kadamakudy Grama Panchayat and the Role of NRHM in Ameliorating the Health Hazards

Kerala is the state which stands first among the Indian states in terms of Human Development Index. Kerala has become a model Indian state viewed in terms of low birth rate, death rate, infant mortality rate, maternal mortality rate, higher life expectancy at birth, favourable sex ratio and achievements in public health. But now Kerala is facing the second generational health problems including high morbidity rates, life style diseases, problems of ageing, entry of private sector which escalated health cost (mediflation), deterioration in the quality of health services, health issues associated with environmental problems, etc. Kerala was one of the last states to start work on NRHM, the mission was launched in 2005 but Kerala joined the movement only in August 2006. But when it did, it brought a sea-change in the public health delivery system in the last four years. The NRHM in Kerala is viewed as the ideal movement for good health. The aims of NRHM in Kerala include provision of comprehensive health care services to the community with special thrust to rural areas, reduction in Infant Mortality Rate, reduction in Maternal Mortality Ratio, reduction of Total Fertility Rate for population stabilisation, provision of client centred, accessible, quality health services to the needy population, environmental and water sanitation and surveillance, prevention and control of communicable and non communicable diseases.

Environmental hazards and water sanitation problems remain a serious threat towards human health in several, water logged and low lying areas in Kerala. Under the aegis of NRHM steps are taken to moderate health threats associated with environmental and water sanitation problems. The case of Kadamkudy Panchayath in Ernakulam district stands as an illustration.

Kadamkudy Panchayath is a cluster of eight islands with a total area of 12.29 sq. km with a population of 15824. The Panchayat is classified as a *difficult rural area* since it exhibits all the characteristics of a difficult rural area as inaccessibility to health services and existence of drivers of health problems including scarcity of drinking water, lack of sanitation facilities, etc. The island community differs in their local geography, infrastructure facilities available and activities undertaken. The intensity of problems also differs in different seasons and during different time of the day. Lack of bridges to interconnect the islands and the city makes people's access to medical services infrequent. People entirely depend on boats, life is hard and emergency health care is a problem. Also unavailability of night boat services adds to the vulnerability of these islanders. Access to safe drinking water is less and sanitary and toilet using habits of the people are poor. Primary data collected from among the islanders reveal that during rainy season fever of unknown origin usually spreads swiftly across the villagers. The children are vulnerable to diarrhea and dysentery continually. Other diseases like jaundice and urinary tract infection is also observed. Analysis of the major health- related problems gave the result that water borne and vector borne diseases are common. The people also face other problems including lack of drinking water facility, lack of proper toilets, unhygienic sanitation, etc.

NRHM has provided facilities including immunisation, awareness campaign on proper sanitation, awareness on the prevention of various diseases, diagnosis, antenatal care, promoted institutional deliveries, etc. A sample of hundred residents in the Panchayat was interviewed on the effectiveness of NRHM. More than fifty opined that NRHM has improved their quality of life. Accredited Social Health Activists visit the island regularly and provide them with preventive healthcare. Awareness camps related to proper sanitation is attended by fifty per cent of the people. Healthy habits related to water including drinking boiling water is now practiced by many of the people. Immunization programme has also been widely practiced and many of the islanders made their children use it. Sanitation measures were also adopted. The special initiative started by NRHM includes the setting up of a floating dispensary. Floating dispensary was set up as an innovative step to bring healthcare professionals and services to the people. The medical team of the dispensary is visiting all the eight islands as per the prescheduled plan and is providing medical services for about two hours in each jetty. Now the service is available to each island two or three times a week. The dispensary in emergency can be used as an ambulance. Primary data reveals that around forty per cent of the people of the island have shifted their treatment to floating dispensary. Thus, under the aegis of NRHM, efforts are being made to moderate the traditional health hazards and to improve the health status of the island community.

Section V

Conclusion

The environment which sustains human life, is also a profound source of ill- health for many of the world's people. The environmental health threats stem mostly from traditional problems such as a lack of clean water, sanitation, adequate housing, and protection from mosquitoes and other insects and animal disease vectors. Effective governmental interventions can moderate the health hazards as is evident from the role played by National Rural Health Mission in ameliorating the health hazards in an island community, Kadamkudy. The major traditional environmental health hazards faced by the island community include inaccessibility to medical services due to lack of transport facilities, deficiency of proper sanitation facilities, inadequate accessibility to safe drinking water, etc., resulting in frequent attack of water borne and vector borne diseases. NRHM is taking effective intervention steps in moderating these health hazards and promoting healthy life of the people.

References

Beaglehole R., Bonita R. (1997) *Public health at the crossroads: achievements and prospects*. Cambridge, United Kingdom, Cambridge University Press.

Cairncross S, O'Neill D, McCoy A. and Sethi D. (2003) *Health, Environment and Burden of Disease: A Guidance Note*, London DFID.

Last A. (1995) *A Dictionary of Epidemiology* (third edition) New York, Oxford University Press.

Litsios S. (1994) *Sustainable development is health development*, World Health Forum.

United Nations (1948) *Universal Declaration of Human Rights*, New York, UN.

United Nations (1993) *The United Nations Programme of Action from Rio*, New York.

World Health Organisation. (1997) *Health and Environment in Sustainable Development: Five Years after the Earth Summit*. Geneva: World Health Organisation.

Warford J.J. (1995) *Environment, health and sustainable development: the role of economic instruments and policies*, Bulletin of World Health Organisation.

World Commission on Environment and Development (1987), Report to United Nations General Assembly.

WHO (1993) *Global Strategy: Health, Environment and Development: Approaches to Drafting Country side Strategies for Human Well-being under Agenda 21*, Geneva, WHO.

9

Development and Conservation with Special Reference to Wetlands

Unnikrishnan N.

Introduction

Wetlands are one of the most important ecosystems on earth. They are considered as lands transitional between terrestrial and aquatic systems where the water table is usually at or near the surface or the land is covered by shallow water. Wetlands are ecotones or transitional zones that occupy an intermediate position between dry land and open water. The Ramsar Convention (1971) defines wetlands as areas of marsh, fen, peat land or water, with water that is static or flowing, fresh, brackish or salty including areas of marine water, the depth of which at low tide does not exceed 6 meters. It may also incorporate riparian and coastal zones adjacent to the wetlands and islands or bodies of marine water deeper than 6 meters at low tide lying within the wetlands.

Wetlands are having many important functions which support life on earth. They are the major source of water. They are considered as kidneys of nature. Wetlands remove or retain the sediments and excess nutrients in water. The nutrients and toxins are removed, stored and transformed by the wetlands. All the pollutants settle in the marshes and different types of water bodies. This ecosystem is home to innumerable number of aquatic organisms, plants and animals. It supports aquatic biodiversity. Ground water recharge is another important function of wetlands. The underground water is the main source of water for plants and also it is the source of drinking water for humans. Wetlands control flood conditions. They provide place for the spreading of flood water. The intensity of drought conditions is reduced by wetlands. This ecosystem also prevents salt water intrusion. Wetlands are also important as carbon sinks and absorb large quantities of carbon dioxide.

Wetlands are one of the most important life supporting systems on earth. It is one of the most productive ecosystems. Major portion of agriculture is being done in wetlands. All the foodgrains are cultivated in wetlands. Fishing and aquaculture is the livelihood for thousands of people. Wetlands provide cheaper and eco-friendly means of transportation. Backwater tourism is a livelihood for many people. All over the world wetlands are places of tourism and recreation.

Bio Diversity

Biodiversity is the degree of variation of life forms within a species— ecosystem, biome or on entire earth. All the different plants, animals and microorganisms found in the world are of a geographical area. There are three levels of biodiversity. They are genetic diversity, species diversity and ecosystem diversity. The variation in genes within a species is called genetic diversity. Different varieties of brinjals are example. Species diversity refers to different species of living organisms on earth. The different types of habitats on earth are considered as ecosystem diversity. Wetlands forests, desert, grass lands, etc., are examples.

The wetlands are rich in biodiversity. They are discussed under the following headings.

Plant Diversity

Wetland ecosystem is very rich in aquatic plant diversity. The flora includes Mangroves, Mangrove associates, medicinal plants and other important aquatic species. Many mangrove species are found growing in our wetlands. *Avicennia marina, A.officinalis, Bruguiera gymnorrhiza, Rhizophora apiculata, R.mucronata, Sonneratia caseolaris, Kandelia candal, Acanthus ilicifolius, Excoecaria agallocha* are some of the common species. *Cerebera odollam, Ardisia liltoralis, Anona glabra, Derris trifoliata, Morinda citrifolia* etc. are some of the ımportant mangrove associates. The wetlands are also an important habitat of medicinal plants. *Eclipta postrata, Premna cerratifolia, Bacopa monneri, Barringtonia racemosa, Monochoria vaginalis, Hygrophila schulli* are some of the examples. *Aponogeton appendiculatus* is a rare hydrophyte which is endemic to the Vembanad wetlands and included in the red data book for Indian plants. Different species of water lilies and many species of bladder wort, *Utricularia* are common in wetlands. *Pandamus odorifer* (screw pine) is an important fibre yielding plant of this ecosystem. The spathe of the flowers of this plant (*Thazhampoo*) was a famous deodorant and also subject of many poems. *Calophyllum inophyllum* is an important tree growing in wetlands and its seeds were used for oil extraction. The flora also includes a number of hydrophytes.

Azolla is an important pteridophyte which is widely used as a biofertilizer, is common in wetlands.

Avian Diversity

The wetlands are famous for its bird diversity. A number of migratory birds visit this area during summer months. The diversity of resident birds is also rich. The Kumarakom bird sanctuary is on the banks of Vembanad lake. The vast paddy fields and the lakes provide food and roosting places for the birds. The visit of migratory birds was the major criteria considered for declaring the Vembana-Kole wetlands, Ashtamudi and Sasthamkotta as Ramsar sites.

The Vembanad wetland is considered as an Important Bird Area ((IBA) by International Bird Conservation Network. A total number of birds recorded from this region are 232. (Sreekumar 2007–2012). Among these 110 are wetland and wetland dependant birds. About 62 of the wetland birds are migratory, coming from different countries during winter season. Some of the important species visiting our wetlands are, Great Cormorant *(Phalacrocorax carbo)*, Open Billed Stork *(Anastomus oscitans)*, White ibis (*Threskiornis melanocephalus*), Glossy Ibis (*Plegadis falcinellus*). Spoonbill (*Platalea leucorodia major)*, Lesser Whistling teal, (*Dendrocygna javanica*) Cotton teal (*Nettapus coromandelianus*), Northern Pintail Duck (*Anas acuta*), Spot Billed Duck (*Anas poecilorhyncha*), Gargany (*A.querquedula*), different kinds of Sandpipers, Shank, Godwit, Plovers, Gulls and Terns, Osprey (*Pandion haliaetus*), Steppe eagle (*Aquila nepalensis*), Booted eagle (*Hieraaetus pennatus*), Wagtails, Spot Billed Pelican (*Pelecanus philippensis*), Painted Stork, etc. Indian Shag (*Phalacrocorax fuscicollis*), Little Cormorant (*Phalacrocora niger)*, Egrets, Night Heron (*Nycticorax nycticorax*), Moorhen, Pond Heron (*Ardeola grayii*) are some of the common resident species. The Oriental Darter (*Anhinga melanogaster)* is an important and rare resident species breeding here.

Fish Diversity

The fish diversity of our wetland system is very rich. About 61 species of fishes (Padmakumar, 2003) including shell fishes are reported from the Vembanad wetlands itself. *Etroplus suratensis, E.maculatus, Horabngrus brachysoma, Wallago attu, Channa striatns,* Mullet, Catfishes, *Puntius* sps., etc., are some of the important species found growing in Kerala wetlands. The giant fresh water prawn (*Macrobrachium rosenbergii*) is a species of great demand. A number of people depend on inland fishing for their livelihood. Some of the fish species are considered as very good aquarium varieties.

Amphibians and Reptiles

About 15 amphibians are identified from our aquatic environment. Different types of frogs are the important members of this category. The exact number of the amphibians is not yet known. Studies are going on in this regard.

The wetlands are home for different types of reptiles such as snakes, Monitor lizard and Tortoise. Python, Cobra, Viper and different types of water snakes are common here. Python is listed in the schedule I of Indian Wildlife Act.

Mammals

Some of the important mammals found in the wetlands are the Otter, Civet, Toddy Cat, Mongoose, Fruit bats etc. Among these the smooth coated Otter *(Lutrogale perspicillata)* is a rare species.

Molluscs and Other Minor Animals

Different types of molluscs and a number of minor organisms are also important components of this ecosystem. Live calm (*Villorita cyprinoids*) is common in the shallow waters of the Vembanad lake. They yield shells which is the raw material for white cement. Shell mining is a livelihood for a number of people.

Development

The present day concept of development is the construction of multi line roads, huge bridges, large buildings, aerodromes, dams etc. Large areas of wetlands are filled or reclaimed for these types of developments. When a dam is constructed vast areas of forest get submerged. Destruction of hills due to soil mining affects water sources and also habitats of different types of plants and animals. All these result in habitat fragmentation and habitat loss, causing extinction of species. Silent Valley is a classical example of a forest area which was saved from destruction. A hydroelectric project was planned there but due to protest from people from various walks of life, the government dropped that project. Later this area was declared as a National Park.

Major Threats to Wetlands

The wetlands all over the world are facing serious threats. The area of wetlands is shrinking very fast. Our wetland ecosystem is not an exception to this. The major threats to this ecosystem are:

(a) Reclamation and construction activities

(b) Pollution from sewage and industrial effluents

(c) Pollution from chemical fertilisers, herbicides and pesticides

(d) Unscientific tourism activities

(e) Plastic pollution

(f) Over exploitation of resources

When back water tourism was started, different areas of the lake ecosystems are

Another threat to our wetlands is the pollutants carried by our rivers. For example, five major rivers drain to the Vembanad lake. All sewage water from the towns situated on the banks of these rivers reach the Vembanad lake. Effluents from various industries also drain to the lake. Another important threat to the wetland is the agrochemicals. Vast areas of the wetlands are being used for paddy cultivation. Large quantities of chemical fertilizers, pesticides and herbicides are used here for crop protection. All these reach the water bodies and pollute them.

Unscientific tourism activities are another pressure on the wetland ecosystem. All the wastes generated in the house boats including plastic, latrine waste, oil, etc., are reaching the lake water causing serious problems. Over exploitation of the resources of the ecosystem is another threat. Clay mining, shell mining and unscientific fishing methods are examples.

The bio-diversity of the wetlands is seriously affected by these threats. According to authentic reports the fish diversity of the wetland ecosystem is drastically reduced. (Padmakumar, 2002) There is also reduction in the quantity of fish caught from the system. For example, previously many commercially important fish species were found in the Vembanad wetlands. (Padmakumar, 2003). Many species are disappeared and many are on the verge of extinction. This is mainly due to habitat loss, cutting of mangroves, pollution due to agrochemicals, sewage and industrial effluents.

Studies (Sreekumar, 2001-2011) showed that there is variation in number and change in the distribution pattern in the avian fauna of wetlands. For example, the Vembanad lake was used by thousands of migratory ducks, as roosting place. But due to the movement of house boats and speed boats in the lake they are shifted to different places. There is also reduction in the number of species in recent years. Recently egrets were found dead and the study of their bodies showed that it may be due to pesticide poisoning. Birds are one of the major attractions for tourists. Reduction in food, pollution and loss of roosting places seriously affect the bird life.

The effect of the previously discussed threats on the life of other organisms like amphibians, reptiles, mammals, molluscs and on thousands of other minor organisms are yet to be studied. The biodiversity of our wetlands are facing serious threats. So there is an urgent need for conservation activities to protect this very important ecosystem.

References

Sreekumar B. 2001-2011. *Reports of Vembanad Water Bird Count.* Kerala Forests and Wildlife Department.

Unnikrishnan N. 2011. *Hydrophytes and Wetland Dependent Plants of Kuttanad. A Decade of Vembanad Water bird Counts* (ed. Prasanth Narayanan and Sreekumar), Kerala Forest and Wildlife Department.

10

Cropping Pattern Changes : A Threat to Sustainable Development

Maneesh B.

Introduction

The most notable feature of Kerala's agricultural development is the emergence of cash crops as a dominant sector over the five decades. The data analysis shows that the proportion of area under foodgrains declined from mid-seventies and an increasing role of cash crops over food crops seen. The nature of changes in area indicates that paddy land has been diverted either to other crops, mainly cash crops or to non-agricultural purposes such as sites for construction of building, brick-mining and infrastructural facilities such as roads, railway, canals etc. The shift in cropping patterns from food crops to cash crops and also the shift from eco-friendly subsistence farming to profit-induced cultivation using chemical fertilisers and poisonous pesticides have accelerated the pace of biodiversity loss. The results have been an acute shortage of drinking water in summer, falling water tables, soil erosion and climatic changes. Thus, in short, the shifts in cropping pattern in favour of cash crops and the consequent reduction in area under food crops are is a big issue of concern that has long term implications for the food security and ecological and environmental balance of the State.

Special Features of Kerala

Kerala was formed on 1st November, 1956, consequent on the reorganisation of States on linguistic basis. It is a narrow strip of land about 585 km in length located at the southern tip of the Indian peninsula between the Arabian Sea on the west and Western Ghats on the east. The land slopes from east to west. Based on topography, the state may be divided broadly into three regions, namely, lowland, midland, and highland. In the lowland region bordering the Arabian Sea, the soil in most places is sandy, but the wetland comprising rolling hills and valleys provides a variety of crops. The soil here is mostly laterite. The highland region is almost entirely covered with forests and is best suited for plantation crops like tea, coffee, and rubber (Government of Kerala, 2006a).

The State gets copious rainfall from the south-west monsoon during June-August and from the north-east monsoon during October-November.

Rice is the staple food of the people of Kerala. Now, the sate is highly deficient in the production of its staple food. The traditional crops of Kerala are, besides rice, coconut, arecanut, jack, mango, banana and plantain, pepper, ginger, and turmeric. The plantation crops like rubber, tea, coffee, and cardamom are grown mainly in the highland regions.

Kerala implemented land reforms as early as in 1970. Therefore, landlordism disappeared and the cultivating tenants became owners of their leased-in holdings, subject to the ceiling provisions.

Kerala has made notable achievements in health standards as reflected in the low infant mortality rate, low maternal mortality rate, low birth rate, low death rate, and high life expectancy that are far ahead of the national averages. The large size of the population, high levels of education and backwardness of industrialisation have thrown up a large army of unemployed persons, the majority of them having qualifications of secondary level and above.

Special Features of Kerala Agriculture

Kerala is fairly rich in natural resources, which are essentially needed for agricultural development. The high rainfall and climate is eminently suited for a variety of cash crops and plantation crops.

Kerala has its own specificities owing to the special feature of agriculture sector in the State. Some of its special features are:

(i) Highly fragmented and small size of holdings except the plantation sector,
(ii) Homestead farming with mixed crops yielding high income,
(iii) Larger area under commercial crops, especially capital intensive perennial tree crops,
(iv) Export orientation of crops, such as spices, cashew, rubber, coffee, tea, etc.
(v) High credit and hired labour intensive cultivation and
(vi) Higher indebtedness of farmers.

Some of these unique features are now found to be the handicaps of the sector, in the open trade environment which emerged after the formation of World Trade Organisation (WTO). Following trade liberalisation, while exports of agricultural commodities from the state declined, there was rise in imports which led to fall in domestic prices of commodities and rise in price volatility. This intensified the problems already faced by the agricultural sector of the State due to high cost of cultivation, stagnant productivity etc. (Joseph and Joseph, 2005 and Jeromi, 2005).

During the last few years, the problem aggravated due to deficiency in rainfall, sharp decline in prices, lower production and the consequent increase in debt burden of the farmers. As a result, close to 2,000 farmers committed suicide in the State (Government of Kerala, 2006b).

In spite of significant advances in industrial and service sectors, agriculture continues to be the largest provider of employment and livelihood both at the national and state levels. In Kerala, agriculture contributed around 12 per cent of GDP in 2011 (Government of Kerala, 2011).

Stagnant Agricultural Income

The contribution of primary sector to the state domestic product (SDP) has been declining fast since 1980-81. Throughout 1960s and 1970s, primary sector was the dominant sector of the state economy contributing more than 50 per cent of the State Domestic Product. While analyzing the sectoral distribution of state income during the first ten years of the 21st century it can be seen that the contribution from primary sector is decreasing and that of the tertiary sector is increasing. The contribution of primary sector declined from 57.5 per cent in 1970-71 to 15.12 per cent in 2010-11 (Table 10. 1). The share of the tertiary sector

Table 10.1
Sectoral Distribution of SDP from 1960-61 to 2010-11
(Percentage)

Year	*Agriculture (1)*	*Primary (2)*	*Secondary (3)*	*Tertiary (4)*	*Total (2+3+4)*
1960-61	40.00	55	17	28	100
1970-71	51.21	57.5	12.2	30.3	100
1980-81	33.84	39.23	24.38	36.39	100
1990-91	32.38	35.98	23.92	40.10	100
2000-01	16.23	22.2	21.9	55.9	100
2005-06	13.84	17.2	23.8	59	100
2006-07	13.53	17.1	25.0	57.9	100
2007-08	12.68	16.6	26.4	57.0	100
2008-09	12.14	15.79	22.84	61.35	100
2009-10	11.47	15.36	23.15	61.49	100
2010-11	11.21	15.12	23.10	61.78	100

Source: Government of Kerala (Various Years), Economic Review, State Planning Board, Thiruvananthapuram.

Table10.2
Growth of Agricultural Incomes in Kerala from 1980-81 to 2010-11

(At Current Prices)

Year	*Agricultural Income (Rs. in Crores)*	*Percentage contribution to state income*	*Annual average growth rate*	*SDP (Rs. in Crores)*	*Annual average growth rate*
1980-81	1311	33.84	-	3823	-
1990-91	3518	32.38	168.34	12173	218.41
2000-01	10678.2	16.23	203.53	63813	424.21
2001-02	10264.9	15.39	-3.87	67963	6.50
2002-03	10407.2	14.53	1.38	75860	11.61
2003-04	10382.6	13.00	-0.23	84734	11.69
2004-05	16980.5	14.23	63.54	95572	12.79
2005-06	18949.14	13.84	11.59	109554	14.62
2006-07	20821.01	13.53	9.88	126842	15.78
2007-08	22216.33	12.68	6.70	145235	14.50
2008-09	24404.58	12.14	9.84	167469	15.30
2009-10	26424.21	11.47	8.27	181289	14.57
2010-11	28432.10	11.21	8.22	201239	14.21

Source: Government of Kerala (Various Years), Economic Review, State Planning Board, Thiruvananthapuram.

made a steep jump from 36.39 per cent in 1980-81 to 61.78 per cent in 2010-11. This means that the producing sector, consisting of the primary and secondary sectors, contributes only around 40 per cent to the state domestic product. The steep decline in the contribution of primary sector started after the introduction of new economic policy (Maneesh, 2011).

The agricultural sector which is the significant part of the primary sector has also been showing the same tendency to decelerate. The contribution of the agricultural sector has declined from 33.84 per cent in 1980-81 to 11.21 per cent in 2010-

11 (Table10. 2). Over the years agricultural income has recorded lower annual average growth rate compared to the growth of SDP.

Thus the relative contribution of primary sector particularly agricultural sector has been continuously declining, after the neoliberal reforms.

Land Use Pattern

Before analysing the cropping pattern, an examination of land use pattern in Kerala is provided.

Kerala has distinct bio-physical characteristics that vary across the state and contribute to its population and land use dynamics. Based on these characteristics, the state can be divided into six major zones— low lands and coastal plains, Malabar midlands, Palaghat region, southern midlands, Foothills and Eastern highlands (George and Chattopadhyay, 2001). During the past three decades, the agriculture sector of Kerala has undergone wide ranging changes in terms of ownership of land, cropping pattern, cultivation practices, production and intensity of cultivation. In earlier periods, the choice of cropping pattern was guided by agronomic considerations and consumption needs of farmers, but now it seems that mainly market forces determine the emerging trend (Mahesh, 1999).

The land use pattern of Kerala for the past few decades is given in Table 10.3.

Out of the total geographical area of 38.86 lakh hectares, net area sown is about 56 per cent in 2010-11. Agriculture and forest area account for over 84 per cent of the land area. The most notable feature of the land use pattern is the rise in net sown area between 1960-61 and 1970-71 from 50.07 per cent to 56.13 per cent of the total geographical area and the corresponding increase in gross cropped area from 60.88 per cent to 75.57 per cent. The proportion of net area sown as well as gross cropped area has remained almost stagnant, since then. Land put to non-agricultural uses has increased from 5.43 percent to nine per cent between 1960-61 and 2010-11 period. It

Table 10.3
Land Use Pattern of Kerala from 1960-61 to 2010-11

(in Hectares)

Sl. No.	*Category*	*1960-61*	*1970-71*	*1980-81*	*1990-91*	*2000-01*	*2010-11*
1.	Total Geographical Area (TGA)	3858523 (100)	3858523 (100)	3885497 (100)	3885497 (100)	3885497 (100)	3886287 (100)
2.	Forests	1056143 (27.37)	1055733 (27.36)	1081509 (27.83)	1081509 (27.83)	1081509 (27.83)	1081509 (28)
3.	Land put to non-agricultural uses	209486 (5.43)	267565 (6.94)	269824 (6.94)	297381 (7.65)	381873 (9.83)	361695 (9)
4.	Barren and uncultivated land	146120 (3.79)	73805 (1.91)	85770 (2.21)	58308 (1.50)	29318 (0.75)	17912 (0.5)
5.	Permanent Pastures and Grazing land	4439 (1.15)	27800 (0.72)	5432 (0.14)	1912 (0.05)	164 (0.00)	96 (0)
6.	Land under miscellaneous tree crops	202194 (5.24)	140235 (3.64)	63875 (1.64)	34375 (0.88)	15409 (0.40)	4423 (0.1)
7.	Cultivable waste	140898 (3.65)	81275 (2.11)	129032 (3.32)	94608 (2.43)	59257 (1.53)	98014 (3)

(Contd.)

(Contd. Table 10.3)

Sl. No.	*Category*	*1960-61*	*1970-71*	*1980-81*	*1990-91*	*2000-01*	*2010-11*
8.	Fallow other than current fallow	66409 (1.72)	23242 (0.60)	26886 (0.69)	26466 (0.68)	33988 (0.87)	45374 (1)
9.	Current fallow	60961 (1.58)	22866 (0.59)	43579 (1.12)	44164 (1.14)	77853 (2.00)	76945 (2)
10.	Net area sown	1931773 (50.07)	2165902 (56.13)	2179590 (56.10)	2246774 (57.82)	2206126 (56.78)	2180679 (56)
11.	Area sown more than once	409427 (10.61)	750186 (19.44)	705250 (18.15)	773206 (19.90)	815556 (20.99)	488026 (13)
12.	Total Cropped Area	2341200 (60.68)	2916088 (75.57)	2884840 (74.25)	3019980 (77.72)	3021682 (77.77)	2668705 (69)
13.	Cropping Intensity	122	135	132	134	137	122

Source: Government of Kerala (Various Years), Economic Review, State Planning Board, Thiruvananthapuram.

Notes: Figures in brackets are percentage of total geographical area.

may be noted that there is a substantial reduction in the area under miscellaneous tree crops, barren and uncultivable land and permanent pastures and other grazing land. The intensity of cropping does not seem to have risen during the past decades even though some fluctuations were observed in the decades in between. The cropping intensity which was 122 during 1960-61 became 137 during 2000-01 and is declined to 122 again during 2010-11. Stagnation of net sown area, existence of large areas of wasteland, fallow land, etc., causes concern from economic, social and environmental angles.

Cropping Pattern

The cropping pattern in the state is quite different from the national scene owing to the topography and climatic conditions of Kerala. Perennial crops dominate the cultivated area in the State. Over the years, the share of perennial crops has been gradually increasing. Table10.4 shows the change in the area under different crops during 1960-61 to 2010-11.

The Table10.4 shows the cropping pattern of major crops in Kerala from 1960-61 to 2010-11. From the Table, it is clear that

Table 10.4
Share of Area under Major Crops in Total Cropped Area in Kerala (Per cent)

Crop	*1960-61*	*1970-71*	*1980-81*	*1990-91*	*2000-01*	*2010-11*
Rice	32.66	29.83	28.88	18.22	11.50	8.77
Coconut	21.44	24.71	23.68	28.69	30.98	29.18
Rubber	5.24	6.15	8.24	12.72	15.70	19.69
Pepper	2.43	3.42	3.75	5.58	6.59	6.43
Cardamom	1.22	1.63	1.87	2.22	1.37	1.56
Cashewnut	2.32	3.52	4.89	3.83	2.85	1.83
Tapioca	10.21	10.17	8.76	4.77	3.68	2.80
Coffee	0.72	1.08	2.00	2.48	2.80	3.18
Tea	1.60	1.29	1.25	1.15	1.22	1.38

Source: Government of Kerala (Various Years), Economic Review, State Planning Board, Thiruvananthapuram.

the area under major cash crops, namely coconut, rubber, pepper, coffee, tea and cardamom accounted for 60 per cent of the gross cropped area in the State. The area of two major food crops-rice and tapioca, declined drastically to the tune of 8.77 per cent and 2.80 per cent respectively in 2010-11. It may infer that the relative contribution of rice to the total cropped area consistently declined in Kerala.

Agriculture sector in Kerala, unlike other states in the country has historically been dominated by commercial crops such as rubber, tea, coffee and spices. Hence this sector has been more open to market forces-both domestically and internationally. With more market orientation and better profitability of cultivation, the share of commercial crops in total area under cultivation in the state has been rising at the expense of food crops such as rice and tapioca (Jeromi, 2005). Thus overtime, the cropping pattern was more tailored to the demands of the world market.

The most notable feature of Kerala's agricultural development is the emergence of cash crops as a dominant sector over the five decades. The most significant segment in this category is the plantation crops consisting of rubber, tea, coffee and cardamom. Among these crops, rubber emerged as the most significant crops with largest area in the state. The area was 5.24 per cent in 1960-61 to 19.69 per cent in 2010-11. Similarly the coffee was 0.72 per cent to 3.18 per cent in 2010-11, Cardamom 1.22 per cent to 1.56 per cent and tea from 1.60 per cent to 1.38 per cent in 2010-11. Another Cash crop, Pepper, also increased from 2.43 per cent to 6.43 per cent in 2010-11.

The data analysis shows that the proportion of area under food grains declined from mid-seventies and an increasing role of cash crops over food crops. The nature of changes in area indicates that paddy land has been diverted either to other crops, mainly cash crops or to non-agricultural purposes such as sites for construction of building, brick-mining and infrastructural facilities such as roads, railway, canals etc. The factors influencing the shift included large increase in cost of cultivation of rice without corresponding increase in its price, relative price changes in favour of competing crops, problems of the managing labour, State Policies relating to land tenure, etc. The shift in cropping patterns from food crops to cash crops and also the shift from eco-friendly subsistence farming to profit-induced cultivation using chemical fertilizers and poisonous pesticides have accelerated the pace of biodiversity loss. Massive conversion of low-lying areas for non-agricultural purposes has led to a distortion of the balance of wetland ecosystems in ecologically fragile region. The conversion of paddy fields into areas to cultivate crops such as bananas and ginger has serious implications in Kerala. Large scale filling of paddy fields and leveling of hills have affected the ecosystem of the region. The results have been an acute shortage of drinking water in summer, falling water tables, soil erosion and climatic changes.

Thus, in short, the shifts in cropping pattern in favour of cash crops and consequent reduction in area under food crops is an issue of great concern that has long term implications for the food security and ecological and environmental balance of the State.

References

1. George, P.S. and S. Chattopadhyay (2001), Population and Land Use in Kerala, In Growing Population, Changing Landscape - Studies from India, China and, the United States, National Academy Press, Washington D.C.

2. Government of Kerala (2006a), *Kerala Human Development Report 2005,* State Planning Board, Thiruvananthapuram.

3. Government of Kerala (2006b), *Draft Approach Paper for Kerala's Eleventh Five Year Plan*, State Planning Board, Thiruvananthapuram.

4. Government of Kerala (2011), *Economic Review*, State Planning Board, Thiruvananthapuram.

5. Jeromi, P.D. (2005), *Agriculture Sector in Kerala and Issues Relating to Credit,* RBI Staff Studies, S.S. (DEAP), 2/2005, Reserve Bank of India.

6. Joseph, Brigit and K.J. Joseph (2005), *Commercial Agriculture in Kerala After WTO*, South Asian Economic Journal, No. 1, June 6.

7. Mahesh, R. (1999), *Causes and Consequences of Changes in Cropping Pattern: A Location Specific Study*, Discussion Paper No. 11, CDS, Thiruvananthapuram.

8. Maneesh, B (2011), *Agrarian Crisis – Causes and Consequences: A Study based on Selected Cash Crops in Kerala*, Thesis submitted to the University of Kerala, Thiruvananthapuram.

11

Eco-Feminism : The Role of Women in Environmental Management and Conservation

Kala Devi V.

Women particularly those living in rural areas or mountains have special relationship with the environment. All women have relationship with environment but in urban areas the approach is different, and women are not on the forefront of the race for protection and preservation of the resource. Ecofeminism means "a philosophical and political movement that combines ecological concerns with feminist ones". The term was coined by the French writer Francoise d'Eaubonne. Ecofeminism argues that there is a connection between women and nature that means every woman is closer to nature than men. Ecofeminism is more focused on the actual, specific interactions with the environment. This closeness, therefore, makes women more nurturing and caring towards their environment. Vandana Shiva, is credited with bringing ecofeminism into public consciousness by her reports of the Chipko movement. Chipko movement also led to the formation of anti-alcoholism.

Women's Connection with Environment

Women, Environment and Development debate (WED) began in the early 1970s. In Mexico-City, in 1975, at the First World Conference on Women, Vandana Shiva introduced the issue of women and the environment. Women have a vital role in environmental management and development. Their full participation is, therefore, essential to achieving sustainable development. It illustrates women and environment sustainability. Feminisation of agriculture means women are responsible for farm work and related domestic food production. The dependence on nature and the environment for survival is common among third world women. Dependence creates a deeply rooted connection between women and their surroundings. The dependency of women on natural resources, based on their responsibilities, creates a specific interest that may be different from the interests of men.

Role of Women in Conservation of Environment

Biomass plays a crucial role in meeting daily survival needs of the vast majority of the rural households. Production and processing of biomass agriculture, forestry and minor forest produce and village crafts based on biomass as raw materials are also the biggest sources of employment. Development imperatives have inevitably led to some destruction of the biomass through deforestation and environmental degradation. Traditionally, women have been responsible for subsistence and survival for water, food, fuel, fodder and habitat, though they rarely get the credit for nurturing these life support systems. The challenge is to re-establish the symbiosis between communities, women and natural resources and reverse the trend of the negative impact of existing developmental paradigms. Women have always been the principal conservers of bio-diversity. Even today they perform duties such as seed selection, multiplication and conservation. The on-farm conservation traditions of rural and tribal women, with reference to agro-biodiversity are well known.

Women have dealt with non-monetised biomass based subsistence economy of the household, i.e., firewood, cow dung, crop wastes, organic manure, etc. The environmental degradation took place due to men dominance over women, and women's large investment in environmental sustainability; some have theorised that women would protect the Earth better than men. The experience reveals to them that soil water and vegetation, necessary for their day-to-day living, requires, care and good management. Environmental degradation is related not only to the biosphere alone, but to the social sphere as well. Keeping in view of the inherent capabilities of women in the management it is needed that women entrepreneurship, development, educational and vocational training in various fields, communication skills, creativity and innovation, quality management and control, inventory and production management needed to be strengthened throughout the length and breadth of the country. To achieve this, resources and strength of women need to be channelised to develop their full potential so as to take their rightful place as equal partners in all spheres.

The role of women in land ownership and property management is significantly pointed out in ecofeminism. Specifically in developing countries, there is a great deal of inequality when it comes to land ownership. Traditional practices and bureaucratic factors often prevent women's access to natural resource development and management. Women's access to control of natural resources, land ownership and property management is a developing issue and is the subject of continuous debate in both the environmental realm and women's rights movement. In developing areas of the world, women are considered the primary users of natural resources (land, forest, and water), because they are the ones who are responsible for gathering food, fuel, and fodder. Shouldering this responsibility leads them to learn more about soil, plants, and trees and not misuse them.

Environmental Change and Women

Women's perspectives and values for the environment are somewhat different than men's. Women give greater priority to protecting and improving the capacity of nature, maintaining farming lands, and caring for nature and environment's future. Women struggle against alarming global trends, but they are working together to effect change. By establishing domestic and international non-governmental organisations, many women have recognised themselves. They showed to the world that they not only have the right to participate in environmental dilemmas but they have different relationship with environment including different needs, responsibilities, and knowledge about natural resources. This is why women are affected differently than men by environmental degradation, deforestation, pollution and overpopulation. Women are directly affected by environmental issues, so they become more concerned about environmental problems.

Ecological Movements Initiated by Women

Chipko Movement-(Women tree-huggers in India)

Chandi Prasad Bhatt and Sunderlal Bahuguna started and strengthened the Chipko Movement to prevent tree felling to safeguard the lifestyles of women which were dependent on the forests. Deforestation could qualitatively alter the lives of all village residents but it was the women who agitated for saving the forests. The slogan "ecology is permanent economy."

Green Belt Movement—Wangari Maathai

It aims to bring environmental restoration along with society's economic growth. It works for rapidly diminishing forests as well as empowering the rural women through environmental preservation, with a special emphasis on planting indigenous trees.

Navdanya Movement—Vandana Shiva

'Nine Seeds Movement' seeks to empower local Indian farmers to move away from growing any genetically modified organism (GMOs) on their land and return to organic, chemical-free practices.

Known women environmentalists are: China: Mei Ng, India:Vandana Shiva, Kenya: Wangari Muta Maathai, Russia: Maria Cherkasova, United States: Rachel Carson.

Relevant Legal Provision on Environment

India is one of the few countries of the world that made a specific reference in the constitution to the need for environmental protection, control and preservation. The Constitution (42nd Amendment) Act of 1976 has made it a Fundamental Duty to protect and improve the natural environment. Article 51 (a) provides that it shall be the duty of every citizen of India to protect and improve the natural environment including forests, lakes, rivers and wildlife and have compassion for living creatures. Article 21 of Constitution guarantees the right to life; a life of dignity, to be lived in a proper environment, free from danger of disease and infection. Besides these are number of Directive Principles, which give indirect emphasis for protection of environment.

In addition to Indian Constitutional aspect, certain special legislations are also available in India for environmental protection such as:

- The Air (Prevention and Control of Pollution) Act-1981.
- The Water (Prevention and Control of Pollution) Act, 1974.
- The Wildlife (Protection) Act, 1972.
- The India Forest Act, 1927.
- The Forest (Conservation) Act, 1980.
- Environmental Protection Act, 1986

Research Studies Conclude Some Suggestions

- The protection of women decision-makers, planners, advisers and managers related to environmental management should be increased.
- Environmental education should be expanded in rural areas.
- Women when once mobilised play a significant role in environmental protection.

• The potential of Science and Technology should be utilised to solve environmental related problems and ease women's workload inside and outside the home.

• The central government should develop a strategy to eliminate various obstacles—constitutional, legal, administrative, social and economic in nature to women's full participation in sustainable development.

• The Government, Non-Governmental Organisations, Environmental Conservation agencies and the common man should recognise and mobilise women as active participants to protect and enrich the natural resources that sustain us.

• In spite of all these aspects there must be promotion of disseminating the gender relevant knowledge and valuation of women's role through formal and non-formal education.

References

Agarwal, B., (1997) *The Gender and Environment Debate: Lessons from India in Visvanathan,* N. (ed), *The Women, Development and Gender Reader,* Zed Books, London.

Drengson, A., (2001) *The Trumpcter: Education for Local and Global Ecological Responsibility: Arne Naess's Cross-cultural, Ecophilosophy Approach* [online], available at http://www. ecofem. org.html (accessed December 2001).

Gaard, G., (2001) '*Women, Water and Energy: An Ecofeminist Approach*', *Organisation and Environment*, Vol. 14, No. 2, June 2001, pp. 157-172.

Matthews, H., (2001) '*The Graphic Connection Between Women and the Non-human*', *Journal of Ecofeminism* [online] available at http:// www.ecofem.org/journal

Visvanathan, N. (ed), (1997) *The Women, Development and Gender Reader,* Zed Books, London.

12

Ecological Discourses on Thiruvathira

Yamuna, D.S.

Ecology, a term coined in 1873 by the German Zoologist and Philosopher Ernst Heinrich Hackel, refers to the relations of organisms to one another and to their surroundings (Oxford, 2001). The ecological discourses on literary and cultural studies locate the interconnections between man's cultural and literary preferences and his natural environment. Such a discourse understands man as a part of a greater whole. The land, the air, the vegetation, animals, insects and even the solar system are considered to be deeply implied in human lives. It takes a more holistic view of the world, where the human beings live in, and seeks to apply to all living beings. The entire ecosystem including humans, function as a whole. An examination of the folk festivals in Kerala with their rustic backdrops often exhibits an ecological understanding of their natural environments.

Thiruvathira is a seasonal folk festival in Kerala celebrated by women. It celebrates the solar manifestation of the winter solstices mingled with household agricultural activities. The misty weather and moonlit nights bring in the festive mood. In a poem written by P. Kunjuraman Nair, the famous Malayalam poet, there is the description of the weather and nature who are preparing themselves for the Thiruvathira celebrations. The poet envisions that each and every natural phenomenon in the winter month of Dhanu (December –January) enthusiastically welcome the festival just as the womenfolk who engage in celebrating it.

The *Thiruvathira* celebrations begin ten days before the day of thiruvathira star in the month of Dhanu. The biotic and abiotic lives in the rustic world are glorified during the occasion. Each day of the festival begins with women moving towards the village pond in a procession before dawn with lanterns and materials for bathing and make up, mostly home made. As they reach the water body it will still be dark and cold. They burn heaps of dried leaves for light and slowly steps into the cold water one by one. Once in the water, they form a circle and begin a dance, tapping rhythmically on the water and splashing it. The process is accompanied by a song which is meant to wake the water up. After invoking the water goddess to join them in the celebration, the rhythm of beats and splashes in the water and that of their songs heighten as they enjoy sporting in the water till the sun comes up (Putheri, Balan, 6). Here, the waterbody itself becomes a companion to them in their rejoicing.

As Jasleen Dhamija rightly points out, our folk art forms are closely intermingled with our day to day activities in terms of the objects we use in our home (1). Being a festival of rustic women, cooking becomes a part of the celebration. Dishes made of fruits and other vegetation available during the season, form their special diet. Not just their agricultural produces but even certain small herbs that grow as weeds in their farm land play a key role in the festive activities. A collection of ten medicinal herbs, together nomenclatured '*Dasapushpam*' are important to the midnight ceremony of 'pathirapoochudal' when women ritualistically deck their hairs with these flowers. Women also plant the saplings of these herbs and water them as part of the ritual. The herbs that alleviate most of the ailments in their daily life are venerated assigning them a sacred status.

An instance of nature worship can be cited here. All the ten plants possess medicinal qualities. The essence of 'Karuka' (couch grass) is used to cure the diseases that affect the brain cells and the spinal cord. 'Vishnukranti' (Dwarf Morning Glory) has medicinal roots that can be used to purify blood, improve memory and also to prepare hair oil. It also cures stomach pain in children. The essence of 'Poovankurunila' (Little Iron Weed) reduces body temperature and cures urinary problems. 'Kayunni' enhances hair growth and improves eyesight. The essence of 'Mukkutti' (Little tree plant) relieves cough. 'Thiruthali' is used in treating infertility. 'Cherula' (Mountain knot grass) cures renal diseases. And 'Uzhinja' is used to lessen the throes of child birth (Jolly, 160-61).

The ceremonial planting and watering of the ten types of medicinal plants in the ritual 'pathirapoo chudal' refers to the intimacy between man and his natural environment.

The various games women engage in during the time, in fact, turn out to be a carnivalisation of the animal life around them. 'Thumbi thullal', one of the popular games dignifies the dragon fly. Swarm of tiny flies with their charming translucent wings merrily flying up and down near the water bodies is a regular sight in rustic Kerala. The game begins with songs sung by women sitting on the ground, forming a ring and clapping in rhythm with the singing. The song addresses the dragon fly, inviting the creature to join them. As the pace of singing intensifies, one of the women begins to quiver imitating the movements of the fly. The game ends in jeers and laughter. The game obviously precipitates a collective consciousness that has successfully comprehended the interconnections between natural phenomena and the human world.

Other entertainment programmes like 'Chozhikali', 'Kummattikali' and 'Pulikali' too incorporates animal themes into the festival. Wild beasts such as bear and tiger are imitated here. Often it is the boys who dress up to look like these beasts and dance imitating their movements. The relationship with the non-human nature is understood here not as extrinsic to man's identity but as essential in defining what it means to be human.

The most interesting fact of the celebration is the 'Thivathirakali' or Thiruvathira dance performed by women in their courtyards. The dancers form a ring around the lighted traditional wick lamp. They execute graceful movements in a circular pirouetting pattern accompanied by clapping and singing. The rhythms very often, closely follow the movements of the elements of nature. "The songs sound like a flowing river-sometimes it moves swiftly, sometimes they hurtle down like waterfalls, sometimes they have docile movements and at times they are serene" (Thiruvathira pattukal).

The dance takes place in the natural backdrop of mist and twilight. The presence of nature is intimately felt by the participants "We have been enjoying the sweetness of the mist covered moon-lit nights. As we gradually get close to the full moon night we can feel a systematic change in the aura all around" (qtd. in Sivadas Varma). Here we find that instead of creating an artificial theatrical space, the natural environment itself has been so integrated into the festival as to form its natural theatre. Theatre, thus, is not just a backdrop, but becomes an essential part of the performance.

The song sung during the Thiruvathira performance is a rich reportaire of folk songs that reveal a holistic view of the interconnection between human lives and his natural surroundings. The invocation of gods and goddesses turns out to be the deification of nature and its elements. Goddess Saraswathi is a maiden who was born out of a golden lotus in the golden pond. She wears tulsi flowers. The local goddesses Perandur Karthiyayani is described as one seen in the river bank. She is a lady with long thick dark hair and with fire and moon on her forehead. Lord Siva of Nagakula resides in the pond amongst lotus flowers and sits in the river. He wears Ummam flower and ash and takes food in the stem of aracanut leaf.

One of the songs picturizes how women amuse themselves while taking collective bath in the village pond. They play games swimming in the water. Another song is in the form of a conversation with a little bird. The bird comes from Guruvayoor, the land of Sri Krishna's temple. When it is asked to describe the news from there, it gives a detailed description of how jasmine plants are planted there, how they are watered, how the Varyar plucked the flowers to fill the basket, how he collected strings from the plantain and made thousand garlands to be offered to Lord Krishna.

There are also songs on planting, watering and flowering of plants. In 'Onnanam Kunnin mel oredimannin mel", there is an account of the Paala plant being planted atop the hill, watered and tendered carefully. The sprouting of each leaf and bud is watched curiously. In the song 'thrisavaperur madilakath' ('Inside the compound wall in Trisavaperur') the elanji tree with its yellow flowers in bunches has been depicted. Songs on the cultivation and harvesting of agricultural produces like cucumber, pea, coconut and paddy are also found in plenty.

As a female folk festival, Thiruvathira becomes a spontaneous expression of women's creativity which arises from an elemental consciousness of the changing moods of nature and their response to them. The mundane routine chores of everyday are pushed aside and women get busy creating a happy new world-establishing their companionship with the larger world of animate and inanimate forms around them.

References

Compact Oxford Dictionary, Thesaurus and Word power Guide. New York : Oxford University Press, 2001.

Dhamija, Jasleen. *Indian Folk Arts and Crafts.* New Delhi : National Book Trust, 1970.

http | | www.culture.shoppe.com/products/thiruvathirapattukal-thiruvathira-songs-traditional-Kerala-audio-cd.php.

Kunjuraman Nair, P. "*Ayakkatha kath.*" *Pookkalam* (Kottayam: S.P.SS, 1964) p. 375.

Putheri, Balan. *Thiruvathira :Eitheehyangalum Pattukalum.* Malappuram: Balan Putheri, 1999.

Jolly, C.I. *Keralathile oushadhasasyangal- Thrissur*: Current, 2009.

13

Physico-chemical Characteristics of Water Sample from Parvathi Puthanar Canal in Thiruvananthapuram District, Kerala

Geetha R. Nair

Abstract

Parvathi Puthanar is a man made canal that runs through the west coast of Trivandrum District. Periodic evolution of water quality of the Parvathi Puthanar is of great importance in the present study. The various parameters such as temperature, pH, total alkalinity, acidity, carbon dioxide, dissolved oxygen, primary productivity, chloride, chlorine, and calcium, etc., in the water sample and organic carbon in the soil were analysed.

Key words-Parvathi Puthanar, Physico-chemical characteristics, Primary productivity.

Introduction

Human population growth and industrial development have been the major havoc to the biotic environment. Water qualities in the upstream stretches of water bodies of Kerala are generally good and potable, the quality deteriorates as the water bodies transverse through the thickly populated lowland areas. It is due to several reasons such as discharge of waste water, dumping of solid waste, application of agrochemicals and also due to other anthropogenic activities.

The present study was conducted in the pre-monsoon and monsoon period.

Materials and Methods

The present attempt is to analyse the water sample collected from two different locations of Parvathi Puthanar Canal, viz. Chakkai bridge and Vallakadavu. Samples were collected during March, 2012 to June 2012. The distance between the collection sites were approximately 10 kms.

The sample is collected in polyethylene bottle of two litre capacity. The containers are washed with concentrated HCl and synthetic washing agents are used for eliminating fats. In addition to water sample, soil samples were also taken from the collection site. Two kilograms of soil samples were collected from the bottom of the river. The samples are then dried in air, grinded in a mortar, sieved and fine particles were packed in polythene bags. The samples were analysed in the laboratory. The following parameters were analysed by standard methods given in APHA. (Sharma, 2003).

Result and Conclusion

The present study was conducted in pre-monsoon and monsoon period (March 2012 to June 2012). The present study reveals that water temperature was highly fluctuated by the season. In March, the temperature value ranges from 34 to 32.5. The highest value reported in site A and lowest value reported in site B. In April, the range is between 32 to 30, where a maximum value is exhibited by the site A minimum of site B. In May, the temperature value ranges 26 to 22. The highest value reported in site A and lowest in site B. In June, the value range is between 24 to 22 where maximum value is exhibited by site A and minimum of site B. The present study shows that high temperature value during pre-monsoon and low during monsoon.

The temperature affects the chemical and biological reactions of water. A rise in water temperature accelerates chemical reactions, reduces solubility of gases amplifies taste or odour and elevates metabolic activity of organism. The slight variation in temperature in two stations is due to the difference in the time of sample collection. Temperature controls the occurrence and abundance of algal diversity. (Dwivedi and Pandey, 2002) and moderately high temperature favours the active multiplication of protoplasm resulting in low transparency. (Kang and Anand, 1978).

The results of pH showed slight variation in each sampling period. In March, the pH value ranges from 6.4 to 6.9. The highest value reported in site B and lowest value reported in site A. In April, the range is from 6.5 to 6.4. The highest value reported in site B and lowest in site A. In May, the temperature shows similarity in both site A and site B. In June, the pH ranges from 4.2 to 4.8, where maximum value is reported in site B and minimum of site A. The present study shows that high pH during pre-monsoon and low during monsoon. These findings agreed with the study of Kaur *et. al.* (1999). The pH of water is alkaline in nature. The slight variation in pH of two stations is due to high anthropogenic activities like washing clothes, sewage, bathing, etc.

Alkalinity of water is its capacity that neutralises a strong acid and is characterises a strong acid and is characterised by the presence of all hydroxyl ions capable of combining with hydrogen ions. In the present study, the phenolphthalein alkalinity is zero indicating the absence of carbohydrates. The carbohydrate is absent in both pre-monsoon and monsoon season.

In March, the bicarbonate content ranged from 40 to 60 mg/litre. The maximum bicarbonate content was observed in site B and minimum is at site A. In April, the range is between 65 to 95 mg/litre, where a maximum value is exhibited by site A and highest bicarbonate value is at site B. In May, the value ranges from 130 to 105 mg/litre. The highest value reported in site A and lowest bicarbonate in site B. In June, the value ranges from 140 to 165 mg/litre. The highest bicarbonate content is present in site A. The present study reveals the highest bicarbonate concentration during monsoon and lowest during summer.

The trend of bicarbonate is as that of alkalinity. Alkalinity also may due to the contamination by leaching process through the surface water during rainy season (Singh *et .al.*, 1999).

The acidity of the water is its capacity to neutralise a strong base and is most due to the presence of strong mineral acids, weak acids and weak bases. In the present study, the methyl orange acidity is zero. The methyl orange acidity are absent in both pre-monsoon and monsoon period. In March, total acidity varies from 1.25 to 2.5 mg/litre. The highest value reported in site B and lowest is at the site A. In April, the total acidity was maximum in site B, and lowest in site A. In May, the range is between 5 and 3.5, by site A and lowest by site B. In June, it ranges from 10 to 5 mg/litre, where maximum value is exhibited by site A and minimum in site B. The present analysis of acidity shows a maximum value during monsoon period and minimum during pre-monsoon period. This analysis is agreed with the result of Dwivedi and Pandey, (2002).

The result of carbon dioxide showed slight difference in pre-monsoon and monsoon. In March, it shows a range between 8.4 to 12 mg/litre. Maximum carbon dioxide value reported in site B and minimum is at site A. The maximum and minimum value of carbon dioxide during April is 17.0 and 14.4 in site B and A. In May, the highest value 22.0 reported in site A and lowest value in site B. In June, the range is between 24.0 to 22.18 where a maximum value is exhibited by site A and minimum of site B.

Free carbon dioxide dissolved in water is essentially the only source of carbon that can be assimilated and incorporated into the body of all aquatic autotrophs. Once fixed it can further be utilised by the organisms of other categories. The trend indicates the free carbon dioxide content is minimum during the monsoon period.

Dissolved Oxygen (DO) is necessary for life of aquatic systems. In March, the DO concentration varies from 8.466 to 6.4832 mg/litre. The lowest level was reported in site B and highest in site A. In April, it ranges from 8.84 to 9.600 mg/litre. In May, site A shows high value of dissolved oxygen 11.65 and lowest value 9.448 by site B. In June, the highest value is 14.266 mg/litre for site A and 13.272 lowest for site B.

The DO may be due to the decomposition of organic matters and is an indication of high microbial activity. Many factors such as turgidity, day length and biological activity influence DO dynamics in estuaries and basic water (Reid and Wood, 1976). DO indicates physical, chemical and biological activities in a water body. DO affects the solubility and availability of many nutrients (Wetzel ,1983).

The primary productivity of two stations was recorded in the Table13.1. In March, the gross productivity of site A exhibits maximum value (0.0813 mg of c/1/hr) and minimum is by site B (0.0467 mg of c/1/hr). In April, the gross productivity of site B exhibits maximum value (0.1084 mg of c/1/hr) and site A shows minimum value (0.0813 mg of c/1/hr). In May, maximum value of gross productivity exhibited by site B (0.1426 mg of c/1/hr) and minimum value exhibited by site A (0.1421 mg of c/1/hr). In June, the gross productivity ranges from 0.400 to 0.362 mg of c/1/hr. The maximum value exhibited by site A and minimum value by site B.

The net productivity of two stations were recorded. In March, net productivity of two sites is same (0, 0813 mg of c/1/hr). In April, the maximum net productivity exhibited by site B (0.142 mg of c/1/hr) and minimum exhibited by site A(0.1108 mg of c/1/hr). In May, the net productivity ranges between 0.2233 to 0.2675 mg of c/1/hr, where the maximum net productivity exhibited by site B (0.2675 mg of c/1/hr) and minimum net productivity exhibited at site A (0.2233 mg of c/1/hr). In June, the maximum net productivity exhibited by site B (0.2892 mg of c/1/hr) and minimum by site A (0.2413 mg of c/1/hr).

In natural fresh water chloride concentration quite low. In March, the content ranged from 1.478 to 1.621 mg/litre. The minimum chloride content was noticed in site A and maximum was in site B. In April, the chloride varied from 0.8026 to 1.4023 mg/litre. The maximum chloride content was in site B and minimum in site A. In May, the chloride content varied from 0.6118 to 1.1024 mg/litre, where the minimum chloride content was noticed in site A and maximum was in site B. In June, the chloride content ranged from 0.224 to 0.82 mg/litre, where maximum value reported in site B and minimum is at site A.

The chlorine content of canal is also varies due to influence of rain. The chlorine content in March ranged from 0.81 to 0.88

Table13.1
Physico-chemical Parameters of Site A

Sl. No.	*Parameters*	*Unit*	*March*	*April*	*May*	*June*
1.	Temperature	°C	32.5	30	22	21
2.	pH		6.9	6.4	4.8	4.8
3.	Total alkalinity	Mg/l	60	95	105	140
4.	Acidity	Mg/l	2.5	3.5	3.5	5
5.	Carbon dioxide	Mg/l	12	17.0	20.2	22.18
6.	Dissolved Oxygen	Mg/l	6.4832	8.84	9.448	13.0272
7.	Gross productivity	Mg of c/1/hr	0.0467	0.1084	0.1426	0.362
8.	Net Productivity	Mg of c/1/hr	0.0813	0.142	0.2675	0.2892
9.	Chloride	Mg/l	1.621	1.4023	1.1024	0.82
10.	Chlorine	Mg/l	0.88	0.6225	0.1662	0
11.	Calcium	Mg/g	3.0671	1.8041	0.6201	0.2094
12.	Organic carbon in soil	Mg/g	0.0127	0.0082	0.0064	0.0010

Table 13.2
Physico-chemical Parameters of Site B

Sl. No.	*Parameters*	*Unit*	*March*	*April*	*May*	*June*
1.	Temperature	°C	34	32	26	24
2.	pH		6.4	6.5	4.8	4.2
3.	Total alkalinity	Mg/l	40	65	130	165
4.	Acidity	Mg/l	1.25	2.5	5	10
5.	Carbon dioxide	Mg/l	8.4	14.4	22.0	24.0
6.	Dissolved Oxygen	Mg/l	8.466	9.600	11.65	14.266
7.	Gross productivity	Mg of c/1/hr	0.0813	0.0813	0.1421	0.400
8.	Net Productivity	Mg of c/1/hr	0.0813	0.108	0.2233	0.2413
9.	Chloride	Mg/l	1.478	0.8026	0.6118	0.224
10.	Chlorine	Mg/l	0.81	0.661	0.497	0
11.	Calcium	Mg/g	1.0081	0.8023	0.2604	0.2004
12.	Organic carbon in soil	Mg/g	0.0124	0.0128	0.0074	0.0042

mg/litre, where the maximum chlorine content noticed in site B and minimum was in site A. In April, the minimum chlorine content was exhibited by site A (0.661 mg/litre) and maximum was exhibited by site B (0.6225 mg/litre). In May, the range is between 0.0897 to 0.1662 mg/litre, where maximum value is exhibited by site B and the minimum by site A. In June, the chlorine content is zero in all sites. The chlorine content in this canal may be due to high anthropogenic activities.

In March, the calcium ranges from 1.0081 to 3.0671 mg/litre. The lowest value reported in site A and highest in site B. In April, the calcium value ranged from 0.8023 to 1.8041 mg/litre, where maximum value exhibited by site B and minimum value exhibited by site A. In May, the range is between 0.2604 to 0.6201 mg/litre, where maximum value is exhibited by site B and the lowest by site A. In June, the calcium varies from 0.2004 to 0.2094 mg/litre. The lowest level was reported in site A and high level in site B. The present analysis shows that high calcium content in canal during summer and low during monsoon.

The organic carbon content of soil of two sites indicates variation. In March, it ranges from 0.0124 to 0.0127 mg/g. Maximum value reported in site B and minimum is at site A. In April, it ranges from 0.0082 to 0. 0128 mg/m, where maximum reported in site B. In May, the maximum value was observed in site A (0 .0074 mg/g) and minimum value was observed in site A (0. 0042 mg/g) and minimum in site B (0.0010 mg/g).

The present analysis indicates that certain remedial measures are taken for the conservation and sustainable management of the ecosystem.

References

1. Aaradhana, P.S. (1998). *Environmental Management*. Rajat Publications. Delhi :127.

2. APHA (American Public Health Assosciation). (1980). *Standard method for the examination of water and waste water* (15th edn.). Amer. Health Asso. Inc., New York: 1134.

3. Diwedi. B.K. and Pandey G.C. (2002). *Physico-chemical Factors and Algal Diversity of Two Ponds* (Girijqulcundi and Maquhara Pond) Faizabad India Poll Res 21 (3) :361-370.

4. Kant, S. and Anand V. K. (1978). *Inter relationship of Phytoplankton and physical factors on Mansabal Lake, Jammu.* Indian Z.J. Eco. 134-140.

5. Kaur, H. Dhillion S.S. Bath K.S. and Mander G. (1999). *Correlation of rotifers with physic-chemical factors at Harike reservoir*. Punjab. India Daya Publishing House, New Delhi: 336.

6. Reid, G.K. and Wood. D. (1976). *Ecology and Inland Waters and estuaries*, D Van Norstand Company New York : 678.

7. Sharma, B.K. and Kaur H. (1997) *Environmental Chemistry*, Krishna Prakshasan Media (p) Ltd : 185.

8. Sharma, P.D. (2003) *Ecology and Environment* (7th Edn), Rasthogi Publication Meerut, India 580-583.

9. Singh, S.K. and Chowdhary (1999). *Study of Physic-chemical Parameters of Ground Water of Nagpur District, Some Co-relations,* 28th Annual conventions of IWWA, Jodhpur Proceedings: 99-102.

14

Indoor Gamma Dose in the South West Coast of Kerala

Rani. K. Pillai, Ben Byju S., Arunima S., Lekshmi R., Vishnu Prasad A.K., P.J. Jojo

Abstract

We are all exposed to ionizing radiation from natural sources in three different pathways namely: external, ingestion and inhalation. The external sources are cosmic rays and naturally occurring radioactive isotopes of the ^{40}K, ^{238}U, and ^{232}Th decay series, some or all of which can be found in the ground, in construction materials, and in air. Cosmogenic radionuclide's are produced through the interaction of cosmic rays with atoms in the atmosphere, and do not contribute significantly to external gamma radiation doses. High background radiation levels are found in many parts of the world including south west coastal region of Kerala. This higher concentration is due to primordial radioactive nuclides in soil. Indoor external gamma dose measurements are important as most individuals spend about 80 per cent of their time indoors. Indoor gamma radiation dose rates were measured in 120 residential buildings along south west coast region of Kerala from Trivandrum district to Alappuzha District using $CaSO_4$: Dy Thermo luminescent dosimeters. Active measurements of gamma dose were done using a GM tube based survey meter while fixing and retrieval of detectors from locations. A good correlation was found between the survey meter and TLD measurements. The observed annual dose rates were found to vary from 21112 µGy/y, to 415 µGy/y. Indoor doses were found to vary with the nature of flooring materials used.

Key words: Primordial Radionuclide's, TLD, GM tube based survey meter.

Introduction

Natural radiation is ubiquitous ever since its creation. Radioactive elements found in nature, classified into three categories: Primordial, Cosmogenic and Human produced. Primordial continues from the creation of earth. They are typically long lived, with half lives of the order of millions of years. Some Primordial radio nuclides are ^{40}K, ^{238}U, and ^{232}Th decay series. Cosmogenic radio nuclides such as ^{10}Be,^{26}Al,^{36}Cl, etc., formed as the result of cosmic ray interactions with matter, do not contribute significantly to external gamma radiation doses. Human produced radio nuclides like Tritium, Iodine 131, Cesium 137 are formed due to human actions, is minor amounts compared to other. Background radiations levels are a combination of Primordial and Cosmogenic radiation. This level is fairly constant over the world, being 8-15 ìrad/hr. High background radiation levels are found in many parts of the world including southwest coastal region of Kerala. This higher concentration is due to primordial radioactive nuclides in soil. One such mineral, Monazite, is a highly insoluble rare-earth mineral that occurs in beach sand together with illuminate. The main radionuclide's in monazite are from ^{232}Th decay series, Uranium and its progeny ^{226}Ra. Indoor external gamma dose measurements are important as most individuals spend about 80 per cent of this time indoors. There are several dwellings in the region with unusually high levels of indoor radiation levels.

The present study aims at the external dose measurements in dwelling in the southwest coast region of Kerala. There are several studies reported for measurement of indoor gamma dose levels to assess the dose to the population (Lin *et al*., 1987;

Nambi *et al.*, 1987; Yu *et al.*, 1992; Chen *et al.*, 1993; Bacci *et al.*, 1988; Rybach *et al.*, 2002). In the Southwest Coast of Kerala there were few published studies on measuring terrestrial gamma radiation dose rate (Sunil A *et al.*, 2011, M.P. Chougaonkar *et.al*, 2004). Most of the environmental radiation studies performed in Southwest Coast of Kerala concentrated on measurements of indoor radon concentrations and radon exhalation from soil.

Materials and Methods

Selection of Houses for the Survey

The selection of houses was in proper order, chosen for the measurement. Altogether hundred houses were selected along the coastline from Thiruvananthapuram District to Alappuzha District for the investigations. There were six locations namely, Varkala, Paravoor, Eravipuram, Chavara, Karunagappally, Kayamkulam which are the coastline region of southwest coast of Kerala. Averages of twenty houses were selected from each location. Dwellings for this study were chosen near the coast, at increasing distances from the coast and span of 200 m throughout the study area. About ten dwellings were selected from the Normal background radiation (NBRA) region in eastern side of Kollam and Thiruvanthapuram district in random. While choosing the monitoring location, the construction materials used in the house were also considered. Majority of the houses under survey were constructed with brick walls, while the remaining houses were either wooden or thatched walls with or without being plastered and painted. Most of the houses were made of concrete roof, remaining were thatched, tiled and either asbestos cement or galvanised iron (GI) sheets. Most of the houses were cement flooring. Some are tiles, granite, and marble.

Indoor Gamma Ray Dose Using TLDs

Indoor gamma dose, inside the houses, was monitored using Thermo Luminescent Dosimeters (TLDs). Dysprosium doped calcium sulphate ($CaSO_4$:Dy) phosphor is one of the most efficient phosphors prepared for use in wide-spread in various applications of radiation dosimetry as its sensitivity dependent upon the concentration of Dy. The method of preparation of $CaSO_4$: Dy phosphor is described elsewhere (Yamashita et al., 1971). Prepared TLDs were heated at 400°C for 6 hr to erase the previous dose history. The processed phosphor was filled in brass capsules, wrapped with identification label and sealed in PVC. The thickness of the brass capsule has been standardised for achieving an almost energy-independent response within the energy range of the terrestrial radiations. Performance characteristics of the TLD phosphor have been described in an earlier publication (Nambi *et al.*, 1986). The period of monitoring of TLDs was three months. During installation and retrieval of TLDs, ambient gamma dose was measured using an environmental radiation dosimeter. After the exposure for about three months, the TLDs were retrieved and analysed for the dose they recorded during the exposure period. The dose values evaluated were normalised to 365 days to obtain the dose per year. The dosimeters were properly calibrated at BARC, Mumbai. The measurement was done with a PC-based TL analyser. All the measurements were performed with a continuous flow of nitrogen gas maintained at constant flow rate.

Outdoor Gamma Ray Dose Using Survey Meter

Spot surveys for the outdoor external gamma ray doses were also carried out using GM Tube based Survey meter of type UR705 (Nucleonix, India) consisting of GM tube and microprocessor-based digital display. The active gamma dose measurements were made at ground level and approximately 1 m height from the ground, inside and outside the dwellings, during the deployment and retrieval of the dosimeters.

Results and Discussion

The distribution of the dose due to gamma rays (indoor) during three months in different location was observed using TLDs. During the time of deployment and retrieval of TLDs, Gamma ray dose were also measured using Survey meter. It has been found that the external gamma dose rates based on TLDs in the location varies from 415 μGy/y to 11419 μGy/y and based on Survey meter in 1 m height is from 1314 μGy/y to 21112 μGy/y, in ground, from 1402 μGy/y to 31886 μGy/y. The TLD readings were found in good correlation with the Survey meter readings (R=0.8). Table 14.2 lists the maximum, minimum, mean values, standard deviation, skewness and kurtosis coefficients of the seven location using TLDs. Table 14.3 lists

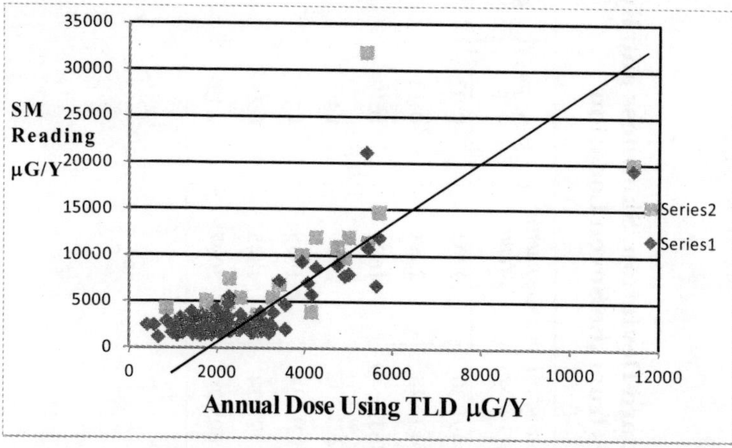

Fig. 14.1: Correlation between the gamma dose as measured by TLDs and Survey Meter

the same for survey meter. The correlation graph is shown in the Fig.14.1.

The skewness of the data represents the symmetry of the given distribution. From the analysis of the results for TLDs no one gets the skewness of zero. But from the observation of some location, skewness was nearly zero i.e.,—0.07,—0.61, —0.19 shows slightly skewed. The data for TLD as well as survey meter in the Normal Background Radiation Region (Varkala, NBRA) shows a platykurtic kurtosis (< 0), indicates that the central peak of the dose distribution is lower and broader as compared with the normal distribution having its tails shorter and thinner. But the remaining indicate the distribution was leptokurtic kurtiosis (0 >).

The data collected gave the information of the variation of dose rates throughout the southwest coast of Kerala. In the Normal Background Radiation Region (NBRA) the dose rate slightly differ with respect to the building material, mainly flooring material. Some building materials (like some ceramics)

Table 14.1: Maximum, Minimum, Mean Values, Standard Deviation, Skewness and Kurtosis Coefficients of the Dose Rate using TLDs from the Seven Location

Name of location	*Maximum*	*Minimum*	*Arithmetic Mean*	*Standard deviation*	*Geometric Mean*	*Skewness*	*Kurtosis*
Varkala	3265	1713	2443	491.30	2394	-0.07	-1.37
Paravoor	3569	1755	2633	497.48	2588	-0.12	0.61
Eravipuram	2646	663	1749	463.0549	1680	-0.19	0.94
Chavara	11419	856	3462	2218.12	2929	1.97	5.88
Karunagapally	5635	415	1935	1211.99	1635	1.65	3.23
Kayamkulam	2769	1375	1877	377.24	1845	1.23	1.85
NBRA	3217	1663	2164	605.26	2097	1.12	-0.59

Table 14.2: Maximum, Minimum, Mean Values, Standard Deviation, Skewness and Kurtosis Coefficients of the Dose Rate Using Survey Meters from the Seven Location

Name of location	*Maximum*		*Minimum*		*Arithmetic Mean*		*Geometric mean*		*Standard Deviation*		*Skewness*		*Kurtosis*	
	IM	GD	IM	GD	IM	GD	IM	GD	IM	GD	IM	GD	IM	GD
Varkala	26.28	2438	1447	1485	1930.85	1978.60	1907.77	1960.41	308.26	270.94	0.40	-0.19	0.10	-0.67
Paravoor	2190	2628	1577	1577	1890.58	2065.92	1879.99	2038.93	206.05	349.32	-0.35	0.22	1.01	-1.01
Eravipuram	2716	3767	1051	1402	1975	2313	1916.93	2235.31	474.28	628.74	-0.19	0.73	-0.83	0.36
Chavara	21112	31886	2278	2190	6531.56	8083.76	5185.06	6362.13	5042.68	6629.14	1.71	2.25	2.80	6.24
Karunaga pally	7008	9373	1577	1927	3352.68	3898.09	3119.33	3575.65	1409.90	1856.46	1.45	1.66	1.97	2.57
Kayamkulam	2716	3154	1314	1402	1978.42	2109.75	1934.42	2066.23	442.84	459.79	0.54	0.88	-0.56	1.51
NBRA	2540	3504	1840	1840	2277.40	2558.00	2265.26	2506.23	244.19	542.74	-0.38	0.29	-0.98	-0.54

are known to have slightly higher natural background radiation than others. This change analysed in the Fig.14.1 and this is represented in the Table 14.1 But the fifth type of building material (Mud) shows high value compared to normal value because those houses were near to Varkala Beach. In Varkala beach the Survey meter readings were 200 μR/hr. When compared the SM reading with TLD reading, got a correlation of 0.59.

Table 14.3: Indoor Dose Rates having Different Building Material

Sr. No	*Type of building material*	*Dose rate using TLD μGy/y .*	*Dose rate using survey meter μGy/y*
1.	Cement	2268	2155
2.	Granite	1971	2109
3.	Marble	2539	2041
4.	Mosaic	2524	2212
5.	Mud	2864	2323
6.	Ordinary Tile	2691	2047
7.	Vitrified Tile	3012	2361

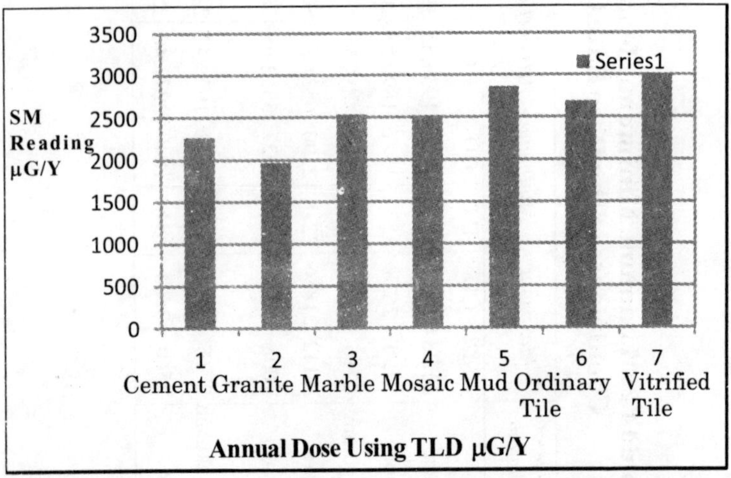

Fig. 14.1. Variation of Dose Rate With Respect to Building Material.

Conclusions

Everyone in the world is exposed to natural background radiation. Some areas of the world were lower than this average (like the value you reported), and some were much higher. The indoor gamma ray dose rate in the HBRA areas (Karunagappally) surveyed is similar to those reported in the earlier studies in the region. Remaining locations expect Chavara shows indoor gamma ray dose rate observed satisfies the reported value in Non Background Region.

Acknowledgement

The presented work is a part of the research work carried out in Centre for Advanced Research in Physical Sciences, Department of Physics, Fatima Mata National College, Kollam. We thankfully acknowledge Dr E.V. Wilson (Head of the Department), technical and scientific assistance from the research lab. We are also thankful to the residents living in the study area for their cooperation during the field work.

References

Chen C.J., Weng P.S., Chu T.C., 1993. Evaluation of natural radiation in houses built with blach schist. Health. Phys. 64, 74–78.

Bacci C, Fureta C, Rispoldi B, (1988). *Experimental observation on thermo luminescent dosimetry used in environmental monitoring.* Radiat. Eff. 105, 159–165.

Lin,Y.,M. Lin, P.H. Chen, C.J. Huang, (1987). *Measurement of terrestrial gamma radiation in Taiwan, Republic of China. Health.Phys.* 52, 805–811.

M.P. Chougaonkar, K.P. Eappen, T.V. Ramachandran, P.G. Shetty, Y.S. Mayya, S. Sadasivan, V. Venkat Raj, (2004). *Profiles of doses to the population living in the high background radiation areas in Kerala,* India Journal of Environmental Radioactivity 71, 275–297.

Nambi K.S.V., Bapat V.N., David M., Sundaram V.K., Sunta C.M., Soman S.D., (1986). *Natural background radiation and population dose distribution in India.* BARC report.

Nambi K.S.V., Papat, V.N., David, M., Sundaram V.K., Sunta C. M., Soman D., (1987). *Countrywide environmental radiation monitoring using Thermoluminescence dosimeters.* Radiat. Prot. Dosim. 18, 31–38.

Rybach L., Bachler D., Bucher B., Schwarz G., (2002). *Radiation doses of Swiss population from external sources. J. Environ. Radiat*. 62, 277–286.

Sunil A., Ben Byju S. and Jojo P. J., (2011). *External gamma dose to the population in high background radiation area in Kerala,* International Journal of Fundamental Physical Sciences.

Yamashita T., Nada N., Onishi, Kitamura S., (1971). *Calcium sulfate activated by Thulium or dysprosium for thermoluminescence dosimetry*. Health Phys. 21, 295-300.

Yu K.N., Guan Z.J., Stokes M.J., Young E.C.M., (1992). *The assessment of the natural radiation dose committed to the Hong Kong people. J. Environ. Radiat*. 17, 31–48.

15

Dimensions of Global Environmental Politics

K.C. Sreekumar

Environmental problems of the world should be looked at from the perspective of global politics. Actually this is being necessitated by a plethora of opinions put forward in support of and against the very nature of environmental crises of the globe and the policies pursued by different nations to tackle those crises by environmentalists, politicians and the media all over the world. To unravel the complexities of environmental politics one has to ask a few pertinent questions and try to answer them. How and when did environmental issues assume significance? What are the major global environmental issues? What are the measures adopted by different nations to solve the problems? What are the political dimensions of environmental agreements?

Environmental pollution is an age old phenomenon. Advancement of science and technology has hoodwinked the selfish Homo sapiens to meticulously and unscrupulously exploit the nature. Being fratricide from the very beginning, man savored the pleasure of harnessing weapons which had its brunt on the nature, especially with the dawn of the nuclear age which actually brought him to the brink of the abyss. Can he now sprout wings as a hopeful Kazantzakis would make us believe?[1] People like Bertrand Russell, who disproved Rousseau's conception that 'thinking man is a depraved animal', lamented about the immorality of the unbridled destruction of nature which leads to environmental crises. The world at that time was not mature enough to lend its ears to them. The world was roused from its slumber in 1974 when two scientists—Rowland and Molina sounded the warning bells of ozone layer depletion. Still there were many doubting Thomases amidst environmental scientists, politicians, businessmen and industrialists. They considered it as science fiction or just ridiculous nonsense.

However, the United Nations opened its eyes towards the problem and the UN Environmental Programme funded a study by the World Meteorological Society to find out the connection between chlorofluorocarbons (CFCs) and ozone depletion. In 1976, the U.S. National Academy of Sciences (NAS) released a report that confirmed the scientific credibility of the ozone depletion hypothesis. Albeit the environmental scientists all over the world were alerted it was not until 1985 that a consensus on the existence of ozone depletion emerged, thanks to the discovery of a hole in the ozone layer above the Antarctic. In that year Farman, Gardiner and Shanklin, scientists of the British Antarctic Survey, published results of abnormally low ozone concentrations above Halley Bay near the South Pole. Later it was noted by hundred scientists from ten countries that the ozone layer in the northern Hemisphere had been reduced by up to three per cent between 1969 and 1986. Thus, slowly environmental problems began to get the attention of the world.

The magnitude of the environmental crisis becomes clear just by a glimpse of the list of global environmental problems. Climate change is one of the most glaring environmental problems about which volumes have been written. It is defined as a change in the statistical properties of the climate system when considered over long periods of time, regardless of cause. It is very often used to refer to climate change caused by human activity, as opposed to changes in climate that may have resulted as part of earth's natural process. Naturally it is used to mean global warming. While global warming refers to surface temperature increases, climate change includes global warming and everything else that escalating greenhouse gas levels will affect. Greenhouse effect is a natural phenomenon whereby various atmospheric gases keep the earth's temperature high enough to sustain life. These gases include carbon dioxide (CO_2), methane nitrous oxide and halo carbons. These permit radiation from the sun to pass through but then absorb the radiation reflected back from the earth's surface. This helps in trapping heat in the atmosphere. In the absence of natural greenhouse effect the average global temperature would become 33 degrees centigrade lower.[2]

A 2007 report by the Intergovernmental Panel on Climate Change (IPCC) assessing the work of 2,500 scientists, economists, and policy-makers from more than 120 countries brought out the fact that human beings have been the primary cause of global warming since 1950. There were alarming reports of greenhouse gases from human pollution sources reaching a very high level and causing severe droughts, floods and heat waves in 2011. A report titled "State of the Climate in 2011", compiled by nearly 400 scientists from 48 countries, stated that 2011 was among the 15 warmest year since documentation began in the late 1800s, and that the Arctic warmed at about twice the rate of lower latitudes with sea ice at below average levels. It is observed that during the last century global mean surface temperature rose by about 0.6 degrees centigrade. It is projected to increase by between 1.4 and 5.8 degrees (relatively to 1990) by 2100.[3]

Environmental degradation is one of the ten threats officially cautioned by the High Level Threat Panel of the UN. The UN International Strategy for Disaster Reduction has defined environmental degradation as "The reduction of the capacity of the environment to meet social and ecological objectives, and needs."[4] It is the deterioration of the environment through exhaustion of natural resources such as air, water and soil, the destruction of ecosystems and the extinction of wildlife. The horrendous face of environmental degradation is visible in the fact that in the poorest regions of the world more than 11 million children die before reaching the age of five. This is caused by preventable illnesses.

Fresh water depletion is a casualty of environmental degradation. It has to be remembered that life on earth is dependent on the availability of fresh water. Only 25 per cent of all of the water on earth is fresh water and 69 per cent of this fresh water is frozen in ice caps located on Antarctica and Greenland. By that we mean that only 30 per cent of the 25 per cent of fresh water is available for consumption. Scarcity of fresh water is going to increase in future due to population growth, spreading of urbanisation, higher standards of living, and climate change. Global temperature will rise in the coming years due to climate change and temperature increase; in turn, it would cause the decreasing of the length of the snow season in the winter and increasing of the intensity of snowmelt in warmer seasons. All these can affect the earth's water supply adversely and make living condition worse.

Environmental degradation includes land degradation which is undesirable change or disturbance to the land. It has to be kept in mind that 40 per cent of the world's agricultural land is seriously degraded. Land degradation is caused by a host of factors such as deforestation, destroying the fertility of the soil through intensive cultivation, unscientific use of artificial manures and pesticides, overgrazing, inappropriate irrigation, quarrying of stone, sand, ore and minerals, unplanned urbanisation, etc.

Pollution poses a serious threat to environment. It can be caused by chemical substances, sound, heat or light. Pollution caused by plastic waste, chemical sludge and other debris is also very dangerous. It has been noted that even the Himalayas have been littered by plastic. Though the industrial revolution caused much environmental pollution the public awareness about the dangers of it assumed global proportions only with the dawn of the nuclear age. The effect of radioactive contamination caused by nuclear testing will last hundreds of thousands of years. The Fukushima nuclear disaster paved the way for worldwide discussion on the rationality of using nuclear fission reactors to generate electricity from nuclear fuel for civilian purposes. Advocates of nuclear energy are of the opinion that nuclear power is a source of sustainable energy. It reduces carbon emissions and increases energy security. Unlike fossil fuels nuclear power produces no air pollution. They assure that the risks of storing the nuclear waste are negligible and the adoption of latest technology would further reduce the risk.[5] On the other hand the opponents highlight the high risk involved in nuclear power. According to them these threats include health hazards and environmental pollution caused by uranium mining, processing and transport, the risk of nuclear weapons proliferation or sabotage and the question of disposing the nuclear waste.[6] It is estimated that about 400 million metric tons of hazardous wastes are generated each year.

Attempts to Problem Resolution

Taking into consideration the question of resolving global environmental problems one has to think globally. This is so because very little could be contributed by local areas, regions or even states to find out solutions for global issues. Although the policies pursued by various states to find out solution to the global problem are not insignificant here one has to emphasise the steps taken by nations collectively. A look at the history of environmental agreements between nations shows that multilateral environmental agreements (M.E.As) existed even before the UN Conference on the Environment held at Stockholm in 1972.[7] These were mainly concerned with issues like wildlife conservation and maritime pollution. The Stockholm conference, gave global dimension to such issues as well. It was the U.N.'s first major conference on environmental issues. It has much significance as far as global environmental politics is concerned.

In 1977, the USA, Canada, Norway, Sweden and Finland (collectively known as the Toronto Group) together urged UNEP to consider remedial action. Since nothing positive took place they unilaterally decided to ban non-essential aerosol uses of CFCs. In 1985, 20 nations, including most of the major CFC producers, signed the Vienna Convention, which established a framework for negotiating international regulations on ozone-depleting substances. This Convention could not impose a target to reduce CFC production despite the fact that it was ratified by all the UN members as well as the European Union. It had no legally binding reduction goals for the use of CFCs. These were actually laid out in the Montreal Protocol of 1987. After the discovery of the ozone hole it only took 18 months to reach a binding agreement in Montreal. It came into force on January 1, 1989. It was designed to protect the ozone layer by phasing out the production of numerous substances believed to be responsible for ozone depletion. By this Protocol the European Community and Japan agreed to reduce CFC production by 50 per cent of 1986 levels by 1999 and to freeze Holon production of 1986 levels by 1992. The ozone layer would recover by 2050 if the Protocol is adhered to. Even Kofi Annan had high expectations, about it, is clear from his words that "perhaps the single most successful international agreement to date has been the Montreal Protocol."[8] The treaty provided a timetable on which the production of substances like the CFCs, HCFs was to be phased out and ultimately eliminated. The Parties to the Protocol were required to base their future decisions on the available scientific, environmental, technical, and economic information. Panels were drawn from worldwide expert communities to assess such information. There is disagreement between the developed and developing countries regarding the monitoring of CFCs and HFCs.

Developed countries hold the view that since the rise in the emission of super-greenhouse gases is a consequence of the phasing out of CFCs and HCFCs under the Montreal Protocol, the same agreement should monitor them. On the other hand, the developing countries like India, China and Brazil, are of the opinion that the emission and regulation of greenhouse gases fall under the purview of the United Nations Framework Convention on Climate Change (UNFCCC). While the developed countries following the Kyoto Protocol report their HFC emission data to UNFCCC the parties to the Montreal Protocol have no such obligation. It has to be noted that the developing countries are afraid of the high cost of transition from HFCs to a safer option.

A Multilateral Fund was created for the implementation of the Montreal Protocol. Its main objective is to assist developing country parties to the Montreal Protocol whose annual per capita consumption and production of ozone depleting substances (ODS) is less than 0.3 kg to comply with the control measures of the Protocol. The Parties to the Montreal Protocol who meet these criteria are referred to as Article 5 countries. Funds are used for purposes like financing the conversion of existing manufacturing processes, training personnel, paying royalties and patent rights on new technologies, and establishing national ozone offices. It is the first treaty with a financial mechanism managed democratically by an Executive Board with equal representation by developed and developing countries. All countries in the United Nations, the Cook Islands, Holy See, Niue and the European Union have ratified the original Montreal Protocol.[9]

According to scientific evaluation of the effects of the Montreal Protocol there is clear evidence of a decrease in the atmospheric burden of ozone-depleting substances and some early signs of stratospheric ozone recovery.[10]

The Rio Earth Summit

It was the Rio Earth Summit that enabled world leaders and non-governmental organisations committed to environmental protection to sit together and thrash out issues concerning global environment. This UN Conference on Environment and Development held at Rio de Janeiro in 1992 reaffirmed the Declaration of the UN Conference on Environment adopted at Stockholm and sought to build upon it. Its declared goal is worth noting in connection with environmental politics. It consisted of a "*new and equitable partnership* through the creation of new levels of cooperation among states, key sectors of societies and people..." [emphasis added]. Here it is recognised that a new partnership and equitable partnership are required for the protection of the integrity of the environmental and developmental system. The politics involved in the use of the term 'equitable partnership' will become more visible after analysing later developments.

It proclaims that, in accordance with the UN Charter and the principles of international law, States have the sovereign right to exploit their own natural resources in pursuance of their own environmental and developmental policies. It is pointed out that along with this right the States have certain obligations as well. Accordingly, the States should ensure that the activities carried out within their jurisdiction are not causing damage to the environment of other States or of areas beyond the limits of national jurisdiction.[11] This is openly violated quite often. Most of the environmentally polluting activities that take place within a State would definitely affect the global environment. That is why we say that even localised activities can have global consequences as far as environment is concerned. Principle 3 of the Declaration recognises the need for equitably meeting the developmental and environmental needs of not only the present but also of the future generations. And that makes sense of the concept of sustainable development. It is also recognised that the third world countries are in an environmentally vulnerable position. The least developed nations require special priority.[12] The conservation, protection and restoration of the health and integrity of the Earth's ecosystem require cooperation of all States. At the same time it is pointed out that, since different States contributed differently to environmental degradation different States have differentiated responsibilities also. It is gratifying that the developed countries expressed their awareness about the way in which their societies have degraded the environment in their pursuit of achieving development. Considering their technological and financial superiority also they recognise their responsibility to play leading role in securing global sustainable development. Principle 8 emphasises the need for reducing and eliminating unsustainable patterns of production and consumption and promoting appropriate demographic policies. The need for developing international law regarding liability and compensation for adverse effects of environmental damage caused by activities of States, within their jurisdiction to areas beyond that is also pointed out. No one would dispute the spirit of these words. But the picture of the politics involved becomes clear only after a study of the manner in which nations cooperated in all this.

The polluter should pay as per the principle is mentioned in Principle 16. Accordingly, States have the obligation to promote the internationalisation of environmental costs. This is in conformity with the principle that the polluter should bear the cost of pollution. About activities that may have considerable trans-boundary environmental effect the States should give prior and timely notification and relevant information to potentially affected States.

The Rio Summit proclaims that warfare is destructive of sustainable development and asks the States to respect international law providing protection for the environment in times of armed conflict. That these good intentions are thrown to the winds during times of war is a common knowledge. Today there is no international organisation that is powerful enough to enforce such regulations. Even now, God is with the powerful army.

The Kyoto Protocol

The Kyoto Protocol to the United Nations Framework Convention on Climate Change (UNFCCC) was adopted by Parties to the UNFCCC in 1997, entered into force in 2005. The treaty follows the main principles agreed in the original 1992 UN Framework Convention. The main aim of the Kyoto Protocol is to contain emissions of the main anthropogenic greenhouse gases (GHGs) in ways that reflect underlying national differences in GHG emissions, wealth, and capacity to make the reductions. It is worth noting that this Protocol sets binding obligations on industrialised countries to reduce emissions of greenhouse gases. The European Union and all UN members, except Andorra, Canada, South Sudan and the United States, are Parties to the Protocol. The United States signed but did not ratify the Protocol and Canada withdrew from it in 2011.

As part of the Kyoto Protocol, many developed countries have agreed to limitations/reductions in their emissions of greenhouse gases in two commitment periods. The first commitment period applies to emissions between 2008 and 2012, and the second commitment period applies to emissions between 2013 and 2020. It is observed that the Kyoto Protocol's first round commitments are the first detailed step taken within UN FCCC. The first period emission reduction commitments expired on 31 December, 2012. So the protocol was amended in that year to accommodate the second commitment period, but this amendment has (as of January, 2013) not entered into legal force. However, developed countries were permitted to do emissions trading until late 2014 or 2015 to meet their first-round targets.[13]

The 37 countries with binding targets in the second commitment period are Australia, all members of the European Union, Belarus, Croatia, Iceland, Kazakhstan, Norway, Switzerland, and Ukraine. Belarus, Kazakhstan and Ukraine have stated that they may withdraw from the Protocol or not put into legal force the Amendment with second round targets. Japan, New Zealand, and Russia have participated in Kyoto's first-round but have not taken on new targets in the second commitment period. Other developed countries without second-round targets are Canada (which withdrew from the Kyoto Protocol in 2012) and the United States (which has not ratified the Protocol).

The Protocol recognises the development needs of the developing countries and hence emissions in accordance with their needs are permitted. These countries are not given any binding targets. According to the treaty the credit or discredit of contributing around 77 per cent of emissions between 1750 and 2004 goes to the developing countries. It was pointed out that carbon dioxide emissions per person in developing countries (2.9 tonnes in 2010) are, on average, lower than emissions per person in developed countries (10.4 tonnes in 2010). Under the Protocol, only the Annex I Parties have committed themselves to national or joint reduction targets. The non-Annex I Parties are mostly low-income developing countries. Annex I Parties can use a range of sophisticated "flexibility" mechanisms to meet their targets.[14]

Emissions Cuts

The UNFCCC parties proposed many emission cuts during negotiations. The G77 and China were in favour of strong uniform emission cuts across the developed world. It was proposed that those countries which could achieve more than their fixed goals in their first period can "bank" their unused allowances for use in the subsequent period. The European Union demanded that it should be permitted to make a collective commitment that allowed some EU members to increase their emissions, while others cut theirs. It was the most vulnerable nations – the Alliance of Small Island States (AOSIS) – that demanded deep uniform cuts by developed nations, so that emissions could be reduced to the greatest possible extent. Regarding assessing the quantity of emissions that have to be controlled different countries proposed different indicators. However, the final targets negotiated in the Protocol were the result of last minute political compromises. The targets closely matched those decided by the chairman of the negotiations, Raul Estrada.

Financial Commitments

The Protocol also reaffirms the principle that the developed countries should financially and technologically assist other countries for climate-related studies and projects. Here it has to be remembered that the Kyoto Protocol agreed to finance concrete adaptation projects and programmes in developing countries that are Parties to the Protocol.

Provisions for Implementation

Arriving at an agreement on many issues became difficult due to disputes between the European Union which favoured a tougher implementation and the United States, Canada, Japan and Australia who wanted the agreement to be less demanding and more flexible. The required decisions could be taken only in the Bonn meeting of 2001. This time the European Union agreed to give certain concessions like allowing more use of carbon dioxide sinks and thus managed to get the agreement of Russia and Japan.

The first Meeting of the Parties to the Kyoto Protocol (MOP1) along with the 11th conference of the Parties to the UNFCCC (COP11) was held in Montreal from 28 November to 9 December 2005. As of February 2012, 190 countries and one regional economic organisation (the EC) have ratified the agreement, representing over 61.6 per cent of the 1990 emissions from Annex I countries.

The American and Canadian Opposition

As stated earlier the US did not ratify it. It was the Byrd-Hagel Resolution that stood in the way of ratification. This resolution which had the unanimous support of the US Senate prevented ratification of any international agreement that (1) did not require developing countries to make emission reductions and (2) "would seriously harm the economy of the United States".[15] President George Bush had the opinion that the Kyoto treaty exempted 80 per cent of the world, including major population centers such as China and India, from compliance, and that it would cause serious harm to the US economy. This provoked him to oppose it. He did not change his views despite the opposition to it by almost all the major political leaders of the world. Here one has to take into account the fact that the US accounted for 36 per cent of emissions in 1990.

In the case of Canada it was committed to cutting its greenhouse emissions to six per cent below 1990 levels by 2012, but in 2009 emissions were 17 per cent higher than in 1990. So Canada simply withdrew from it. Japan and Russia also stated in 2011, that they would not take on further Kyoto targets.

Achievements

Thanks to the Protocol total aggregate GHG emissions for all Annex I Parties including the United States taken together decreased from 19.0 to 17.8 thousand teragrams CO_2 equivalent, a decline of six per cent during the 1990-2008 period. The factors that contributed to this decline include the economic restructuring in the Annex I Economies in Transition (the EITs). It is estimated that there was an emission fall of 40 per cent in the EITs over the period 1990-1999, due to the collapse of central planning in the erstwhile Soviet Union and east European countries. The large scale contraction in their heavy industry-based economies resulted in reductions in the fossil fuel consumption and emissions. Emissions growth in Annex I Parties has also been limited due to the successful policies and measures adopted. It is now expected that the annual emissions in 2020 would reach 18.9 thousand Tg CO_2 eq, which is an increase of 0.6 per cent on the 1990 level. A very important positive development is that the non-Annex I Parties, which belong to the low-income group, are making efforts to amend and update their environmental legislation to include global environmental concerns.

Assessing the Protocol

The World Bank commented that the Protocol had only limited effect on curbing global emissions growth. One reason for this is that the treaty had provided only limited financial support to developing countries to assist them in reducing their emissions and adapting to climate change. Some of the criticism of the Protocol has been based on the idea of climate justice. This is centred on the balance between the low emissions and high vulnerability of the developing world to climate change, compared to high emissions in the developed world.

In the 2012 United Nations Climate Change Conference, held at Doha, an agreement was reached to extend the Protocol to 2020 and to set a date of 2015 for the development of a successor document, to be implemented from 2020. The Kyoto second commitment period applies to about 15 per cent of annual global emissions of greenhouse gases. Other results of the conference include a timetable for a global agreement to be adopted by 2015 which includes all countries.

Environmental Politics

Global environmental politics "is the study of the cooperation and conflict among governments that surround environmental degradation, natural resource use, and other human generated impacts on the earth and the efforts to address them."[16] It involves the study of why and when international conflicts arise over environmental issues and why and when efforts to resolve them succeed or fail.[17] If we look at the global environmental issues and the measures adopted by nations of the world to tackle these issues, from this perspective, we would get a picture of global environmental politics. Though environmental problems are affecting the whole mankind, the assessment of the gravity of these problems, the need for tackling these issues, the measures to be adopted for that, etc., provide bones of contention. There is considerable difference between the developed nations and the developing nations regarding all these. There are differences among nations disregarding whether they are developed or developing. Very often national interests are projected over and above the interests of mankind. Again, we can see national interests being determined by MNCs. Thus, while pressure groups influence decision making inside nations, among nations the same role is played by powerful nations or groups of nations. A clear picture of the various dimensions of global environmental politics emanates from certain facts described and discussed below.

It has to be noted that the Vienna Convention failed to impose a target to reduce chlorofluorocarbons (CFCs) production due to the opposition of the European community which produced 45 per cent of the world CFC. Though the industrialised nations represent only 25 per cent of the world's population they consume almost 90 per cent of the CFCs. Their per capita consumption is more than twenty times higher than in less industrialised nations.[18] This rather provoked the developing nations to bargain action on environmental issues of political concern to the developed nations against action on economic, trade, debt, and equity issues of concern to developing countries.[19] The developing countries took the stand that since they were not responsible for creating the problem they were not going to meet the expenses of resolving the problem. They insisted that either they should be allowed to continue using CFCs or they should be provided with financial and technological assistance to develop substitutes.

Two binding agreements were signed in the UN Conference on Environment and Development (UNCED), held in Rio de Janeiro in 1992. The US signed but refused to ratify the

Convention on Biological Diversity. Though the US signed and ratified the UN Convention on Climate Change it refused to ratify the Kyoto Protocol to that agreement which contained actual abatement obligations. Its lack of ratification of the Basel Convention on the Control of Trans-boundary Movements of Hazardous Wastes and their Disposal (1989) and related treaties on trans-border movement of other toxic materials suggests that it managed to avoid important global environmental obligations before Rio.[20]

The US under President George W. Bush tried to "unsign" the Kyoto Protocol. The country's "unwillingness to participate delayed the protocol's entry into force and weakened the agreement because besides the US it needed the participation of almost all industrialised countries, many of which also refused to go along until their obligations were made more flexible and less onerous."[21] Since there was no serious action by the US to decrease emissions other countries, like Canada, also were unwilling to meet their Kyoto obligations. This US unilateralism on environmental issues is a proof to the fact that the US leads internationally on issues on which it has previously regulated domestically.[22] The European Union (EU) on the other hand has 'established some of the strongest and most innovative environmental protection measures in the world.'[23] It has taken initiative in many issues such as climate change, chemical regulation, product standards, and bio safety.

In the case of the developing countries 'there is a generally acknowledged and easily identifiable sense of shared identity and common purpose.'[24] It is noted that in spite of the "growing disparities among the developing countries between rapidly industrialising countries such as China, India, Malaysia, and Brazil, and debt-ridden countries that have experienced little or no growth since the 1980s, such as most of sub-Saharan Africa, Vietnam, Myanmar, and Nicaragua, developing countries share a common view of the relationship between global environmental issues and North-South economic relations."[25] In the UN Conference on Human Environment (UNCHE), held in Stockholm in 1972, the South stood as a unified group and actively took part in the negotiations. The South, through the G-77, could effectively force the UN General Assembly in 1974 to legitimise its demand for the creation of a New International Environmental Order. At the first UNFCCC Conference of the Parties in Berlin, the G77 was able to push for a mandate (the "Berlin mandate") where it was recognised that:

- developed nations had contributed most to the then-current concentrations of GHGs in the atmosphere,

- developing country emissions per-capita was still relatively low,

- and that the share of global emissions from developing countries, would grow to meet their development needs.

During negotiations, the G-77 represented 133 developing countries. China was not a member of the group but an associate. It has since become a member.

However, it was at Rio that the South got an opportunity to seriously engage itself in the global environmental issues. From then on the South effectively influenced the global environmental agenda, particularly with a view to emphasise sustainable development. Writers like Jessica Tuchman Mathews are of the opinion that since the developed countries require the active cooperation of the developing nations to solve the global environmental problems the latter can be expected to exercise the leverage, this situation offers to the fullest extent they can.[26] I would say that this is rather a North-centric perspective. Before saying that the South would make use of the leverage provided by the 'situation' we have to think about what and who were most responsible for the creation of the 'situation'. Mukund Govind Rajan argues that actually it is the North that is in a superior bargaining position. This is so because the South being very weak in many aspects, 'requires the North's cooperation to solve their environmental and developmental problems.'[27]

It won't be out of place here to mention that many developing countries held the view that the environmental concerns of the

North were aimed at thwarting the developmental aspirations of the South. So the South vigilantly stood to protect its environmental interests. Its negotiation strategy was formulated around two main goals: (1) to ensure adequate environmental space for its future development, and (2) to "modify global economic relations in such a way that the South obtains the required resources, technology, and access to markets which would enable it to pursue a development process that is both environmentally sound and rapid enough to meet its needs and aspirations."[28] According to many observers the environmental politics comprises "a struggle between the developing and developed countries to define sustainable development in a way that fits their own agendas. The developed countries, most of which are relatively rich, put environment first. By contrast, the developing countries, most of which are poor and still struggling to meet basic human needs, put development first."[29] The South has firm conviction that the polluter–pays principle put forward by the Rio Summit has been increasingly diluted during the last two decades. It has been pointed out that there is an escalating pattern of pushing implementation of multilateral environmental agreements increasingly Southward, including in the climate, desertification, and biodiversity regimes, by seeking relatively fewer changes in behaviour patterns in the North and relatively more in the South – even though it was Northern behaviour that gave rise to many problems from the very beginning.[30]

The Berlin mandate was recognised in the Kyoto Protocol that developing countries were not subject to emission reduction commitments in the first Kyoto commitment period. However, the large potential for growth in developing country emissions made negotiations on this issue tense. In the final agreement, the Clean Development Mechanism was designed to limit emissions in developing countries, but in such a way that developing countries do not bear the costs for limiting emissions. The general assumption was that developing countries would face quantitative commitments in later commitment periods, and at the same time, developed countries would meet their first round commitments.

Conclusion

At the Rio+20 United Nations Conference on Sustainable Development held at Rio de Janeiro in June 2012, the Stockholm Resilience Centre, a Swedish research institute, reported that the earth's environment has planetary thresholds or boundaries. The Centre holds the view that the earth always do not react to change, gradually. Reaching a tipping point can cause uncontrollable and unforeseeable events that would be disastrous to the global economy. The Centre has developed a scientific model to quantify the planetary boundaries or thresholds that mark the point at which humanity must take action to maintain the health of the earth's environment. (See the following Table 15.1).

The model shows that the earth has already exceeded planetary thresholds in three areas: climate change, biodiversity

Table 15.1

Earth System Process	*Parameters proposed*	*Boundary*	*Current status (as of 2009)*	*Preindustrial value*
Climate Change	Atmospheric carbon dioxide concentration (parts per million per volume)	350	387	280
Rate of Biodiversity loss	Extinction rate (number of species per million species per year)	10	>100	0.1 – 1
Nitrogen cycle	Amount of nitrogen removed from the atmosphere for human use (millions of tonnes per year)	35	121	0

Table 15.2

Humankind's ecological footprint	*The Planet's limit*
18.2 billion hectares	12 billion hectares

loss, and the nitrogen cycle. Moreover, as these earth system processes are interconnected and interrelated, focusing on any single one alone and ignoring the others is ineffective. It is clear from the Table that in the case of climate change the proposed boundary for atmospheric carbon dioxide concentration is 350 parts per million per volume. That was surpassed and it touched 387 parts per million in 2009. As far as biodiversity loss is concerned the proposed boundary is an extinction rate of about ten species per million per year. This now exceeds 100 species. How alarming it is! For the nitrogen cycle, the proposed boundary for the amount of nitrogen removed from the atmosphere for human use is about 35 million tonnes per year. This value has now reached 121 million tonnes. One should not forget to note that before the Industrial Revolution not a single tonne was removed from the atmosphere.

The concept of *ecological footprint* also has to be discussed here. 'The ecological footprint of a country is calculated by combining the area of land needed to satisfy demand for natural resources and the area of land needed to produce its food. The area includes agricultural lands, oceanic fishing grounds, forested areas that absorb carbon dioxide, and the land used outside the country to produce its food and supply of raw materials (natural resources).'[31] Mankind is using natural resources 1.5 times faster than the earth can replenish them. The following Table gives a clear picture:

It is clear from the Table15.2 that for maintaining the sustainability of the planet, we have to make sure that mankind's ecological footprint should not exceed 12 billion hectares. But it has already reached 18.2 billion hectares. The gravity of the situation is well understood even by spiritual organisations like Sukyo Mahikari which asked its members to become pioneers in starting an environmental revolution.[32]

As I observe the trajectory of the global environmental politics I strongly feel that a North-South divide politics would not only thwart the cause of global sustainable development but it would also pose challenges to the very survival of the Homo sapiens. However, under the dark clouds of the politics of difference we see a silver lining in the universal agreement that the environment has to be protected and that development has to be sustainable. We are happy to note that in the Rio+20 Conference the Member States decided to initiate a process to develop a set of Sustainable Development Goals (SDGs), which will build upon the Millennium Development Goals (MDGs) and converge with the post 2015 development agenda. Borrowing from Paulo Coelho I would suggest that every nation, irrespective of its being developed or developing has to know that it is going through a decisive moment in the history of humanity and that it needs to change itself before it can transform the world. Yes, as Bertrand Russell says, let us remember our humanity and forget the rest.

References

1. The old rabbi, in the '*The Last Temptation of Christ*' says: "Man cannot sprout wings unless he has first reached the brink of the abyss!"
2. Neil Carter, *The Politics of the Environment: Ideas, Activism, Policy* (Cambridge University Press, New York, 2007), p. 249.
3. Intergovernmental Panel on Climate Change, Aviation and the Global Atmosphere, http://www.ipcc.ch/pub/av(E).pdf).
4. For details see: "Environmental degradation" in Wikipedia.
5. http://en.wikipedia.org/wiki/Nuclear_power_ debate #cite_note-10.
6. *Ibid*, No.12.
7. Neil Carter, *The Politics of the Environment: Ideas, Activism, Policy* (Cambridge University Press, New York, 2007), p. 242.
8. http://en.wikipedia.org/wiki/Montreal_Protocol#cite_note-2.
9. http://en.wikipedia.org/wiki/Montreal_Protocol#cite_note-14.
10. http://en.wikipedia.org/wiki/Montreal_Protocol#cite_note-18.
11. Principle 2 of the Declaration.
12. Principle 6.
13. International 'emissions trading' allows developed countries to trade their commitments under the Kyoto Protocol. They can trade

emissions quotas among themselves, and can also receive credit for financing emissions reductions in developing countries.

14. The flexibility mechanisms are International Emissions Trading (IET), the Clean Development Mechanism (CDM), and Joint Implementation (JI). IET allows Annex I Parties to "trade" their emissions (Assigned Amount Units, AAUs, or "allowances" for short).

15. http:://en.wikipedia.org/wiki/Kyoto_Protocol#cite_note-110.

16. Ronald B. Michell, *International Politics and the Environment*, (Sage, London).

17. *Ibid.*

18. Richard Bonedick, *Ozone Diplomacy* (Cambridge, M.A, Harward University Press, 1991, pp.148-9.

19. Jim MacNeill, Pieter Winsemius and Taizo Yakushiji, *Beyond Independence* (Oxford, Oxford University Press, 1991), pp. 68-69.

20. Regina S. Axelrod, Stacy D. Vandeveer, and David Leonard Downie (eds.), *The Global Environment: Institutions, Law, and Policy* (CQ Press, Washington, DC, 2011), p.193.

21. *Ibid.*

22. *Ibid.*, p.194.

23. *Ibid.*, p. 213.

24. Adil Najam, "*The View from the South: Developing Countries in Global Environmental Politics*", in Regina S. Axelrod, Stacy D. Vandeveer, and David Leonard Downie (eds.), *The Global Environment: Institutions, Law and Policy* (CQ Press, Washington, DC, 2011, p. 239.

25. Gareth Porter, Janet W. Brown, and Pamela S. Chasek, *Global Environmental Politics,* 3rd ed. (Boulder, Colo.: Westview, 2000), 179.

26. See for details: Jessica Tuchman Mathews (ed.), *Preserving the Global Environment: The Challenge of Shared Leadership* (London, W.W. Norton and Company, 1991).

27. Mukund Govind Rajan, *Global Environmental Politics: India and the North-South Politics of Global Environmental Issues* (Delhi: Oxford University Press, 1997), p. 5.

28. Chris Mensah, "The Role of Developing Countries", in Campigio, L., et.al., (ed.), *The Environment after Rio: International Law and Economics* (London: Graham and Trotman, 1994), pp. 33-53.

29. Tariq Osman Hyder, "Looking back to see forward", in I.M. Mintzer and J.A. Leonard, *Negotiating Climate Change: The Inside Story*

of the Rio Convention (Cambridge: Cambridge University Press, 1994), p. 205.

30. Anil Agarwal and Sunita Narain, *Global Warming in an Unequal World: A Case of Environmental Colonialism* (Centre for Science and Environment, New Delhi, 1991).

31. Oshienushisama, "Pioneering environmental revolution", *Sukyo Mahikari International Journal,* January 2013, No.126, p.12.

32. *Ibid.*, p.16.

16

Environmentalism in India : Issues and Initiatives

Rajeevan R.

India is a unique country with tremendous natural diversity associated with all kinds of climates and rich flora and fauna. The human societies in this state have been evolved within magnificent environment. It is very rich in biodiversity and considered to be one of the 12 centres of the origin and diversity of several plant species in the world. In India, we have about 77000 known species. These include about 53000 species of insects, 1200 birds, 453 reptiles, 372 mammals, 5000 molluses and 2500 fish. The actual number of species of plants and animals must be much higher since information regarding other flora and fauna is patchy and many biologically rich areas like North East Hills and Western Ghats have not been fully explored.

Traditionally, India is considered as a land of respect to the environment. The Vedas, Puranas, Upanisads and many more ancient scripts contain the message of protecting and worshipping the environment. For thousands of years while praying to Goddess Durga the devotees say 'so long the earth has mountains, forests and trees, human race will survive.' The Hindu belief that all beings are a manifestation of one essential being called

'Brahman'. "Suffering of one life form is the suffering of other life forms, to harm other beings is to harm oneself" formed the basis of Chipko movement[1]. In our country people worship mountains, trees, rivers, animals and birds. So we have a natural affinity towards our environment.

But as a part of the environmental degradation taking place all over the world, India also experiences degradation of its natural resources, mainly due to the mounting demands of ever increasing population and rapid industrialisation. Large areas of forests are promptly cleared and sources of fresh water were poisoned due to industrialisation. Eco-friendly village life was converted to towns and cities. Agricultural lands were destroyed for huge buildings, residential complexes and industrial estates. The increased demand for food and industrial needs leads to the disappearance of forests. Weeds and pests have multiplied to an enormous number. Natural biotic communities are shrinking due to denudation of vast forest area. Many plant and animal species are becoming extinct. Most of the waterways, rivers, inland and coastal waters are polluted. The resources of the lithosphere have been mined and used in order to sustain industries.

The indiscriminate increase of human population in India is resulting over exploitation of natural resources. The resource support given to 125 crore Indian population definitely has an adverse effect on its coastal and marine systems, fresh water systems, agricultural systems, forest systems and soil systems. India with its huge population is facing the crisis of fast declining of natural resources. More than half of our eco-system is considered degraded as a result of mismanagement of the nature and a failure to invest and reinvest in their productivity, health and sustainability.

One of the serious environmental crisis in India is deforestation. The growing demand for farm land, especially to grow lucrative cash crops and increased export of forest products to affluent industrialised countries is causing deforestation. This deforestation leads to floods, soil erosion, silting up of rivers and eventual desertification. Thus deforestation, a substantial cause of ecological disruption arises largely from the needs of modern industries in affluent countries or from "wasteful patterns of resource use for the conspicuous consumption of moneyed elites" everywhere.[2] For instance, in the hilly region of Kumaun which – thanks to its dense and sprawling forest – was once the scene of Jim Corbett's legendary encounters with tigers, "the man-eaters of Kumaun" and other ferocious animals, large scale deforestation has taken place by urban-based contractors in search of easy money. This has generated the famous "chipko" (stick to the trees to prevent felling) movement.

The "Chipko movement", popularised by Sunderlal Bahuguna, is the most powerful environmental movement in India. Bahuguna stressed the need for the protection of soil and water by implementing ban on felling trees in Himalayan region at the UNEP meeting held in London in June 1982. He along with a team of dedicated workers, undertook a track on foot for 3000 km from Srinagar (Kashmir) to Siliguri (West Bengal). The movement attracted conservationists from several western countries like France, Germany, Sweden and Switzerland.[3] The "Appikko Movement,"[4] the "Narmada Bachao Andolan" against the Narmada Valley project and "Silent Valley Movement"[5] in Kerala are also powerful environmental agitation movements in India.

Deforestation is also taking place due to the converting of large area of forest land to agriculture land to meet the food requirements of the rapid increasing population of India. Together with this crisis, modern scientific and technological experiments are freely applied to the soil for increasing production of foodgrains. The excessive use of chemical fertilisers and deep mechanical ploughing make damage the surface of the soil. It also results in large scale soil erosion. Further the use of chemical fertilisers and pesticides damage the ecological balance of the earth by destroying the smaller species. It also creates large scale poisoning of land and water which directly and indirectly affect the health of all living beings including man. The persistent use of chemical fertilizers and pesticides in Japan is reported to "have poisoned land and water surroundings of major cities."[6]

The agricultural activities of most of the countries, to a certain extent, have been described as a gamble of monsoon. The monsoon has hither to been a largely stable phenomenon all over the world. But there was growing evidence that global warming had put the climate in a different mode and therefore the future could be different from the past. "Any major changes in rainfall patterns will have far reaching consequences for agriculture and water availability"[7] as pointed out by J. Sreenivasan, an atmosphere scientists of the Indian Institute of Science in Bangalore. The scientists at the U.K. Meteorological office too predict that "on a global basis, draught events are slightly more frequent and of much longer duration by the second half of the 21st century relative to the present day."[8] There is also a warning that "two hundred million people are facing a waterless future.[9]

India, with ever increasing population and impact of its activities on natural resources, our environment has been undergoing significant changes especially with the second half of the 20th century. One of the most significant changes brought about by human activities is an increase in the concentration of carbon dioxide and other greenhouse gases in the atmosphere. The citizen's fifth Report of the Centre for Science and Environment (1999), New Delhi revealed that the emission of Carbon dioxide (CO_2) has been held as the most dangerous and most significant greenhouse gas emission causing global warming.

Global warming also affect rainfall pattern. India witnessed an increase in rainfall by five per cent in summer and up to 15 per cent in winter. The level of sea water would rise by 20-140 cm in various parts of the world due to global warming. By the close of the 20th century sea level has already risen by about 30 cm. A rise in sea level which hit the lower coastal regions will take place.

In the guise of development we are making big harm to the environment and its resources. The government on the one side makes legislations and executing environmental friendly schemes and programmes. At the same time government is closing its eyes towards large scale atrocities by people in search of easy money. In the past few years, the judiciary in India including the Supreme Court has taken over the role of an arbitrator and judge of moral and ethical value systems and even the environmental laws of the country. A Supreme Court judge Arijit Pasayat, in 2002 expounded a strong ethical view point when he declared that "by destroying nature, man is committing matricide, having in a way killed mother earth". Here I would like to point out two cases in India, which demands our attention towards the shaping of the need for a humane environment.

1. Nature's Fury in Uttarakhand

The June 2013 flash floods, cloud bursts and landslides in Uttarakhand is the latest warning, nature has given to us. Nature's fury reinforced the fact that preserving the eco-system and the harmonious balance with human beings cannot be compromised. It is argued that the quest for short-term gains and commercial interest have forced the Uttarakhand governments to permit the construction of new commercial complexes adjoining with rivers. Hydel projects have been constructed in the seismic zone and many more are planned. Roads have been built haphazardly by blasting through the vulnerable Himalayas, destabilising them and loosening up boulders, soil and plantations. Radhaben Bhatt, the chairperson of Gandhi Peace Foundation and Sarva Sewa Sangh explained the incident as the result of the corruption nexus between government and private commercial groups. She says "for years, villagers had done afforestation on this land with the state refusing to help in any way, and now it is selling this land to the coke company for Rs.19 lakh per acre. It will cut down all the trees on village land and allow the company to extract six lakh litres of water a day. This is the kind of politician-private company nexus that is destroying the valley.[10]

Uttarakhand was purely an ecofriendly land in the past. Traditionally agriculture, forestry, horticulture and animal husbandry have been the mainstay of sustainable income generating activity in this hilly region. The Chipko movement was strong there in the 1970s, when women hugged trees to protect them from being felled. People's protest on environment preservation was very strong on the construction of Tehri Dam. The Tehri Dam project in the river Bhageerathi, has raised a lot of controversy not only from the point of view of loss of forests and inundating large areas, but also on the rehabilitation of the tribals and local people. The Himalayan ranges lie at a distance 20 to 22 km from the dam site which is located in a potential seismic area. A mild tremor may induce landslides and dam failure. The huge volume of debris may fill the reservoir. Many villages and thousands of people in Tehri District on the downstream side may be adversely affected. Fertile lands may be submerged and silt trapped. The project has been given green signal by the Hon'ble Supreme Court of India.

After the completion of the 1000-MW Tehri dam, 18 more projects are planned across the Alaknanda, Mandakini, Pinder and Ganga. However, in December 2012, following protracted protests by activists, the Union Ministry of Environment and Forests declared the 100 km of Bhageerathi watershed an eco-sensitive zone and banned all constructions activities, including large dams, stone-quarrying, polluting industries, commercial felling of trees, saw mills and so on. The Uttarakhand incident affirms the fact that there is a need to broaden the scope of Eco-sensitive Zones (ECZ) in order to plan for both man and nature. The unbridled approach to exploitation of mountain resources has contributed to the Uttarakhand disaster. Chandra Bhushan, Deputy Director General, Centre for Science and Environment, New Delhi said, "There is a connection between deforestation, construction and the property of soil to retain water. Dams and other constructions reduce the absorbing capacity of soil."[11]

No doubt, the unpredictable ferocity of nature, indiscriminate construction and environmental degradation lead to the Uttarakhand tragedy. The violation of the environmental norms in construction and planning has exacerbated the scale of the disaster.

Another major environmental crisis India faces is the emission of greenhouse gases through its outdated technology in industries and motor vehicles. A more serious but unnoticed problem is the emission of large quantity of carbon dioxide from the chimneys of our rural as well as urban people.

2. Smoking Kitchens

One of the major environmental crisis is the threat of a long run increase in the surface temperature of the earth which is called global warming or greenhouse effect. The temperature increase is now becoming inevitable, posing threats to climate changes. Recognising the precarious situation, most countries have joined an International Treaty; the United Nations Framework Convention on Climate Change (UNFCCC) to consider what can do to reduce global warming. India is a party to UNFCCC, which was adopted in May 1992 and it came into force on March 21, 1994. The objective of the UNFCCC convention is to achieve stabilisation of concentration of green house gases into the atmosphere at a level that would prevent dangerous anthropogenic (human activities) interference with the climate system. The third world nations argued that the chief source of the emission of greenhouse gases is the industries of the developed countries.

In this context, we must have to open our eye to estimate our contribution in this respect. As far as India is concerned, a large section of its population, nearly 75 per cent of rural and 22 per cent of urban households still uses biomass for daily cooking. An estimated 80 per cent of the residential energy in India comes from biomass and much of it is burnt in traditional cook stoves of chulhas. Cooking in rural households and in congested urban slum-dwellings takes place in extremely constricted and badly ventilated living spaces. The toxic smoke and particulates that are emitted from biomass burning have significant and adverse health and socio-economic consequences. The emission from these chulhas also contributes a great share to the greenhouse effect.

The biomass fuels from the chulhas generate indoor air pollution which is responsible for nearly half a million premature deaths annually, predominantly among young women and children. This figure, however, could be as high as 2.5 million, as was found in an extensive study carried out by the Energy and Resources Institute in the mid 1990s, based on exposure of thousands of users carrying personal monitors around the clock and analysis by epidemiologists of data thus generated[12]. The global burden of disease study 2010 ranked indoor air pollution as the leading cause of death and disability-adjusted life years in South Asia.[13]

The toxic products of incomplete combustion of the chulhas of the financially unsound people of the third world countries emit large quantities of green house gases. Attempts are going on in India and other states to improve cook stove technology over the past few years. Further advances are still possible and necessary. What is required to save both human beings and the environment is cutting-edge advanced technology, rather than low technology solutions.

Indian Initiatives towards a Humane Environment

As far as India is concerned environmental conservation is not a new concept. We had a long tradition of love, respect and reverence for nature. Historically, the protection of nature, its flora and fauna formed an ardent article of faith, reflected in the daily lives of people and also enshrined myths, folklore, religion, art and culture. Not only rulers and saints but the common people had respect for the natural environment.

The modern India on a certain extent continues the tradition. Ours is one of the few constitutions of the world, which has provided protection against environmental pollution. Such provisions encourage our judicial system to wage war against environmentally unsound actions of the state. Article 48-A of the Directive Principles of State Policy provides "the state shall endeavour to protect and improve the environment and to safeguard the forests and wildlife of the country." Article 51-A(g) read "To protect and improve the natural environment including forests, lakes, rivers and wildlife, and to have compassion for living creatures." Article 21 of the Fundamental Rights provides "right to life and personal liberty" to all persons living in India. This right includes the right to have a "living environment" congenial to human existence. Any activity, which pollutes the environment and makes it unhealthy, is a violation of this right.

The Indian Prime Minister Indira Gandhi was the only visiting head of the state who participated in the UN Conference on Human Environment held in Stockholm (Sweden) on 5-10 June 1972. This was the first UN Conference which seriously discussed the environmental issue. It declared environment and the related issues of pollution, ecological decay or resource depletion as matters of overwhelming global concern. The conference attended by 113 countries, drew up 26 principles calling upon all governments to co-operate in protecting and improving the natural environment.[14] The Conference declared June 5 as the World Environment Day to undertake and make people more aware of the need for environmental protection all over the world.

Soon after her arrival in New Delhi, Indira Gandhi constituted the National Council of Environmental Planning and Co-ordination in 1972, as the apex body in the department of Science and Technology. This was followed by an empowered committee; the Tiwari Committee was set up in 1980. On the recommendation of this committee, the Department of Environment was set up in 1980 as the focal agency in the administrative structure of the central government for planning, promotion and co-ordination of environmental programmes. This department became part of the new ministry of environment and forests in 1985.

The Ministry of Environment and Forests is the apex body under the government of India for planning, promotion and co-ordination of environmental and forestry programmes. The ministry has also been designated as the nodal agency of United

Nation's Environment Programme (UNEP), South Asia Co-operative Environmental Programme (SACEP), International Union for Conservation of Nature and Natural Resources (IUCN), International Centre for Integrated Mountain Development (ICIMD) and European Union. The ministry also functions as nodal agency and participates actively in all international programmes in connection with environment and release annual financial contributions to all the programmes in this respect.

With the spirit of realising a humane environment, India extends its full support to environmental awareness campaigns, encourage peoples involvement and participation in environmental activities, formation of eco-clubs, production of films and audio-visuals on environmental issues and supports environment friendly products. The Government of India extends its full support for environmental education from primary school to distinguished research institutes. The Ministry of Environment and Forests has made every effort to recognise individuals and groups, which have contributions in this respect. More than ten National awards and fellowships were instituted to eco-friendly contributions.

On the basis of the decisions of the Stockholm Conference of 1972 the Government of India has undertaken various legislative measures also: The Water (Prevention and Control) Act 1974 and the Air (Prevention and Control) Act 1981, two major laws directly dealing with environmental pollution, were passed by the Parliament. The Forest (Conservation) Act 1980 was passed to curb deforestation. The Environment (Protection) Act 1986 was a major step to achieve the goals laid down by the Stockholm Conference. The Act consistently of twenty six sections is divided into four chapters, and extends to the whole of India. The act empowers the central government to take necessary measures to protect and improve environment or for preventing, controlling and abating the environment pollution.

India also proved herself as the spokesnation of environmentalism has taken an active role in global efforts to tackle environmental problems. Indira Gandhi was the lone visiting head of state to participate in the UN Conference on Human Environment at Stockholm in 1972. In the meeting Indira Gandhi stressed the point that "the global community must address the issue of global development in order to move towards an environmentally sound planet." She added that the removal of poverty is an integral part of the goal of an environmental strategy for the world.

P.V. Narasimha Rao, the then Prime Minister of India had the honour of inaugurating the UN sponsored Earth Summit held during June 3-14, 1992 in Rio de Janeiro (Brazil). The Conference attended by 115 heads of states, 10,000 government missions and about 20,000 NGOs was definitely the largest UN sponsored global Conference both in the number of participants and scope of the agenda. This conference adopted Agenda 21, which is a blueprint for a global plan of action for achieving sustainable development. The Commission on sustainable development was set up in 1993 under ECOSOC, United Nations for the purpose of review of progress of implementation of the Agenda 21. India's Ministry of External Affairs plays an important role for providing technical support and for implementation of Agenda 21.

Dr Man Mohan Singh, the Prime Minister of India along with 125 crore Indian people have reason to be happy about the overwhelming support received from poor and developing countries in incorporating the principle of "common but differentiated responsibility" in the draft declaration submitted for adoption in the Earth Summit at Rio de-Janeiro. This United Nations Conference on sustainable Development-2012 was named Rio+20 because the city hosted it 20 years after it first hosted the Summit in 1992. The BRICS nations (Brazil, Russia, India, China and South Africa) especially India and Brazil have worked hard to fight poverty and deforestation. In the Conference, India had a clear vision of development goals, particularly eradicating poverty and hunger from the third world nations.

As India has emerged as the spokes nation of the developing world, responsibility devolves on it to ensure that the rich nations do not get away from their moral and environmental obligations to the rest of the world. Of course that India played a key role in shaping Agenda-21 and its major principle of "common but differentiated responsibilities" for the rich and poor countries in dealing with environmental and development imperatives in the first Rio Summit of 1992. One significant success of the Rio + 20 Summit has also been the restoration of the centrality of the principle of "common but differentiate responsibilities" in the environmental discourse, which had brought equity in the centre of the obligations to save the world.

Conclusion

In the long run, the socio-economic health of a nation depends on and is directly proportional to the health of its environment. A nation, has not able to effectively conserve and manage its natural resources, eventually will have to pay a price for short sighted policies. Now world is slowly realising that sustainability is the most essential aspect of the education. Considering these facts UNO has declared the decade 2005-2015 as decade of education for sustainable development. The United Nations or other international agencies have their own limitations to compel the individual nations to limit environmental pollution. Kyoto, Copenhagen, Rio are all testaments to that. It is the duty and responsibility of every state to reduce or limit the carbon foot print.

As in the case of international agencies, individual nations have also their own issues and inefficiencies to turn to green. India is always at the forefront to fight environmental crisis. But currently India is one among the world's largest carbon emitter. New Delhi not only played leading roles in all international conferences on environment but also hosted such meetings in the state. New Delhi recently hosted the fourth version of the global meet where delegates from 20 countries came to discuss renewable energy. After the meeting Prime Minister Man Mohan Singh reaffirmed India's stand that "rich nations, who emit the bulk of greenhouse gases, also have high per capita income, which gave them the highest capacity to bear the burden and provide a workable solution to fight climatic change." Strangely, India follows neither within its own borders. To cut down green house gas emissions and spur the growth of renewable energy in the country, the Prime Minister in 2008 released the National Action Plan on Climatic Change. But the plan flopped as 22 out of 29 states in the country failed to do their responsibility.

The developing nations like India can also do a lot of things in this respect. For instance it is a big allegation of the North that a large quantity of carbon dioxide emission is taking place from the chulhas of the financially unsound rural population of the third world states. It is also a fact that in India the household biomass fuel generated indoor air pollution which is responsible for nearly a half million premature deaths annually, predominantly among women and children. On the basis of this understanding, the Ministry of New and Renewable Energy launched a national mission for clean cook stoves in 2008. But that initiative has so far been unable to liberate the bulk of our rural women from their chulahs. So a dedicated effort on the side of third world states and their governments to liberate their states from the emission of greenhouse gases through the development and distribution of green technologies. It is also a truth that the developed countries with lesser population consume more resources where as developing countries, with plenty of resources and increasing population, recklessly destroy the natural resources.

International agencies and national governments have their own limits to control pollution. In this instance, the social groups through their collective effort can play a vital role in the wise use and conservation of natural resources and make our tomorrows green. From our experience our non-government organisations are more aware of our environmental issues than the government agencies. NGO's action programmes fulfill the needs of healthy environment and which have more accessibility to the common people than that of government agencies. Thousands of such groups are operating all over India with and without funding from government. These social groups are viewing with great hope and unless we all fight together, we have no right to hope for a better world for our children and grand children.

There is a need to have an eco-protection duty starting from an individual to meet the threat of environmental degradation. Nature and its resources belong to each one of us. Like human beings each species has value for its own sake, an intrinsic value unrelated to human needs. So it is the responsibility of all of us to contribute towards the sustainable use of nature and its resources for the happy life of every being. Small droplets of water together form a big ocean. Together with international agencies and national governments, the NGOs, the civil society and the individuals can make revolutions in this field. Remember, there is no second earth to go to when we make our planet uninhabitable.

References

1. ***Chipko Movement:*** The classic struggle against indiscriminate felling of trees was fought by Amrita Devi in Khejari village near Jodhpur in 1731. In the heroic fight, Amrita Devi, her husband and three daughters along with 363 Bishnoi women sacrificed their lives to save the trees from being felled. In this struggle two or three women hugged the trees and never allowed the axe men to cut the trees. But the cruel men axed the women along with the trees. This movement was again started in 1972 against the cruelties of men against trees. It was started by C.P. Bhatt and later on by Sundar Lal Bahuguna. He undertook a march in the hilly regions and covered over 3000 km appealing to the people to protect the trees from being felled. —K.Raghavan Nambiar (2008), *"Environmental Studies"*, Chennai, Seitech Publications (India) Pvt. Ltd, p. 213.

2. Ignacy Sachs, *"Human Environment"* in Jan Tinbergen (Co-ordinator) (1977), *"Reshaping the International Order"*, London, p. 285.

3. Rajeevan, *"In search of a Humane Environment: The Gandhian Approach"* in Rajeevan R. and Yamuna D.S. (ed) (2009) *The Gandhian Way,"* Icon Publications Pvt. Ltd, New Delhi, p.155.

4. ***Appikko Movement*** – The Chipko movement reached to Karnataka as Appikko movement. Like a migrating bird the idea of chipko flew south to Salkani village of Sirsi taluka in North Kanara district of Karnataka on September 8, 1983. Some 160 men and women

marched eight km to the Kelase forest where the contractor's axe men under orders from the forest department have turned the area into a slaughter house. They hugged the trees and compelled the axe men to stop tree felling. This movement spread to other place of the state. The movement received much support from many other quarters. For instance Prof Madhav Gadgil of Indian Institute of Science, Bangalore could conclude that "contentions of yuvak mandalis, i.e., excessive damage in the course of felling and excessive concentration of trees marked for felling were true". He went on to recommend that such mandalis be involved in conservation programmes. P.D. Sharma (2011) *"Ecology and Environment"*, Rastogi Publications, Meerut, p. 459.

5. ***Silent Valley Movement*** – Silent valley, occupying an area of 8950 hectares at an altitude of 3000 feet in Palakkad district of Kerala, is perhaps the only remaining undisturbed tropical rainforest in Indian Peninsula. This tropical rain forest in Western Ghats is a precious reservoir of bio-diversity where many plant and animal species have survived for centuries. The silent valley movement started with the proposed construction of a river valley project to fetch the need of electricity and irrigation to the people of the area. A number of NGO's and environmentalists supported the movement. With the intervention of "Friends of Trees Society", the controversy of the proposed hydel project was over in 1979 and it was declared as a National Park by the then Prime Minister Rajiv Gandhi in 1985. The environmentalists are always vigilant on this hotspot. S.P. Mishra and S.N. Pandey (2009) *Essential Environmental Studies*, Ane Books Pvt. Ltd, New Delhi, pp.79-80.

6. Allen V. Kneese, "Development and Environment", *Third World Quarterly* (London) Vol.1, No.1, January 1979, p. 88.

7. N. Gopal Raj, "India and the Challenges of Global Warming", *The Hindu,* Thiruvananthapuram, February 5, 2007.

8. George Manbiot, "Rivers Running Dry", *The Hindu,* Thiruvananthapuram October 11, 2006.

9. *Ibid.*

10. Gargi Parsai, "Angry Mountains," *The Hindu,* Thiruvananthapuram, June 30, 2013.

11. *Ibid.*

12. *The Hindu*, Thiruvananthapuram, June 22, 2013.

13. *Ibid.*

14. Jeffrey Haynes (2005) *"Comparative Politics in a Globalized World"*, Polity, Cambridge, p.159.

17

Sustainable Environment: Right of the Citizens and Role of the Court

G. Balachandran and *Hameema M.*

"Our environmental problems originate in the hubris of imagining ourselves as the central nervous system or the brain of nature. We're not the brain; we are a cancer on nature."

Dave Foreman

Humanity is one large family inhabiting its only home, the planet Earth. For man the earth holds everything for it gives him physical sustenance and affords him the opportunity for intellectual, moral, social and spiritual growth. And just as human ingenuity has accidentally caused environmental problems; it can play a huge role in helping us undo the damage. In the long tortuous evolution of human race on this planet a stage has been reached when through rapid acceleration of science and technology man has acquired the power to transform his environment in countless ways and on unprecedented scale.

Today, India is the sixth largest energy consumer in the world. To sustain its current economic growth of five per cent per annum, India will need to generate four per cent more energy annually. In congruence with the growing need for fuel and energy is the need for a strong uniform environmental policy that will be enforced throughout the Indian subcontinent. In a country where corruption overruns the executive branch and plagues public officials, the Supreme Court of India is particularly active in its approach towards molding an ideal body of environmental laws. Remarkably, India enacted significant environmental laws decades ago, and the Supreme Court of India has developed a rich body of law that guarantees a fundamental right to live in a clean and healthy environment. Through the development of Public Interest Litigation, the Supreme Court of India has greatly broadened the procedural right of Indian citizens to present environment-related challenges against the government and its agencies.

Legislative Background

Over the last sixty years the Indian Parliament has taken measures to enact significant environmental regulations. In 1974, the government passed the Water Prevention and Control of Pollution Act (Water Act); its purpose is to "provide for the prevention control of water pollution and the maintaining and restoring of wholesomeness of water." The Water Act established Central and State Pollution Control Boards to oversee the "prevention, abatement, and control of water pollution." The Boards are responsible for conducting site inspections and acquiring information regarding non-compliance with any aspect of the Water Act. Similarly, in 1981 the government enacted the Air Prevention and Control of Pollution Act (Air Act) "to provide for the prevention, control, and abatement of air pollution." Like the Water Act, the Air Act provides for Central and State Control Boards to handle all matters associated with the improvement of air quality.

In response to the Water and Air Acts, the Indian legislature promulgated the Environment Protection Act (Environment Act) in 1986 to cure deficiencies left in India's core body of environmental law. The Environment Act provides the central government with the broad power to take all measures necessary "for the purpose of protecting and improving the quality of the environment and preventing, controlling, and abating environmental pollution." Together, these pieces of environmental legislation provide a framework for the Indian people, as well as the judiciary, to enforce environmental protections.

The Indian Constitution and Fundamental Rights

India's most powerful statement on the environment is a constitutional amendment; Amendment 42 to Article 48A, which includes a provision for environmental protection and states that a clean and healthy environment is now a fundamental duty. Article 48A of the Indian Constitution states, "the State shall endeavour to protect and improve the environment." The key fundamental rights provision of the Indian Constitution, Article 21, guarantees that "no person shall be deprived of his life or personal liberty except according to procedure established by law."

Under this provision, the Court has expanded the "right to life" to include protection from harmful environmental elements. In a seminal decision, Rural Litigation and Entitlement Kendra vs. State of Uttar Pradesh, the Supreme Court of India resolved issues related to environmental and ecological balance as a result of a quarrying operation that mined limestone. In its ruling, the Supreme Court ordered the permanent closure of the quarries. The Court recognised that its judgment would have great financial consequences for the business, but noted it is a price that has to be paid for protecting and safeguarding the right of the people to live in healthy environment with minimal disturbance of ecological balance and without avoidable hazard to them and to their cattle, homes and agricultural land and undue affectation of air, water and environment.

While the Supreme Court did not explicitly refer to Article 48A nor Article 21 of the Indian Constitution, its judgment was in accord with these fundamental environmental rights. In a separate decision by the High Court of Andhra Pradesh, T. Ramakrishna Rao vs. Hyderabad Urban Development, the court expressly invoked Article 21 and noted that the right to a clean environment is a fundamental right when it stated, "the slow poisoning of the atmosphere caused by the environmental pollution and spoilation should be regarded as amounting to a violation of Article 21 of the Constitution." The court further asserted that it is "the legitimate duty of the Courts as the enforcing organs of the constitutional objectives to forbid all actions of the State and the citizens from upsetting the ecological and environmental balance." Thus, the Supreme Court of India and other lower courts have expanded fundamental rights within the penumbra of the Indian Constitution to include environmental protections and have judiciously supported a right to a clean and healthy environment.

Public Interest Litigation

The Supreme Court of India's vehicle for enforcing environmental protection is Public Interest Litigation. Public Interest Litigation is "purely a matter of constitutional law in which the writ jurisdiction of the Supreme Court or any one of the provincial High Courts is invoked ... to enforce ... fundamental rights." This allows any Indian citizen to file a writ of appeal directly with the Supreme Court concerning the protection of a fundamental right. To facilitate judicial access, the Court has declared that a person "may move the Court even by just writing a letter." This relaxation of the locus standi requirements allows public interest attorneys to present cases before the Court when a fundamental right is at stake.

As a result, Public Interest Litigation is the module for major environmental protection advancement through the Indian court system. Through Public Interest Litigation, the Supreme Court has taken steps to recognise that good health is a fundamental right, and "so are conditions that promote good health, such as clean air and water." Ultimately, through a series of cases, the Court determined that there is an obligation to protect the environment that is derived from the protection of fundamental rights.

Current Levels of Pollution

Over the last decade, policy-makers have become alarmed at the impacts of increasing levels of air pollution and climate change upon the Indian subcontinent. In 2004, more than eighty-four per cent of the Indian population inhaled dangerously poor air in the eighty-three cities where air quality monitoring data was available. Data available for Bangalore, India, the IT capital of the region, indicates that the suspended particulate matter (SPM) is nearly triple the national standard. Furthermore, in the capital city of Delhi, vehicle exhaust causes seventy-two per cent of air pollution. Despite the city's efforts to phase out twelve thousand diesel buses, the number of diesel cars has increased by over 420 per cent in the last decade. Most striking, is the fact that "the total number of diesel cars in Delhi is equivalent to adding particulate emissions from nearly thirty thousand diesel buses." According to the World Health Organisation (WHO), Delhi is one of the ten most polluted cities in the world. In New Delhi, the metropolitan center of Delhi, incidences of respiratory disease caused by pollution is twelve times higher than the national average.

Today, India is the sixth largest energy consumer in the world and must import seventy per cent of its oil. This is a dramatic increase from 1990 when India supported sixty per cent of oil demands with its domestic supply. As a result of this demand and consumption, India addresses the issue of energy sustainability via energy diplomacy.

Energy is also vital to India's transportation industry, as the energy demand for this sector is expected to grow 4.4 per cent per year and account "for 20 per cent of the country's total energy consumption in 2025." With regards to oil, India consumed approximately 2.25 million barrels of oil per day in 2005; a figure that is expected to rise to 3.48 million barrels per day by 2015 and 5.29 million barrels per day by 2025. These numbers correspond to an approximate 3.2 per cent increase in energy demand per year. In response to growing energy demands, nine nuclear reactors are under construction to develop civilian nuclear energy. In sum, about 53 per cent of India's total energy (and 70 per cent of India's electric power generation) is derived from coal. Of the remaining sources: nearly 33 per cent is derived from oil; eight per cent from natural gas; five per cent from hydro-electric power; less than one per cent from renewable (solar and wind) sources; and, the remaining one per cent comes from nuclear energy.

Finally, according to the Energy Information Administration, emissions resulting from India's fossil fuel consumption account for fourteen per cent of total global carbon dioxide emissions, and is projected to increase to eighteen per cent by 2025. Thus, as India continues to demand access to energy and relevant technologies, it must address the environmental consequences of such rapid economic growth.

The government's efforts to curb pollution from automobile emissions require significant attention. As wealth increases, encouragement of automobile ownership is at odds with government efforts to curb pollution. In Delhi, the number of diesel cars has maintained a growth rate of 16.6 per cent per year, compared to half that rate for petrol cars, 8.5 per cent per year. The environmental effect of the rise in diesel car sales has been the creation of devastating smog and carcinogenic air. Furthermore, the government fails to encourage auto manufacturers to use cleaner technology. In its efforts to create a tax incentive for the purchase of smaller vehicles, the government inadvertently created a loophole for increasing diesel car sales. In 2006, the Union Minister of Finance reduced the excise duty from twenty-four to sixteen percent. At the same time, it relaxed the engine capacity limits for qualification as a diesel car. As a result, the auto industry responded by developing and promoting a greater number of mid-size diesel vehicles that will fit within the government's definition of a small car. It is estimated that this small "car concession has resulted in price cuts for diesel cars by about Rs. 12,000 to Rs. 25,000." Moreover, India has failed to set fuel economy regulations, "Indian small diesel cars are more than 20 per cent less fuel efficient and 50 per cent more polluting than their counterparts in Europe." This occurs at a time when governments around the world are imposing higher levies on larger automobiles to minimise their environmental impacts.

Over the last decade, India has been blessed with a booming economy and rapid industrial growth. This economic growth has forced India to cope with increased energy demands, new technological growth, and the environmental consequences that accompany movement from a third world country to a developed nation. With continuous development, however, makes greater pollution and greenhouse gas emissions. In 1990, India's greenhouse gas emissions constituted three per cent of the world's greenhouse gas emissions, and rose to four percent by 2000. This one per cent change represents a 4.2 per cent increase in greenhouse gas emissions per annum. While this may seem rapid, the absolute value of these emissions is still one-sixth of the United States' emissions.

As India continues to disperse greater greenhouse gases, there is an international political response pushing for stricter emissions standards. Developing nations view the burden placed upon them to adopt cleaner technology and adapt to international standards with hostility. Developing nations maintain that "industrialised countries owe their current prosperity to years of historical emissions, which have accumulated in the atmosphere since the start of the industrial revolution [while] developing countries have only recently set out on the path of industrialisation and their [greenhouse gas] emissions are still low." As a result of this perception, "these nations have insisted that any multilateral treaty adopted by the international community not hinder their development efforts, perceiving a palpable distinction between opulent rich nation emissions and their necessary development emissions." It is unfair for developed nations to impose constraints and additional burdens upon nations simply trying to "catch up." Furthermore, these additional constraints may hamper economic growth; in fact, limits on greenhouse gases are viewed as a limit on economic growth. India, caught in the middle, will either have to adopt cleaner technologies and ease the financial burdens for small scale industries, or continue to pollute the environment and endanger the climate. While India's Supreme Court is incredibly activist in issuing decisions that aim to protect an individual's right to clean air, water, and the overall environment, there must be a bureaucratic breakthrough. Administrative agencies must break the shackles of corruption and enforce the Court's decisions. The relevant administrative agencies should enforce their environmental mandates and vigilantly require compliance from both large and small scale industries. Furthermore, an overall policy is necessary to define priorities and principles in a strong effort to improve compliance. Yet, it is important to remember that India is on the right path to the extent that the judiciary and legislative branches are addressing environmental protection. As a population giant, India should reconcile its energy demands and economic modernisation with environmental protection.

There is little doubt that both India's and China's increasing energy demands will burden the global market for oil, natural gas, coal and other resources in the foreseeable future. This strain will force industrialised nations, including the western world, to adopt new energy initiatives to sustain their own access and demands for resources. The United States is legitimately concerned that India and China have begun to stockpile oil and scour the world for access to new oil resources. Moreover, as India continues to breed a new middle class, its demand for automobiles also increases. As long as there are cars, there will be a demand for oil.

On an international scale, India's rapid industrialisation creates a demand for greater monitoring and for institutions to handle environmental degradation. To this end, the United Nations Environment Programme (UNEP) must devote greater resources to tackle the connection between industrialisation and climate change with environmental protections. The concern over assuring adequate energy supplies has fostered a strategic relationship between the United States and India. This relationship has led efforts to drill for off-shore hydrates and to support energy efficiency and investment in renewable energy. While it is unclear what long-term impact these initiatives will have, they are important steps towards maintaining the United States' access to energy and assuring that India will have the supply it needs to become a developed nation. In reality, "both nations depend heavily upon domestic supplies of coal for electric power generation and seek to increase their utilisation of natural gas, renewable energy and nuclear power." Furthermore, India was the first country to join the United States in the FutureGen alliance. As part of this initiative, the FutureGen partnership will enable the greater use of coal in an environmentally friendly way. By adopting this technology, India may reduce the density of future greenhouse gas emissions from burning coal. In addition, the United States Department of Energy is working with India to develop an emergency response plan to a potential oil crisis situation.

India is currently experiencing unprecedented economic growth which will potentially lift millions of Indian citizens out of poverty, providing them with a better life. It is imperative that the western world recognise an interest in India's continued growth and assist India in meeting its energy needs while protecting the environment. It is on the shoulders of every developed nation to assist developing countries, such as India, by providing access to cleaner technology, civilian nuclear technology, and initiatives for energy sustainability. The strain that India and China will place on the global marketplace cannot be denied; because of this, it is in the best interest of the nations of the world to address these concerns now, and put measures in place before it is too late.

Environmental Consciousness

In response to increasing environmental consciousness, India has spurned grass root movements and non-governmental organisations attempting to tackle the problem. Since 1980, the Center for Science and Environment (CSE), an independent public interest organisation, has challenged the Indian government "and the public to confront environmental problems and for solutions that government and communities can implement effectively." These types of organisations must continue to disseminate information and educate the public about the environment.

The Role of an Activist Supreme Court

The Supreme Court of India has reacted to perceived bureaucratic failures by taking an activist stance towards the enforcement of environmental regulations. The Court, however, hands down decisions and recommendations that are often too difficult to implement, thus leading to greater confusion in the area of environmental enforcement. Furthermore, the Court ignores the "logistical difficulties associated with implementation of their ideas of environment protection." Most striking is the Court's failure to establish a standard for acceptable pollution; therefore, any level of pollution may constitute a violation.

Moreover, the Court continues to turn a blind eye to current environmental laws, instead creating its own committees and reporting systems. Rather than this activist position, the Court should take steps to support both current environmental regulations and government actors in their enforcement. "The results of such activist actions are clear: if the Court begins to create legislation, it bypasses the democratic means." By creating its own committees, the Court is signaling to the public that legislatively-created committees are inefficient and lack credibility. Furthermore, the Court's criticism of the government and its agencies' actions undermines any confidence in administrative proceedings. There are several facets of the Court's activism that lead to confusion. When the Court chooses to create its own set of rules, the result is two sets of rules for an individual, court-made and legislative. It remains unclear, however, which set of rules should prevail. This issue is further complicated by the Court's power to "review executive and legislative acts." Through these powers, the Court issues decisions without remanding cases to the administrative agency responsible for enforcement. The Court assumes this power because Amendment 42 of the Indian Constitution states that environmental rights are fundamental rights that are squarely within the realm of the judiciary. "However, when the Court begins to rule that fundamental rights are no longer just a means of protecting the citizen against the state, the sanctity of fundamental rights is destroyed." Thus, by taking an extreme activist approach the Supreme Court actually diminishes environmental rights. Yet, despite criticism of the Supreme Court's activist approach, the Court's dedication to environmental issues has increased public and governmental awareness.

Consequently, it is now up to the Indian people to harness this awareness and ensure sustainable environmental protection.

Conclusion

With a population of over one billion people, India will play an increasingly important role in the world's economy and energy markets. As India explores the availability of energy resources in the Middle East, it could impact the geopolitical affairs of the area and shift influences within the region. India is now emerging as the swing state in the global balance of power. In the coming years, it will have an opportunity to shape outcomes on the most critical issues of the twenty-first century: the construction of Asian stability, the political modernisation of the greater Middle East, and the management of globalisation. India matters both on a domestic and an international front; its economic growth will affect Indians and citizens of the world alike. India and the international community would do well to consider these facts and cooperate towards the mutually beneficial goals of environmental protection and energy sustainability.

Index

A

Agricultural system, 15
Agricultural technologies, 137
Agriculture, 36, 64, 138
Ahimsa, 50
Air, 16, 26, 36, 53
Air Act 1981, 171
Airport in Aranmula, 111
Aiyer, C.P. Ramaswami, 99
Alps, 21
Ambiguity, 24
Andes, 21
APHA, 180
APPCDC, 23
Appikko Movement, 221
Arctics, 21
Artha, 49
Arunima S., 31, 187
ASHA, 141
Ashoka (King), 114, 115

B

Bahuguna, Sunderlal, 170
Balachandran, G., 32, 235
Bangladesh, 20
Basmati rice, 64
Beegum, Sabitha, 125
Ben Byju, S., 187
Bhageerathi, 224
Bhakti, 48
Biomass production, 45
Birds, 219
Brahman, 220
BRICS nations, 229
British Antarctic Survey, 198
British colonialism, 92
Bronze Age, 16
Buddhism, 50
Bush, George W., 23
Byju, Ben, 31
Byrd-Hagel Resolution, 208

C

Canada, 44
Capitalism, 37
Capitalist society, 93
Carbon dioxide, 19, 20
Carpini, 78
Case of Banisteriopsis Capi (BC), 61
Caste organisations, 97
CBD, 62
Cetana, 50

CHCs, 141
China, 57, 170, 242
Chipko movement, 167, 170, 220
Chlorofluorocarbon, 19, 198, 210
  emissions, 138
Chozhikali, 175
Christian missionaries, 95
Christian thought, 51
Citizen Fifth Report of Centre for Science and Environment (1999), 19
Citizen participation, 113
Citsvarupa, 50
Civil society, 56, 112
Civilisation, 17
Clean Development Mechanism, 213
Climatic changes, 21
Clintock, Barbara M., 43
Coastal Regulation Zone, 127
Commercialisation of the industry, 139
Conservation of nature, 55
Convention on Bio-diversity (CBD), 60, 61
Cook Islands, 203
Cow Protection Movement, 92
Cropping pattern changes, 155-166
  cropping pattern, 163-165
  growth of agricultural incomes in Kerala, 159
  introduction, 155-156
  land use pattern of Kerala, 161-162
  land use pattern, 160-163
  sectoral distribution of SDP, 158
  share of area under major crops in total cropped area in Kerala, 163
  special features of Kerala, 156-157
  agriculture, 157-158
  stagnant agricultural income, 158-160
CSE, 243
Culture, 17
Cyclones, 20

D

Dasapushpam, 174
Deforestation, 53
Development and conservation of wetlands, 147-153
  amphibians and reptiles, 150-151
  avian diversity, 149-150
  bio-diversity, 148
development, 151
  fish diversity, 150
  introduction, 147-148
  major threats to wetlands, 151-153
  mammals, 151
  mollusks and other minor animals, 151
  plant diversity, 148-149
Devi, V. Kala, 30
Dhanu, 174
Dharma, 49, 50
Digital faith, 75
Directive Principles, 171
Dissolved Oxygen (DO), 183
Drought, 21
Durga, Goddess, 219

E

Earth Summit, 136
Earth surface, 19, 57
East India Company, 95

Eco-feminism, 167-172
  ecological movements initiated by women, 170
  environmental change and women, 169-170
  green belt movement, 170
  Navdanya movement, 170
  relevant legal provision on environment, 171
  research studies conclude some suggestions, 171-172
  role of women in conservation of environment, 168-169
  women connection with environment, 168
Eco-friendly (green) technology, 35, 44
Ecological discourses on Thiruvathira, 173-177
Ecology, 173
Ecosystems, 13, 15
ECZ, 224
Emissions, 57
Energy and Resource Institute, 21
Energy Information Administration, 240
Environment, 14
Environment Protection Act in 1986, 236
Environmental crisis, 13, 17
Environmental degradation, 53-58
  air quality, 54
  water quality is another concern, 54-56
  what is sustainable develop ment, 56-58
Environmental imbalance, 54
Environmental issue, 22
Environmental Protection Act, 1986, 171
Environmentalism in India, 219-233
  Indian initiatives towards a humane environment, 226-230
smoking kitchens, 225-226
Erosion of forests, 55
European countries, 23
European Patent Office (EPO), 63
European Union, 25, 205
Exhaust, 57
Experience of Truth, 48
Exploitation of natural resources, 18
Exploitation of nature, 16

F

Facebook factor, 79
Facebook page, 81
Felling of trees, 17
Feudal swaroopam, 96
Fish harvesting, 138
Flood water, 148
Flora and fauna, 14, 21
Food, 26
Foreman, Dave, 235
Forest act, 1980, 171
Forestry, 138
Fossil fuels-coal, 19
Friends of Earth, 48
Frietag, Sandria, 92

G

Gandhi, Indira, 227, 229
Gandhiji, 49, 53
Gases, 19
GDP, 158
Genesis of environmental problems, 17

German Basel Mission, 100
Gintao, Hue, 113
Global environmental politics, 197-218
 achievements, 208-209
 American and Canadian opposition, 208
 assessing the protocol, 209
 attempts to problem resolution, 201-203
 emissions cuts, 207
 environmental politics, 209-213
 financial commitments, 207
 Kyoto Protocol, 205-207
 provisions for implementation, 207-208
 Rio Earth Summit, 203-205
Global Warming, 18, 19, 20, 222
Global Warming Solutions Act, 2006, 23
Globalisation, 18, 24, 40
Glossy Ibis (Plegadis falcinellus), 150
GM Tube, 190
GMOs, 170
God realisation, 49
Government of India, 228
Government of Kerala, 26
Green economy, 24
Green engines, 46
Green house effect, 18, 19
Green house gases, 21, 23, 205
Green Peace, 48
Green Technology, 26, 35
Green trade barriers, 24

H

Haises, Geard, 92
Hameema, M., 32, 235
Hansen, James, 20
HBRA, 195
Health, 18
Herrera, 79
HFC emission, 202
High Court of Kerala, 127
High Level Threat Panel of the UN, 199
High Tide Level (HTL), 122
Hindu scriptures, 49
Home Rule League in Malabar, 100
HOPE, 84
HUGO, 62
Human civilisation, 43
Human societies, 15
Humanity, 235
Hurricane Katrina, 20
Hurricanes, 20

I

IBA, 149
Ice and snow caps, 20
ICIMD, 228
Independence Day, 103
India, 20, 54, 57, 92, 114, 222, 242
India Forest Act, 1927, 171
Indian citizen, 238
Indian National Congress, 96
Individualism, 38
Indoor air in China, 54
Indoor gamma dose in the south west coast of Kerala, 187-196
 indoor dose rates having different building material, 194
 introduction, 188-189
 materials and methods, 189-190

indoor gamma ray dose using TLDs, 189-190
selection of houses for the survey, 189
outdoor gamma ray dose using survey meter, 190
results and discussion, 190-194
Industrial products, 138
Industrial Revolution, 18, 41, 215
Industrialisation, 16, 19
Industrialised countries, 21
Industry, 36, 137
Institutions in Kerala, 115
International Bird Conservation Network, 149
International coordination of NGOs, 47
International Year of Forests, 55
cost of modern development, 41-42
development, 36
environment, 36-37
problem to crises, 42
religion and spirituality, 48-51
S and T for sustainable development, 45
science, technology and development, 42-44
social sciences and environment, 46-48
sustainable means and use of energy, 45-46
traditional theories of development, 37-40
Invasion of Mysorean army, 95
IPCC, 21, 199
IPRs, 64, 66
Irby, 79
Iron Age, 16
Island Panchayat, 134
IUCN, 228
Iyengar, 77

J

Jaina philosophy, 50
Japan, 50
Jarvis, Jeff, 77
Jojo, P.J. , 31, 187
Judaism, 50

K

Kadamkudy Panchayath, 143
Kala Devi, V., 167
Kapital, Das, 39
Karma, 48, 49
Karuka, 174
Kerala, 28, 29, 31, 54, 96, 108, 110, 115, 173, 187-196, 221
Kerala University, 125
Keynesian model, 40
Kollam Corporation, 124
Kozhikkode, 91, 94
Kumarakom bird, 149
Kumaun, 221
Kureepuzha, 119, 122
Kurup, Peethambara, 27, 53
Kyoto agreement, 25
Kyoto protocol, 23, 25

L

Land, 36, 53
Laws, 46
Lekshmi, R., 31, 187
Leopold, Aldo, 42
Livelihood, 31
Locke, John, 121
Lord Siva of Nagakula, 176

M

Maathai, Wangari, 170
Maidanam, 93, 96
Maldives, 20
Malthus, Robert, 38
Malthus, T.R., 59
Mammals, 219
Man and his environment, 15
Mananchira maidanam, 91-105
Maneesh, B., 29, 155
Marx, Karl, 39
Maternal Mortality Raito, 142
Mathew, Abraham, 28, 107
Mathew, Santhosh, 27
Mayfield, 77
McEvoy, 78
MDGs, 216
Menon, K.P. Kesava, 101
Merkal, Angela, 24
Methane, 19
MNCs, 210
Modern hazards, 137
Moksha, 49
Montreal Protocol of 1987, 202
MOPI, 208
MPSS, 125, 126
Mukkutti, 175
Mulla Periyar Dam, 27
Mullaperiyar dam issue, 71
Multilateral Fund, 203
Multinational corporations, 18
Muralivallabhan, T.V., 26, 35
Muslim community, 100
Mysorean rule, 95

N

Nair, Geetha R., 30, 179
Nair, K Madhavan, 102
Nair, Manju, 29
Nair, P. Kunjuraman, 173
Narmada Bachao Andolan, 221
NAS, 198
National Action Plan on Climatic Change, 231
National Bio-diversity Authority, 69
National Council of Environmental Planning and Co-ordination in 1972, 227
National movement in Malabar, 98
National rural health mission, 133-145
  as an intervention mechanism, 139-142
  interlink between health, environment and sustainable development, 134-137
  health, 134-135
  environmental health, 135
  sustainable development, 136-137
  global burden of environmentally related disease, 136
  traditional and modern environmental health hazards and its impact on development, 137-139
  traditional environmental health hazards faced by an island community in Kadamakudy grama panchayat, 142-144
Natural ecosystems, 13
Natural resources, 53
Nature, 13
NBRA, 189
Neo-classical economists, 39

Neolithic period, 15
NGOs, 46, 47, 48, 63, 120, 231, 232
Nivedhitha, D., 27, 71
Non-Cooperation Movement, 102
Non-formal education, 172
Non-renewable resources, 18
Normal Background Radiation Region, 191

O

Obama, Barack, 24
Ozone depletion, 42, 120
Ozone, 19

P

Pachauri, R.K., 20
Paleolithic period, 15
Panchayati Raj institutions, 112
Parvathi Puthanar Canal, 30, 179-186
Patent Act of 1970, 64
PHCs, 141
Pillai, Rani K., 31, 187
Plachimada Coca-Cola, 111
Planning Commission, 108
Plant Breeders Rights, 67
Plastic bags, 108
Plastic film, 108
Policies, 46
Political Economy, 38
Pollution, 16, 18
of soil and water, 53
Population, 16, 17, 18
Prasad, A.K. Vishnu, 187
Prasad, Vishnu K., 31
PRIs, 141
Productivity, 18
Property rights, 38
Prugh, Thomas, 39
Public Interest Litigation, 238
Public sphere, 91
Public-private partnership, 110
Puranas, 219
PVC, 190

Q

Quan-Haase, 76
Quran, 51

R

Rajan, 28
Rajan, T., 119
Rajeevan, R., 31, 219
Rajesh, M., 27, 59
Rational behaviour, 17
Realisation of Truth, 48
Regulations, 46
Religion, 48
Reptiles, 219
Revolution in Science and Technology, 35
Ricardo, 38
Rio + 20: United Nations Conference, 24, 57
Rio Declaration, 23
Rio Summit, 213
Russell, Bertrand, 43

S

SACEP, 228
Salt pollution, 18
Saraswathi (Goddess), 176
Schemes and policies, 140
Schmickle, 76
Science and spirituality, 35-51
Science and Technology, 172
SDGs, 216

SDP, 158
Shiva, Vandana, 170
Silent Valley Movement, 221
Singh, Man Mohan, 229
Sivadasan, P., 28, 91
Skepticism to trepidation, 71-90
  accepting Tamilians as brothers and sisters, 82
  analysis and findings, 80-85
  asking people to wake up and join the movement, 82
  congratulating the participants, 84-85
  cyber activism leading to real life protests, 83
  giving the scientific facts behind the situation of the dam, 83
  introduction, 72-74
  methodology, 80
  participation of people from different parts of the world, 83-84
  posting the
  clippings from the film dam 999, 84
  comments of elderly, 83
  comments of Tamil youth, 83
  event invitations, 82
  review of literature, 75-80
  theoretical framework, 74-75
Smith, Adam, 38
Social Action Theory, 75
Social media, 71, 82
Social Networking Sites (SNS), 72, 73, 76, 77
Socio-economic fallout, 13
SPM, 239
Sreekumar, K.C., 31, 197
Sri Lanka, 50
Stockholm Conference, 23, 228
Stockholm Resilience Centre, 214
Sukhdev, Pavan, 55
Sultan, Tipu, 95
Supreme Court, 236
Sustainability, 18, 24
Sustainable environment, 235-245
  current levels of pollution, 238-243
  environmental consciousness, 243
  Indian constitution and fundamental rights, 237-238
  legislative background, 236-237
  public interest litigation, 238
  role of an activist supreme court, 243-245
SUTRA, 45

T

Tali Temple, 94, 101
Tehri Dam, 224
Tenth Five Year Plan, 140
Theories of development, 40
Thiruvanathapuram Municipal Corporation, 110
Thiruvathira, 174
Thumbi thullal, 175
TLD, 190
Tourism, 138
Toxic air pollutants, 21
Traditional knowledge,
  intellectual property rights and livelihood sustainability, 59-70
  traditional knowledge and basic livelihood issues, 65

and patenting, 62-63
geographical indications, 64-65
herbal medicine, 66
preservation of bio-diversity using traditional know-how, 69
sustainable agricultural practices using traditional knowledge, 66-68
traditional medicine, 65
traditional knowledge, 60-62
Trees, 55, 219
Triggering the environment, 119-131
assertion for survival, 123-126
TRIPs, 61

U

UN bodies, 14
UN Conference on Environment and Development, 22
UN Conference on Human Environment, 22
UN Environmental Programme, 198
UNAPCTT, 44
UNCED, 47, 210
UNCHE, 211
Undernourished, 17
UNED, 221
UNEP, 24, 108, 228, 242
UNFCCC, 202, 208, 225
United Nations Environment Programme, 22
United Nations, 198
Project, 17
Universal Declaration of Human Rights, 136
Unnikrishnan, N., 29, 147
UNO, 230
Upanisads, 219
UPOV system, 67
Urbanisation, 16
Uttar Pradesh, 237
Uttarakhand, 13, 20, 31

V

Varghese, Titto, 27, 71
Vedas, 219
Vembanad lake, 149
Veranani, Santhosh Mathew, 71
Vicious circle of advertisement, 41
Vienna Convention, 201
Volatile organic compounds (VOCs), 54

W

Waste management, 107-117
innovative waste management programmes, 113-114
major waste management and environment issues in Kerala, 110-112
maladies of Kerala, 108-109
man-made disaster, 109-110
measures for protecting environment, 114-116
deep ecology and green politics, 115-116
promote nature friendly constructions, 115
protect water bodies and invent non-conventional energy sources, 114
regulate the use of plastic and toxic materials, 115
stop deforestation and start afforestation, 114-115

role of civil society in waste management, 112-113
Water, 16, 26, 36, 53
Water Act, 1974, 171, 236
Water and Air Acts, 236
Water sample from Parvathi Puthanal canal in Thiruvanathapuram district, 179-186
introduction, 179-180
materials and methods, 180
result, 180-186
Weber, Max, 74
WED, 168
WHO, 134, 135, 239
Wildlife Act, 1972, 171
World Green House Gases emissions, 23
World Population, 16
World War P, 96
WTO, 22, 157

X

Yamuna, D.S. , 30, 173
Youth, 72, 73-79

Z

Zero-Waste, 45
Zhang, 65, 66
Zhao, 76
Zoology department, 125